EXPAND 2

STUDENT'S BOOK & WORKBOOK

Carla Maurício Vianna
Gisele Aga
João Gabriel Schenferd
Simara H. Dal'Alba

Pearson

Pearson

Head of Product - Pearson Brasil	Juliano de Melo Costa
Product Manager - Pearson Brasil	Marjorie Robles
Product Coordinator - ELT	Mônica Bicalho
Authors	Carla Maurício Vianna
	Gisele Aga
	João Gabriel Schenferd
	Simara H. Dal'Alba
Teacher's Guide	Carla Maurício Vianna
Workbook	João Gabriel Schenferd
	Simara H. Dal'Alba
Extra content	Carla Maurício Vianna
	Luciana Santos Pinheiro
	(Allya Assessoria Linguística)
Editors - ELT	Gisele Aga
	Renata S. C. Victor
	Simara H. Dal'Alba
	(Allya Assessoria Linguística)
Editor (Teacher's Book)	Gisele Aga
Proofreader (English)	Silva Serviços de Educação
Proofreader (Portuguese)	Fernanda R. Braga Simon
Copyeditor	Maria Estela Alcântara
Pedagogical Reviewer	Najin Lima
Quality Control	Viviane Kirmeliene
Art and Design Coordinator	Rafael Lino
Art Editor - ELT	Emily Andrade
Acquisitions and permissions Manager	Maiti Salla
Acquisitions and permissions team	Andrea Bolanho
	Cristiane Gameiro
	Heraldo Colon
	Maricy Queiroz
	Paula Quirino
	Sandra Sebastião
	Shirlei Sebastião
Graphic design	Mirella Della Maggiore Armentano
	MRS Consultoria Editorial
Graphic design (cover)	Mirella Della Maggiore Armentano
	MRS Consultoria Editorial
Media Development	Estação Gráfica
Audio	Maximal Studio
Audiovisual Editor	Tatiane Almeida
Audiovisual	Desenrolados

The publisher would like to thank the following for their kind permission to reproduce their photographs:

Calvin & Hobbes: p. 21. **Cartoonstock:** p. 29. **CRITE, Rohan Allan:** p. 48. **FGV:** p. 25. **Garfield, Jim Davis:** p. 114. **Glasbergen:** p. 115. **iStock:** capa, p. 9, 10, 17, 27, 35, 45, 52, 53, 63, 71, 80, 128. **JumpStart:** p. 15. **Lynn Johnston:** p. 107. **Marketingland:** p. 79. **OECD:** p. 25. **Shutterstock:** p. 80.

Every effort has been made to trace the copyright holders and we apologize in advance for any unintentional omissions. We would be pleased to insert the appropriate acknowledgement in any subsequent edition of this publication.

Dados Internacionais de Catalogação na Publicação (CIP)
(Câmara Brasileira do Livro, SP, Brasil)

Expand 2: Student's Book / Carla Maurício Vianna, Henrick Oprea. -- São Paulo: Pearson Education do Brasil, 2019.

ISBN 978-65-50110-32-1

1. Inglês (Ensino médio) I. Oprea, Henrick. II. Título.

19-25482   CDD-420.7

Índices para catálogo sistemático:
1. Inglês: Ensino Médio 420.7
Maria Alice Ferreira - Bibliotecária - CRB-8/7964

ISBN 978-65-50110-32-1 (Student's Book & Workbook)
ISBN 978-65-50110-33-8 (Teacher's Book)

2019

EXPAND 2

- Unit 1 9
- Unit 2 17
- Review 1 25

- Unit 3 27
- Unit 4 35
- Review 2 43

- Unit 5 45
- Unit 6 53
- Review 3 61

- Unit 7 63
- Unit 8 71
- Review 4 79

Grammar Overview 81
Language Reference 85
Reading Strategies 93
Irregular Verbs 94
Common Mistakes 96
False Friends 98
Glossary 99
Workbook 104
Audio Scripts 136

CONTENTS

	READING	VOCABULARY IN USE	LANGUAGE IN USE 1	EXPAND YOUR READING	LANGUAGE IN USE 2	LISTENING COMPREHENSION
UNIT 1 **Hooked on Social Media** page 9	Informative article: Forget FOMO! We're now more likely to suffer from FOJI, MOMO and JOMO (and it's all social media's fault)	Phrasal verbs and adjectives + *to*	Present perfect	Blog post: How I Overcame Social Media Anxiety	Past continuous and simple past	A radio program about fighting social media addiction
UNIT 2 **The Rocky Road of Good Urban Transportation** page 17	News article: a competition between a driver and a bus passenger to cross London	Prefixes	Modal verbs *can* and *could*	News report: With bikes, transit, Uber unveils urban transportation vision	Zero and first conditionals	News about a self-driving car running over a pedestrian

Review 1 (Units 1-2)
Page 25

	READING	VOCABULARY IN USE	LANGUAGE IN USE 1	EXPAND YOUR READING	LANGUAGE IN USE 2	LISTENING COMPREHENSION
UNIT 3 **Generation Z: Conservative or Liberal?** page 27	Informative article: Conservative or Liberal? For Generation Z, It's Not That Simple	Collocations with *make* and *do*	Relative clauses	Interview about Dr. Jean Twenge's book on the iGeneration	*So* for cause and result	A guide to generations
UNIT 4 **What's Going Abroad Like?** page 35	Informative article: Undiscovered destinations: Now that's what I call off the beaten track	Idioms related to travel	*Have to* and *need to*	Blog post: Why the tourism industry has to change and how you can help it do so	Tag questions	Jason Moore interviews Tim Leffel about the ins and outs of living abroad

Review 2 (Units 3-4)
Page 43

Grammar Review
page 81

Language Reference
page 85

Reading Strategies
page 93

Irregular Verbs
page 94

	READING	VOCABULARY IN USE	LANGUAGE IN USE 1	EXPAND YOUR READING	LANGUAGE IN USE 2	LISTENING COMPREHENSION
UNIT 5 What the Future Holds ▶ page 45	Testimonials: Professors' opinions on what universities will be like 10 years from now	Adverbs: suffix -*ly*	*Will* vs. *be going to*	Survey: Workforce of the Future	*May, might, could*	A testimonial about taking a gap year
UNIT 6 It's Time We Reforested the Agribusiness ▶ page 53	Informative article, facts and figures: Agribusiness issue	Collocations with *get* and *set*	Passive voice	Encyclopedia entry: Agroforestry	Discourse markers	News about Brazil's position as an agricultural powerhouse
Review 3 (Units 5-6) ▶ page 61						
UNIT 7 The Economic Effects of Globalization ▶ page 63	Opinion article: The globalization counter-reaction	Vocabulary related to economy	Present perfect - *since / for*	Infographic: A tale of two economies	Present perfect vs. simple past	An interview about financial crisis
UNIT 8 Spotting Fake News among the Real Stories ▶ page 71	News report: Facebook has a fake news 'war room' – but is it really working?	Vocabulary related to fake news	Verb tense review	Narrative essay: Experience: I write fake news	Embedded questions	A teacher's talk about how to identify real news
Review 4 (Units 7-8) ▶ page 79						

Common Mistakes
▶ page 96

False Friends
▶ page 98

Glossary
▶ page 99

Workbook
▶ page 104

Audio Scripts
▶ page 136

PRESENTATION

STUDENT'S BOOK

Welcome to the *Expand* collection! *Expand* prepares students for the English part of Brazilian exams ENEM and vestibular, which are aimed at testing students' ability to read a wide variety of authentic texts of different genres. *Expand* provides students with listening, speaking, and writing activities that help them to develop their overall knowledge of the language. Each thematic unit contains two reading sections that introduce grammar and vocabulary topics, as well as listening comprehension activities that give students contact with oral text genres.

OPENING PAGE

Each unit starts with an opening page containing:

IN THIS UNIT YOU WILL…

This shows the main objectives for the unit.

> **IN THIS UNIT YOU WILL…**
> - talk about social media addiction;
> - exchange ideas about how one can overcome social media anxiety;
> - learn how to use the present perfect;
> - talk about completed actions in the past using the simple past;
> - describe actions in progress in the past using the past continuous.

LEAD OFF

This section presents three to four questions for content contextualization.

> - How can you relate the picture to the title of this unit?
> - Why is there so much concern about the excessive use of social media nowadays?
> - In your opinion, is social media addictive? Why (not)?
> - Are you a social network addict? How can you tell?

READING PAGES

This two-page section contains the first reading text and activities of the unit. It develops reading strategies and is subdivided into the following stages:

BEFORE READING

This section contains one or two activities that help students to prepare for the text topic, which is presented in the section WHILE READING.

> **READING**
> **» BEFORE READING** *Relating to the topic*
> Read the first paragraph of the online article "How owning a car might soon become as old-fashioned as owing a horse." Then exchange ideas with your classmates whether you agree with the message conveyed or not.

WHILE READING

In this section students read a text and answer a question related to it. Texts are in a variety of different genres and aimed at developing several reading strategies.

> **» WHILE READING** *Identifying the author's tone*
> Read the text and classify the author's tone as mocking, apprehensive, vindictive, or humorous. Underline the fragments that support your answer. *Identifying the author's tone*
>
> The 1914 effect
> **The globalization counter-reaction**
> *Globalization is a highly disruptive force. It provoked a reaction in the early 20th century. Are we seeing a repeat?*
> Buttonwood's notebook
> Jun 14th 2017 | by Buttonwood

AFTER READING

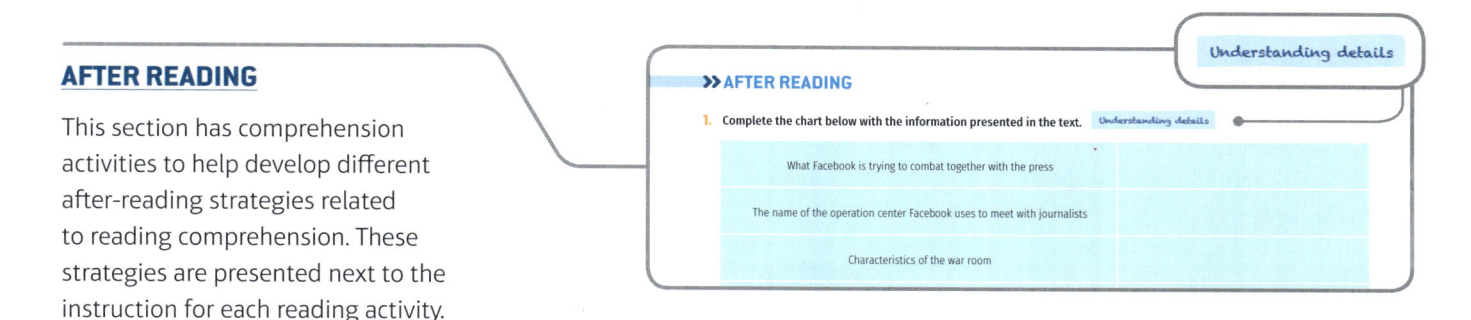

This section has comprehension activities to help develop different after-reading strategies related to reading comprehension. These strategies are presented next to the instruction for each reading activity.

VOCABULARY PAGES

This stage develops students' vocabulary through activities containing vocabulary from the text and related to the topic of the unit.

EXPAND YOUR VOCABULARY

This section contains one to three activities related to the vocabulary presented in the text. It also prompts students to engage in conversational topics based on the text they have read.

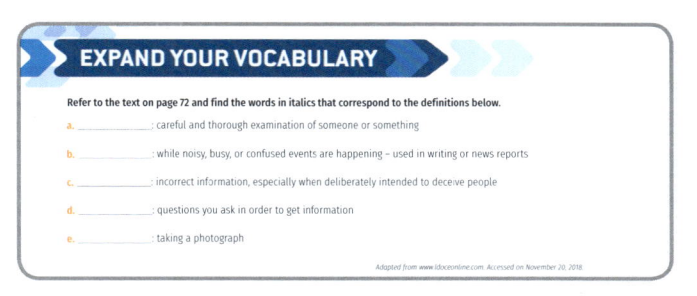

VOCABULARY IN USE

Here students are presented with an example of target vocabulary taken from the main reading text and do activities to develop their vocabulary knowledge.

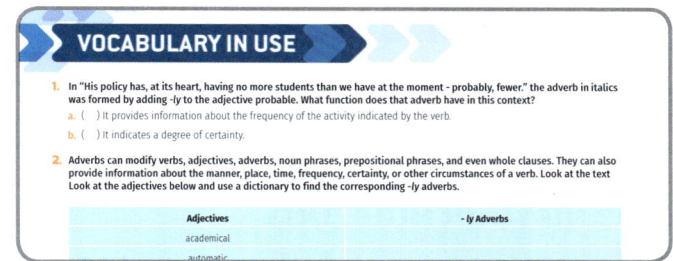

LANGUAGE IN USE 1

This page presents the first grammar topic of the unit. It contains examples from the text and activities that develop students' grammar knowledge in the target language.

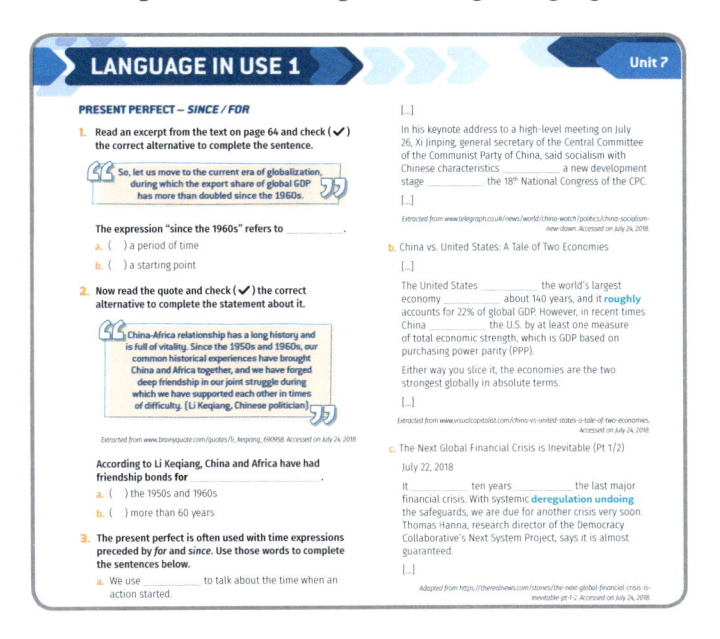

EXPAND YOUR READING

This section contains another text for students to work on both the text genre and comprehension.

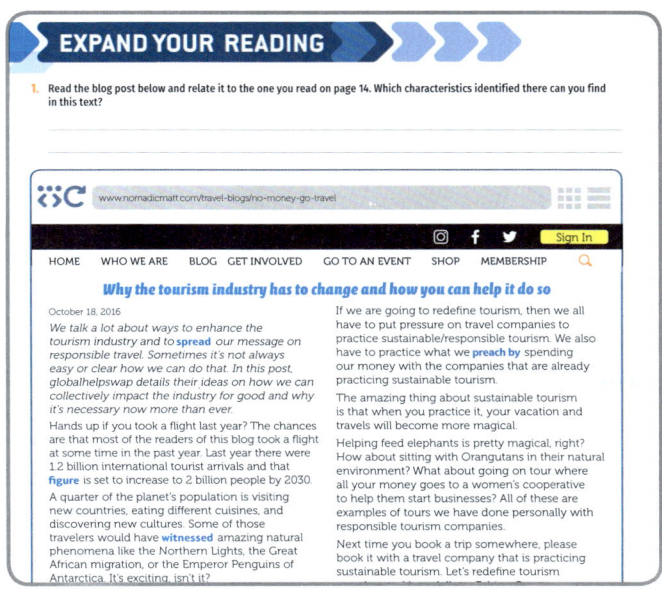

PRESENTATION

LANGUAGE IN USE 2

This page presents the second grammar topic of the unit. It contains examples from the text in *Expand your reading* and activities that develop students' grammar knowledge in the target language.

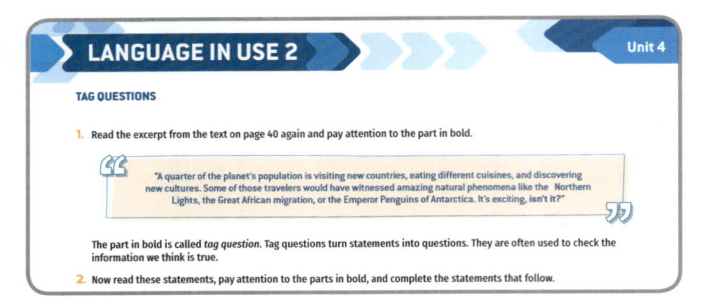

LISTENING COMPREHENSION

This section contains listening activities with authentic texts aimed at developing students' listening skills.

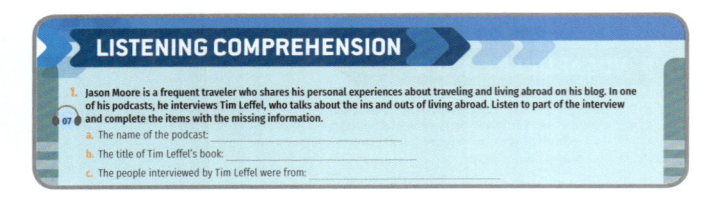

EXPAND YOUR HORIZONS

In this end-of-unit section, students are presented with three statements that allow them to discuss the topic in the listening comprehension section and think critically about it while using the target language.

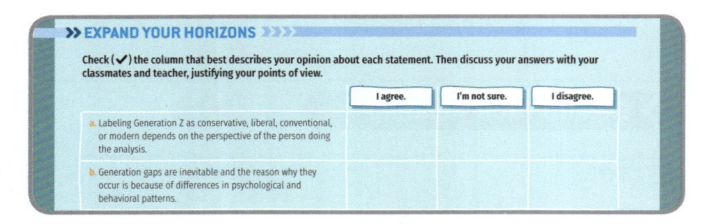

REVIEW

After every two units there is a two-page section for students to review and practice the language they have learned so far.

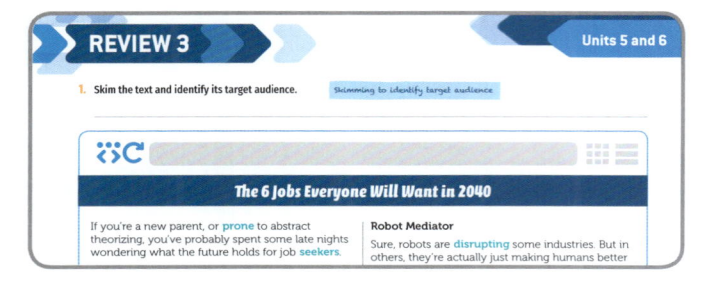

WORKBOOK

Each unit has four pages of reading, vocabulary, and grammar activities. It also has an ENEM or vestibular question in the section AN EYE ON ENEM / VESTIBULAR.

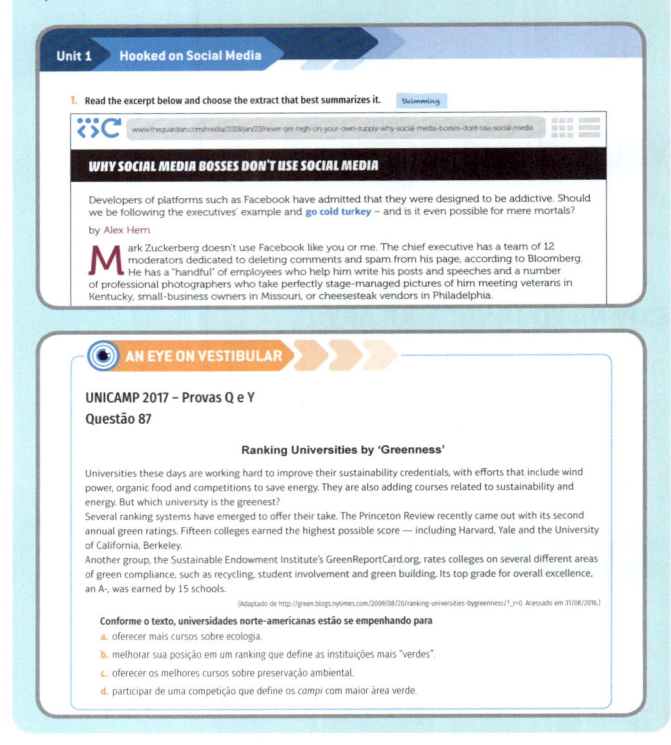

DIGITAL COMPONENTS

Video lessons for all *Language in Use* and *Vocabulary in Use* sections and for exam practice.

Mock test generator with major Brazilian *Vestibular* and ENEM questions to prepare students for these exams.

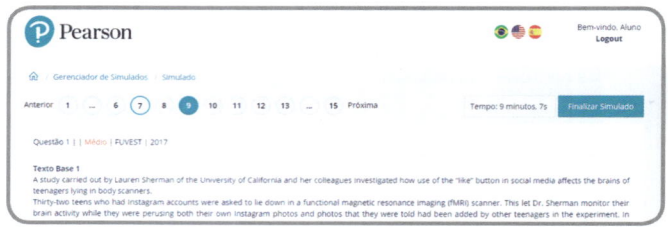

UNIT 1
Hooked on Social Media

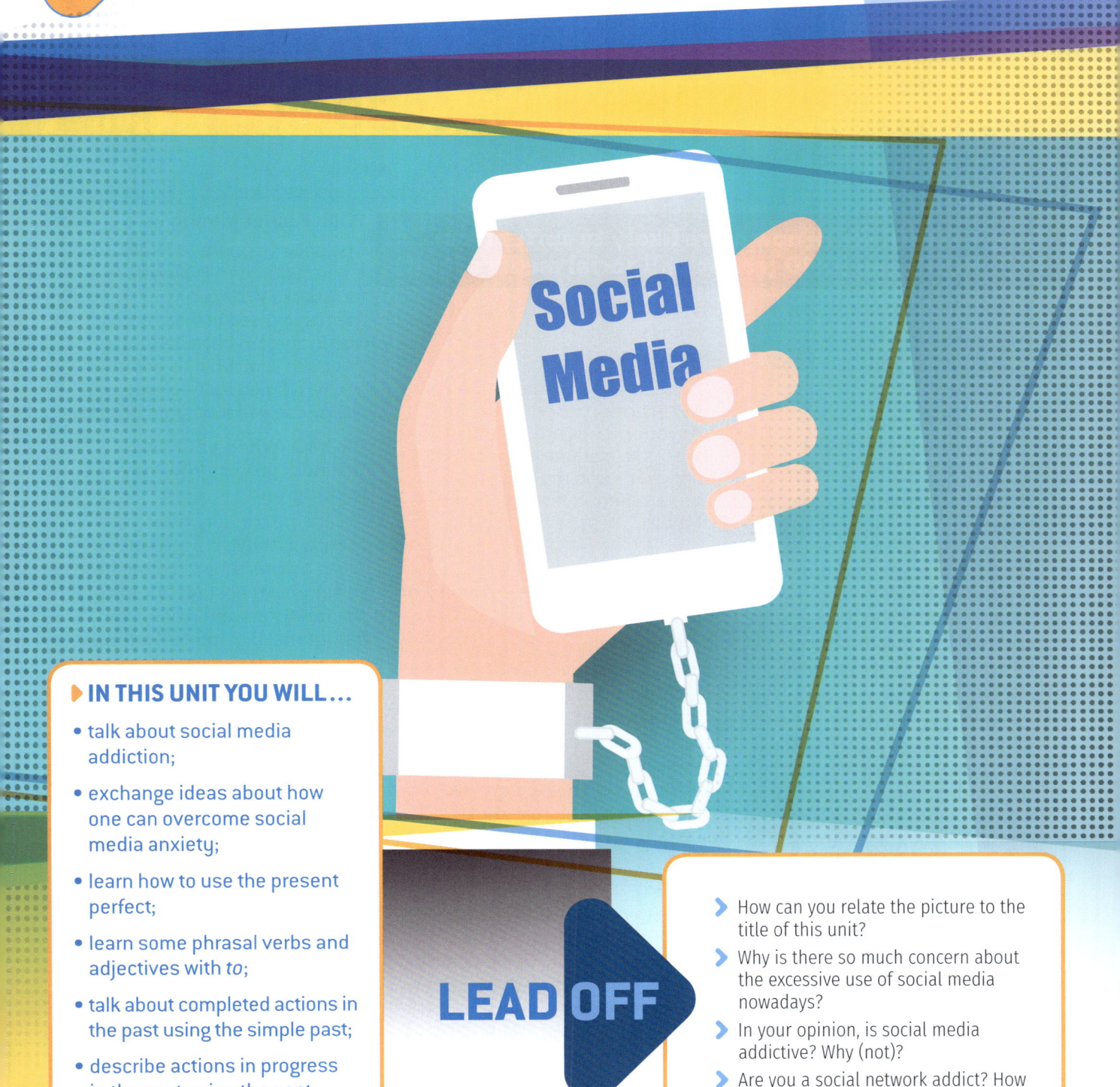

▶ IN THIS UNIT YOU WILL...

- talk about social media addiction;
- exchange ideas about how one can overcome social media anxiety;
- learn how to use the present perfect;
- learn some phrasal verbs and adjectives with *to*;
- talk about completed actions in the past using the simple past;
- describe actions in progress in the past using the past continuous.

LEAD OFF

- How can you relate the picture to the title of this unit?
- Why is there so much concern about the excessive use of social media nowadays?
- In your opinion, is social media addictive? Why (not)?
- Are you a social network addict? How can you tell?

READING

>> BEFORE READING

Look at the picture on the right, which shows some messaging platforms, some apps and brands, and social media, and name the social networks you once were or are a member of. What others would you add to this list?

Activating previous knowledge

_____

_____

>> WHILE READING

Skim the text and identify its probable target audience.

Skimming to identify target audience

Forget FOMO! We're now more likely to suffer from FOJI, MOMO and JOMO (and it's all social media's fault)

By UNITY BLOTT FOR MAILONLINE

PUBLISHED: 07:28 GMT, 22 JANUARY 2016 | **UPDATED:** 09:47 GMT, 22 JANUARY 2016

It was hailed as one of the biggest causes of social anxiety of our generation.

FOMO - **shorthand** for *fear* of missing out - which fell into our collective vocabulary in 2011, is the acute and often unjustified belief that everyone is having more fun than you, and that you're **somehow** being left out of all the fun.

But this affliction, thought to be caused by social media where you see endless status updates and photos of your friends showing off their (**supposedly**) happier, more exciting lives, is just the tip of the worry iceberg.

In fact, FOMO has become such a problem that recent studies suggest it can manifest as a genuine form of social anxiety and even **lead to** an increased risk of alcohol abuse and depression among certain age groups.

But now *commentators* are suggesting that FOMO is just the tip of the iceberg when it comes to social media-related **acronyms**.

There is now a whole *range* of afflictions caused by all the fun your friends are having on Facebook, Instagram, Twitter and Snapchat - and the chances are, you're suffering from at least one of them.

[...]

FOMOMO: Fear of the mystery of missing out

A more extreme case of FOMO that occurs only when your phone is broken or out of battery. According to the Guardian, it means you're afraid of missing out, but not because of what you see on social media - it's what you don't see that's causing you real **angst**.

[...]

MOMO: Mystery of missing out

This is the paranoia that *arises* when your friends don't post anything on social media at all. Instead, you're left with no option but to *scroll* obsessively through your Facebook and Twitter timelines searching for clues.

[...]

FOJI: Fear of joining in

The polar opposite to MOMO; if you suffer from FOJI, you're far less likely to keep your friends updated on Facebook and Instagram because you're not quite sure what to post and you're worried that nobody will like or comment on your photos.

BROMO: When your 'bros' (friends) protect you from missing out

An act of solidarity from your friends. If they've been out the night before, they'll deliberately **refrain** from posting photos of the fun they were having, for fear of making you feel left out.

SLOMO: Slow to missing out

In this case, your anxiety is probably justified. Everybody is having a better time than you, but you're asleep so you don't know it until the next morning when you log into Facebook and find your timeline **littered** with photos of the night before.

JOMO: The joy of missing out

Taking pleasure in 'missing out' by not feeling like you have to be everywhere at once. Instead, you're quite content with staying in bed with a cup of tea and a book.

Extracted from www.dailymail.co.uk/femail/article-3410074/Forget-FOMO-FOJI-MOMO-JOMO-new-anxieties-caused-social-media.html. Accessed on November 19, 2018.

Unit 1

» AFTER READING

1. Check (✔) the statement that defines FOMO. *Understanding main ideas*
   a. ( ) Those who have FOMO are afraid of being without their phones and unable to contact their social media friends.
   b. ( ) Someone who has FOMO believes that other people's lives are more interesting than their own life.
   c. ( ) If someone has FOMO, this person is afraid that his/her friends are having fun, but they are not telling him/her.

2. The author mentions two severe consequences of FOMO. What are they? *Understanding details*
   _____
   _____

3. Read the description of the afflictions caused by social media again. Then read the testimonials below and match them with one of the acronyms. In small groups, say how you think the people feel about the their affliction. *Understanding details and evaluating a text critically*
   a. "When I woke up today, I saw my friends' post on Instagram about a party they went to last night. I'm glad they didn't invite me, because I really needed to stay at home and relax by myself."
   b. "I'm so mad today! My friends went to a concert without inviting me! I am being bombarded with all these pictures on my timeline showing them having a great time."
   c. "OMG! I left my phone at home! Now how will I know where my friends are and what they are doing?"
   d. "I'll post a picture of my healthy lunch. Wait, who wants to know what I eat? Nobody will like my picture. My friends don't care about it. Forget it, I won't post anything."

   ( ) SLOMO   ( ) FOMOMO   ( ) JOMO   ( ) FOJI

EXPAND YOUR VOCABULARY

1. Refer to the text on page 10 and find words in italics that match the definitions below. Then use one of them to complete both blanks in the quote.
   a. _____ : people who know a lot about a particular subject, and who write about it or discuss it on the television or radio
   b. _____ : a number of people or things that are all different, but are all of the same general type
   c. _____ : begins to happen
   d. _____ : the feeling you get when you are afraid or worried that something bad is going to happen
   e. _____ : to move information on a computer or phone screen up or down so that you can read it

   Adapted from www.ldoceonline.com. Accessed on November 19, 2018.

> Internet freedom is not possible without freedom from _____, and users will not be free from _____ unless they are sufficiently protected from online **theft** and attack.
> — Rebecca MacKinnon
>
> *Extracted from www.brainyquote.com. Accessed on November 19, 2018.*

2. In pairs, read the quote again. Do you share Rebecca MacKinnon's opinion? Justify your view.
   _____

VOCABULARY IN USE

1. In the extract "But this affliction, thought to be caused by social media where you see endless status updates and photos of your friends showing off their (supposedly) happier, more exciting lives, is just the tip of the worry iceberg", *showing off* is a phrasal verb (or a multi word verb). Phrasal verbs are...

   a. ( ) made of two words. The first one is a particle (a preposition or an adverb) and the second one is a verb.

   b. ( ) made of two or more words. The first one is a verb and the second (and sometimes third) one is a particle (a preposition or an adverb).

2. Below you will find phrasal verbs with one or more particles. Complete the definitions and examples with the same phrasal verb from the box.

come up with	filter out	log off / out	log on
plug in	run out	sign up	walk out on

   a. _____: to do the necessary actions on a computer system that will allow you to begin using it

   You need to _____ before you start using this software.

   b. _____: to use all of something and not have any more left

   You can borrow my batteries in case you _____.

   c. _____: to connect a piece of electrical equipment to the main supply of electricity, or to another piece of electrical equipment

   I thought my printer wasn't working, but I had just forgotten to _____ it _____. What a relief!

   d. _____: to stop doing something you have agreed to do or that you are responsible for

   From our point of view, it's unethical to _____ a deal.

   e. _____: to do the actions that are necessary when you finish using a computer system

   Is it safe not to _____ of social media accounts on one's personal laptop?

   f. _____: to think of an idea, answer, etc.

   The students were asked to _____ ideas on how to protect themselves from internet addiction.

   g. _____: to put your name on a list for something because you want to take part in it

   They wanted to take an IT course, but it was necessary to _____ for it beforehand.

   h. _____: to remove words, information, etc. that you do not need or want

   I'm searching for a software program that might help me _____ unwanted emails.

   Extracted from www.ldoceonline.com. Accessed on July 6, 2018.

3. In English, some adjectives are usually followed by certain prepositions. Read the extract from the text on page 10 and circle the *adjective + preposition* combination.

   > The polar opposite to MOMO; if you suffer from FOJI, you're far less likely to keep your friends updated on Facebook and Instagram because you're not quite sure what to post [...].

4. Here are some other examples of adjectives that often go with the preposition *to*. Read them and complete the sentences.

addicted	generous	rude	similar

   a. Social networking has such a huge impact on the real world that its craving is considered _____ the cravings for cigarettes and alcohol.

   b. A great number of social media users don't follow netiquettes and are _____ other users.

   c. Ken is so _____ surfing the Net that he doesn't even stop doing that when he is having his meals.

   d. My virtual friends have been _____ me as far as attention is concerned. I could count on their support to listen to me every time I needed it.

5. Finish the paragraph below. Use at least one *phrasal verb* and one *adjective + preposition* combination you learned in this section.

   Some people turn to social media interactions...

   _____
   _____
   _____
   _____
   _____

LANGUAGE IN USE 1

Unit 1

PRESENT PERFECT

1. The excerpt below was extracted from the text on page 10. Read it, paying special attention to the part in bold, and check (✓) the correct answer to the question that follows.

> [...] FOMO **has become** such a problem that recent studies suggest it can manifest as a genuine form of social anxiety [...]

Why is the present perfect tense used in this extract?

a. (   ) To talk about something that had happened at a specific time in the past.

b. (   ) To talk about something that started in the past and continues up to now.

2. Read a fragment about teens and social media addiction and underline other examples of the present perfect tense. Then choose the correct alternative to complete the sentences.

> Teenage social media addiction can be described as a preoccupation and obsession. A teenager with a social media addiction has become so engrossed in the virtual world that it has impacted the real world, causing harmful effects. While many teens engage in social media through platforms such as Facebook, Twitter, YouTube, Snapchat, and others, teens who are addicted to social media see a negative impact on their real-life relationships and responsibilities. [...]
>
> Adapted from www.shepherdshillacademy.org/resources/teens-social-media-addiction. Accessed on July 7, 2018.

a. In the extract above, the present perfect refers to actions that started at a / an _____ (specific / unspecific) time in the past and continue up to the present. They indicate changes that have happened over a period of time and have consequences in the _____ (present / future).

b. To form the present perfect, we use the auxiliary verb - _____ (does / have) or *has* - and the main verb in the past participle. In questions, the _____ (main / auxiliary) verb and the subject are inverted and in negative sentences, we use *not* after the auxiliary verb.

c. The particles *'ve* and *'s* are the contracted forms in _____ (affirmative / interrogative) sentences while *haven't* and *hasn't* are the contracted forms in negative sentences.

d. Some adverbs such as _____ (ever / now), *never*, *already*, *yet*, etc. are commonly used with the present perfect.

3. Use the verbs from the box in the present perfect to complete the text. Refer to the list of irregular verbs on pages 94 and 95 if necessary.

> come   find   see   spark   warn

Neurochemically, smartphone addiction is real - Now what?

We'_____ all _____ it: crowds of people walking with their heads bent, thumbs frantically scrolling, eyes glazed. Smartphones and social media take up hours of time in the average person's day.

Now, scientists _____ a connection between smartphone use and neurochemical imbalances in the brain. [...]

For years, scientists and researchers _____ about the possible negative effects of staring at screens for too many hours a day. From the very first video games to the latest virtual reality experiences, every new piece of technology _____ with pundits questioning their safety.

Yet, no smart device _____ the word "addiction" more than the smartphone. Many recent articles state that smartphone and social media addiction isn't just real, but that it's commonplace.

[...]

Extracted from https://fightaddictionnow.org/blog/smartphone-social-media-addiction-new-face-dependence. Accessed on July 7, 2018.

4. Work in pairs. Use the present perfect tense to answer the questions below. Then report your answers to the class.

a. Have you ever noticed any signs of social media addiction among your friends? If so, how have you tried to help him/her?

b. Have you ever received offensive or intimidating messages through social media? If so, why has that happened?

c. Some schools have used social media for informational and educational purposes. How has that happened at your school? Have you benefited from it?

EXPAND YOUR READING

1. Look at the text below briefly and check (✓) the elements you can see.

a. ( ) menu or navigation bar
b. ( ) publication date
c. ( ) latest update date
d. ( ) icons for network sharing
e. ( ) writer's credentials

---

https://www.belivingbelieving.com/2017/12/27/how-i-overcame-social-media-anxiety-part-1/

beliving & believing

Search...

How I Overcame Social Media Anxiety

[...] Susan 📅 December 27, 2017. 💬 No Comments

Instagram
I love pictures. I always took pictures growing up and when I discovered Instagram I'd post about my family, friends, and myself just living life because I wanted to share what God was doing in my life. I'd also ask people to snap a photo of me because we'd be at a cool monument or on vacation. And a lot of my feed was about highlighting peoples' qualities with a nice picture of them. Then passive aggressive **remarks** started coming: "You think you're pretty, huh?" [...] "Don't be fake." The comments and questions were unnecessary and in **hindsight** it was just a projection of themselves.

But, I had people-pleasing problems. I believed their words even though they weren't true. I didn't know how to navigate through it so the best thing I thought to do was delete all the photos that seemed to make everyone feel uncomfortable. I decided to post **landscapes** and food only. Though I loved sharing about my family, I didn't want others to think I was showing off, so I stopped.

The Problem
I had fear of peoples' opinions of what they believed I was doing while posting photos and sharing testimonies. Social media *exposed* the deep-rooted fear in me – how much I cared about others' negative opinions about me and my life. [...]

Adapted from www.belivingbelieving.com/2017/12/27/how-i-overcame-social-media-anxiety-part-1. Accessed on July 7, 2018.

---

2. Read the text carefully. Based on the layout clues, tone, and content of the text, where do you think it was published? Why do you think so?

3. Read the text once again and underline the correct statements about blog posts.

a. Blog posts often appear on the website in chronological order.

b. Readers can't write comments expressing their opinions about what they've read.

c. Blog posts might include images, hyperlinks, or links to other blogs.

d. Blog posts can be written in many genres such as testimonials, poems, travel diaries, etc.

e. They are very formal pieces of writing and must be arranged in justified alignment.

LANGUAGE IN USE 2

Unit 1

PAST CONTINUOUS and SIMPLE PAST

1. Read the extracts from the blog post on page 14 and check (✓) the correct endings to the sentences about the past continuous.

> I'd post about my family, friends, and myself just living life because I wanted to share what God **was doing** in my life.

> Though I loved sharing about my family, I didn't want others to think I **was showing off,** so I stopped.

a. In both extracts, the past continuous is used to talk about…

( ) finished actions in the past.

( ) actions in progress in the past.

b. To form the past continuous, we use…

( ) *was / were* + main verb in the *-ing* form.

( ) *did / didn't* + main verb in the *-ing* form.

c. The past continuous is frequently used with the simple past with *when* and *while*. In this case, the past continuous describes…

( ) a shorter action or event, while the simple past describes a longer action or situation.

( ) a longer action or situation, while the simple past describes a shorter action or event.

2. Circle the finished actions or states and underline the actions that were in progress in the past in the strips below. Then exchange ideas about the comic strips with a classmate.

Extracted from www.amureprints.com/reprints/results?terms=facebook&feature_codes%5B%5D=jt&release_date_from=&release_date_to=&commit=Search. Accessed on July 8, 2018.

3. Read part of a text by the entrepreneur Jason Zook about his 30-day social media detox and use the verbs from the box in the simple past or past continuous to fill in the blanks.

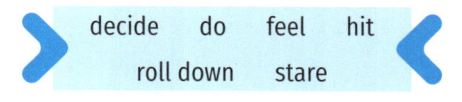

> decide   do   feel   hit
> roll down   stare

Day One of living without social media:

All notifications were turned off. All apps were removed. And I _____ an immediate feeling of freedom living without social media.

I could feel myself wanting to go to Facebook, Twitter, and Instagram, especially on this day because I had just relaunched my personal website the day before (the timing was not only impeccable, it was planned).

After what felt like a few grueling hours, I had spent 30 minutes answering e-mails. One of my first realizations was just how much time can be wasted browsing social networks without knowing it. I could feel myself wanting to sneak a peek at Facebook, so I _____ to get up from my desk and run an errand.

Most of us don't even realize how much we're checking things while driving. I probably glanced down at my phone 20 times during the course of an eight-minute drive. Then I _____ a stoplight. Like a drug addict reaching for his/her fix, I scooped my phone up from the cupholder and swiped it open. It wasn't until I _____ at a barren Home screen, devoid of red notification icons, that I realized what I _____. I closed the phone and put it back in the cupholder. I took notice of how beautiful of a day it was. I _____ the windows and took the moment of beauty in, completely understanding how often I take for granted amazing weather and a moment of stillness.

Adapted from https://jasondoesstuff.com/social-media-detox-recap. Accessed on July 8, 2018.

4. Suppose you were having social media addiction problems and had to disconnect from all social networks for a week. How easy or hard would it be for you and why?

LISTENING COMPREHENSION

1. Read the sentences below. What do those conditions have in common? What do you know about them? Exchange your opinions with a classmate.

smartphone
_____
_____
_____
_____

> **FOMO** (Fear Of Missing Out) is the compulsion to be constantly connected to social media so as not to miss anything.
>
> **Nomophobia** is the fear of leaving your phone at home.
>
> **Sleep texting** happens when people send text messages while they're sleeping.
>
> **Phantom vibration syndrome** occurs when people think their phones vibrate when in fact they do not.
>
> Based on mobileworldcapital.com/2013/09/25/180. Accessed on July 8, 2018.

2. Listen to part of a radio program about fighting social media addiction. Which of the conditions in activity 1 does it talk about?
_____
_____

3. Listen to the second part of the program and mark the statements true (T) or false (F).

a. (   ) British teenagers spend more than twice the time they used to on social media.

b. (   ) About 30% of teenagers are constantly online in the USA.

c. (   ) According to a survey carried out by the Australian Psychological Society, most teenagers suffer from FOMO.

d. (   ) Another study says that using social media at night can affect your sleep.

e. (   ) Although most of the results of studies were negative, the Australian researchers found that using social media can also bring benefits to teens' lives.

4. Read the transcript of both audios on page 136. Have you ever felt the symptoms described in the studies? Do you agree that social media has been affecting teens' lives negatively more than positively? Justify.
_____
_____
_____
_____
_____
_____

>> EXPAND YOUR HORIZONS >>>>

Check (✓) the column that best describes your opinion about each statement. Then discuss your answers with your classmates and teacher, justifying your point of view.

	I agree.	I'm not sure.	I disagree.
a. Smartphone addiction, FOMO, and other disorders are a growing problem nowadays, especially for teenagers.			
b. Social media are, in fact, extensions of being social.			
c. Joining social media isn't necessarily a bad thing if one doesn't make it a priority and manages to spend time doing more important things.			

UNIT 2
The Rocky Road of Good Urban Transportation

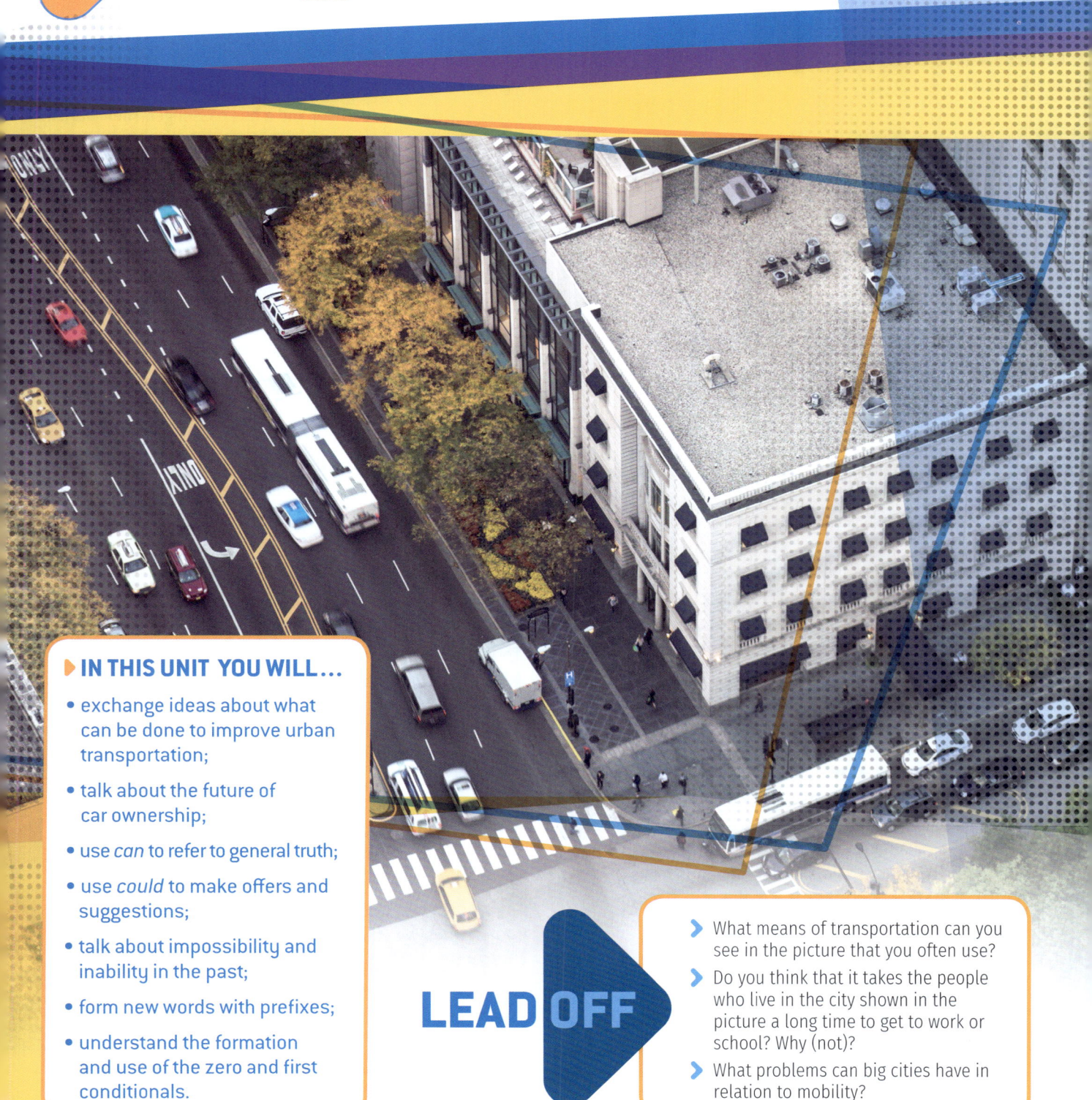

▶ IN THIS UNIT YOU WILL...

- exchange ideas about what can be done to improve urban transportation;
- talk about the future of car ownership;
- use *can* to refer to general truth;
- use *could* to make offers and suggestions;
- talk about impossibility and inability in the past;
- form new words with prefixes;
- understand the formation and use of the zero and first conditionals.

LEAD OFF

- What means of transportation can you see in the picture that you often use?
- Do you think that it takes the people who live in the city shown in the picture a long time to get to work or school? Why (not)?
- What problems can big cities have in relation to mobility?

READING

❯❯ BEFORE READING

Read the first paragraph of the online article "How owning a car might soon become as old-fashioned as owning a horse." Then discuss with your classmates whether you agree with the message conveyed or not.

Relating to the topic

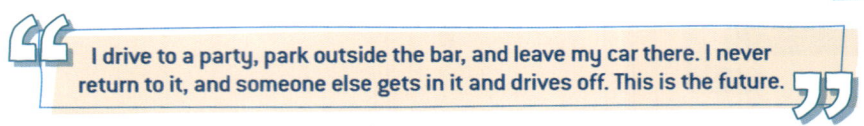

> " I drive to a party, park outside the bar, and leave my car there. I never return to it, and someone else gets in it and drives off. This is the future. "

Extracted from www.independent.co.uk/life-style/gadgets-and-tech/how-owning-a-car-might-soon-become-as-old-fashioned-as-owning-a-horse-a7195836.html. Accessed on September 18, 2018.

❯❯ WHILE READING

Read part of an article that shows a competition to travel across London between a driver and a bus passenger. Then work in pairs and answer the question: Who do you think would like to read it?

Identifying the target audience

DRIVER: 17 MINS 41 SECS

Two-and-a-half million Londoners own cars — but car ownership is declining.

With so many alternative ways of getting around, driving is reserved for those who don't have a choice
5 — such as the elderly or disabled, or those who do it for a living.

[…]

The challenger: Vittorio Frediani, 43, a security driver from South-West London.

10 I'm behind the wheel all day, every day. I see the best and worst of the city roads — and there are definitely more bad than good.

London is becoming impossible for motorists. Roads that used to flow freely have been **narrowed** so
15 much by cycle lanes that there's always solid traffic. London might be cyclist-friendly, but it's becoming car-unfriendly.

I started neck-and-neck with Dan's bike and we followed the same route past Buckingham Palace.
20 Then he veered off onto his (**rather** empty) cycle lane. I felt like my car was surrounded by a swarm of cyclists, cutting me off at every corner. You can't take your eyes off the road for a second, even to check the sat nav. Unlike them, I couldn't cut corners, and instead ended
25 up in gridlock on The Mall. Then I spent another ten minutes in search of a parking space before sprinting to the finish line. What a nightmare!

BUS PASSENGER: 18 MINS 20 SECS

London's public transport system is its beating heart,
30 so heavily do its residents rely on buses, Tubes and trains. But travelling this way doesn't come cheap — with a Tube journey costing £2.90 with an Oyster or contactless card, or £4.90 with cash.

For large families, those on a lower **income** or children
35 travelling alone — who only get free Tube travel until the age 11 — buses are the only way to get around, with a single fare costing just £1.50. However, cyclists can use bus lanes, too, slowing them down.

There are 8,000 buses on 700 different routes in London,
40 and commuters take 1.8 billion journeys every year.

[…]

**The challenger: Vicky Allen, 24, an office manager from South-East London. She's lived in the capital all her life but only started commuting, to a new
45 job in the City, last month.**

I used to work near where I live, so I'm new to this route — and that means I don't have the patience of someone who's done this for years.

There's nothing worse than having to stand the
50 whole way while a bus driver jerks around corners and stops abruptly — it makes me feel sick. The No. 38 bus goes from Victoria to Piccadilly, so my route was straightforward. Buses come every 20 minutes and I got lucky, with one pulling up minutes after
55 I had arrived at the stop. I even got a seat — a miracle in rush hour! — but it soon filled up with grumpy-looking commuters, many of whom were forced to stand.

The journey was smooth until we reached Hyde Park
60 Corner, when we started crawling at a snail's pace. This continued the whole way along Piccadilly — I thought we'd never get there!

I'm not surprised I came last. But it does seem unfair that bus routes are clogged with cyclists —
65 they should stick to their own lanes.

Adapted from www.dailymail.co.uk/news/article-5884743/Ready-steady-GRIDLOCK-SARAH-RAINEY-puts-public-transport-test.html. Accessed on January 4, 2019.

>> AFTER READING

1. Read the questions below and check (✓) the correct alternative. *Understanding main ideas*
Which commuter…

a. was the last one to arrive? ( ) Bus passenger ( ) Driver
b. says London is a difficult city to drive? ( ) Bus passenger ( ) Driver
c. says London is cyclist-friendly? ( ) Bus passenger ( ) Driver
d. refers to two different types of transportation using the same lane? ( ) Bus passenger ( ) Driver

2. Underline the statements that are correct according to the article. *Understanding details*

a. More and more people are using cars in London.
b. Because of the heavy traffic, it was difficult for the driver to take his eyes off the road.
c. It can be expensive to use public transport in London, but buses are considered a quite cheap alternative.
d. The bus passenger believes that the main problem in London is that cars and buses use the same lanes.

3. Discuss the following questions in pairs. Then report your answers to the class.

a. Which commuter from the text on page 18 do you think has the most stressful journey? Why?
b. Why do you think more and more people are looking for alternatives other than cars to commute in London?
c. Which kind of transportation do you think would be the fastest in your city? Justify.

EXPAND YOUR VOCABULARY

1. Match the words in bold with their meanings.

a. "I'm behind the **wheel** all day, every day."
b. "[…] driving is reserved for those who don't have a choice — such as the elderly or **disabled** […]."
c. "Then I spent another ten minutes in search of a parking space before **sprinting** to the finish line."
d. "Buses come every 20 minutes and I got lucky, with one **pulling up** minutes after I had arrived at the stop."
e. "The journey was **smooth** until we reached Hyde Park Corner, when we started crawling at a snail's pace."

( ) running fast for a short distance
( ) the round piece of equipment that you turn to make a car, ship etc. move in a particular direction
( ) happening or operating successfully, without any problems
( ) someone who cannot use a part of their body properly, or cannot learn easily
( ) stopping the vehicle that someone is driving

Adapted from www.ldoceonline.com. Accessed on January 4, 2019

2. Go back to the extract about the driver on page 18 and find a phrasal verb that has the following meaning:

_____ : someone or something that was in a particular situation, state, or place after a series of events, especially when they did not plan it

Extracted from www.ldoceonline.com. Accessed on January 4 2019.

VOCABULARY IN USE

1. Read the following excerpt from the text on page 18 again and choose the best answer to the question.

> London is becoming **impossible** for motorists. Roads that used to flow freely have been narrowed so much by cycle lanes that there's always solid traffic. London might be cyclist-friendly, but it's becoming car-**unfriendly**.

The prefixes *im-* and *un-* were added to the beginning of the words *possible* and *friendly* and formed new words with different meanings. For example, prefixes can create a new word opposite in meaning to the words they are attached to. They can also make words negative. In fact, every prefix has a meaning.

What are the prefixes *im-* and *un-* used for?

a. ( ) To show that someone does a job with someone else.

b. ( ) To show a negative, a lack, or an opposite.

2. Write the words below in the correct column according to their meaning. Then complete the chart with the corresponding prefix.

> encourage   unimportant   amoral   enlarge   enable
> uninterested   atypically   irresponsible   co-create   recreate
> regroup   impolite   co-pilot   endanger   reclaim
> insensitive   illegal   renew   inexperienced

PREFIX(ES)					
MEANING	to make someone or something be in a particular state or have a particular quality	to do something with someone else as an equal or with less responsibility	the opposite or lack of something	again or back to a former state	not or without
EXAMPLES					

3. Read a shared mobility principle and underline three words formed by different prefixes from the ones in activity 2. Then match each prefix with its corresponding meaning.

"2. WE PRIORITIZE PEOPLE OVER VEHICLES.

The mobility of people and not vehicles shall be in the center of transportation planning and decision-making. Cities shall prioritize walking, cycling, public transportation, and other efficient shared mobility, as well as their interconnectivity. Cities shall discourage the use of cars, single-passenger taxis, and other oversized vehicles transporting one person."

Adapted from www.sharedmobilityprinciples.org. Accessed on September 20, 2018.

a. _____ : shows an opposite or negative

b. _____ : between or involving two or more different things, places, or people

c. _____ : too much

LANGUAGE IN USE 1

Unit 2

MODAL VERBS *CAN* and *COULD*

1. Work in pairs. Compare these excerpts from the article on page 18. Then complete the sentences with *can*, *can't*, *could*, and *couldn't*.

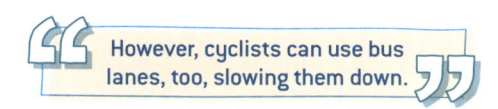

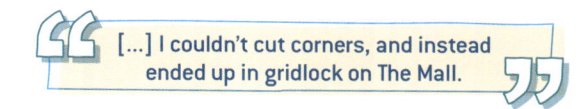

> "However, cyclists can use bus lanes, too, slowing them down."

> "[...] I couldn't cut corners, and instead ended up in gridlock on The Mall."

Can expresses what the speaker believes is a permission, a general truth or a strong possibility.

Could does not express a general truth. The speaker only wants to express a possibility or impossibility.

As seen in *Expand 1*, the modal verb *can* is used in the present. _____ is the past of _____. It is used to talk about an ability in the past or a possibility.

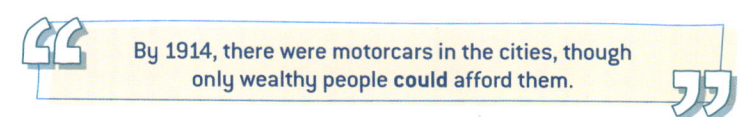

> "By 1914, there were motorcars in the cities, though only wealthy people **could** afford them."

_____ is the short form of *cannot*; _____ is the short form of *could not*. We use *couldn't* when we refer to a past impossibility, a past inability, or a polite present inability.

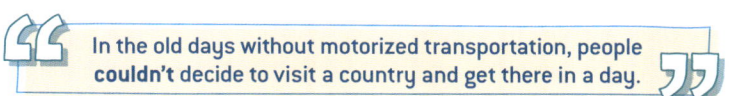

> "In the old days without motorized transportation, people **couldn't** decide to visit a country and get there in a day."

Could is also used to make suggestions and polite offers.

> "You **could** go from Tirano to Chur by train, if you are not in a hurry. The view is amazing. I **could** help you with the train ticket."

2. Read the comic strips below and complete them with the words from the box. There is an extra option.

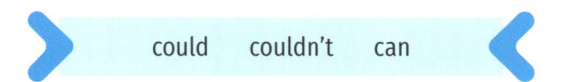

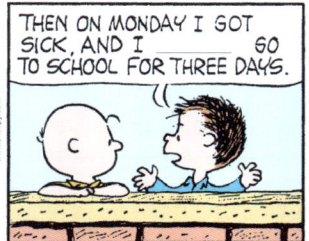

> could   couldn't   can

Comic 1 (Peanuts):
- Panel 1: "NOTHING MAKES ME MORE MAD THAN WASTING A GOOD HAIRCUT!"
- Panel 2: "LAST SATURDAY I GOT A HAIRCUT SO I'D LOOK NICE FOR SCHOOL MONDAY MORNING.."
- Panel 3: "THEN ON MONDAY I GOT SICK, AND I _____ GO TO SCHOOL FOR THREE DAYS."
- Panel 4: "I WASTED A GOOD HAIRCUT!"

Extracted from www.gocomics.com/peanuts/1962/09/21. Accessed on September 20, 2018.

Comic 2 (Nemi):
- Panel 4: "WELL, LEAST ONE OF US _____ GO HOME EARLY."

Extracted from http://www.bullspress.com/produkter-tjanster/produkter-tjanster/nemi/. Accessed on September 20, 2018.

EXPAND YOUR READING

1. Scan the text and answer: Where was it published? Is the full text presented here?

_____

> www.dailymail.co.uk/wires/afp/article-5604689/With-bikes-transit-Uber-unveils-new-vision-urban-transport.html
>
> ## With bikes, transit, Uber *unveils* urban transportation vision
>
> By AFP   PUBLISHED: 18:57 BST, 11 April 2018 | UPDATED: 20:57 BST, 11 April 2018
>
> Uber said Wednesday it plans to add mass transit, bike-sharing, and other options to its mobile app, as it unveiled a vision for urban transportation that goes well **beyond** its **core** ridesharing offer.
>
> Chief executive Dara Khosrowshahi presented the plans during a visit to Washington, where he said the **ride-hailing** pioneer would **seek** a more diversified model offering various transportation options, including car rentals on a partner **peer-to-peer** service.
>
> "More and more, Uber is not just going to be about taking a car, but is about moving from point A to point B in the best way," Khosrowshahi told an event in the newly launched Uber driver center in the US capital.
>
> Khosrowshahi said the Uber app would start including locations for electric bikes from its newly **acquired** bike-sharing group Jump, which **currently** operates in Washington and San Francisco.
>
> Uber also announced a partnership with the peer-to-peer car-sharing service Getaround to allow users to rent vehicles from individual owners, with a launch planned later this month in San Francisco.
>
> The service will be labeled Uber Rent. "You can use your Uber app if you need a car and you want to drive yourself, if you need a car for an hour, a day," the Uber chief said.
>
> For mass transit, the San Francisco startup said it would allow app users to see various options and would **launch** a partnership with e-ticketing service Masabi that would eventually allow the Uber app to be used instead of tickets or passes.
>
> Masabi has partnerships with transit systems in Boston, Los Angeles, Las Vegas, and New York, as well as train and transit operators in Europe.
>
> Khosrowshahi said the new plans would help Uber offer solutions for an increasingly urban world population and reduce the need for car ownership.
>
> […]
>
> Extracted from www.dailymail.co.uk/wires/afp/article-5604689/With-bikes-transit-Uber-unveils-new-vision-urban-transport.html. Accessed on September 20, 2018.

2. Check (✓) the sentences that are true about the news report you have just read.
- **a.** (   ) It is clear, objective, and personal.
- **b.** (   ) Paragraphs are brief, and they often consist of a few sentences or a single sentence.
- **c.** (   ) It counts on quotations, which give the text strength and credibility.
- **d.** (   ) The headline is long, and it does not tell the reader what the story is about.
- **e.** (   ) It does not mention who wrote the article.

3. News reports aim at informing readers about daily facts or events. In pairs, summarize the main information provided in the piece of news above.

_____

_____

_____

LANGUAGE IN USE 2

Unit 2

ZERO and FIRST CONDITIONALS

1. Study the excerpts below. Then match the columns.

Zero conditional

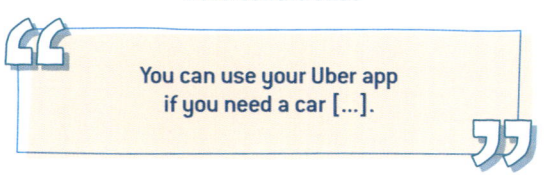

> You can use your Uber app if you need a car [...].

First conditional

> If Uber adds electric bikes to its services, users will have more options to get around.

a. These excerpts express...
b. They are known as...
c. They are often...
d. Conditional sentences consist of...
e. The zero conditional...
f. The first conditional...
g. The zero conditional is formed by...
h. The first conditional is formed by...

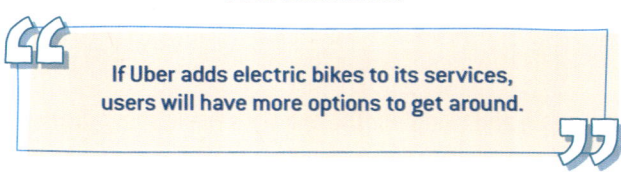

( ) conditional sentences or *if*- clauses.
( ) introduced by the word *if*.
( ) *if* + simple present + simple future, modal verb with future reference, or imperative form.
( ) expresses something that is true now or always.
( ) *if* + simple present or a modal verb + simple present.
( ) an imagined situation or condition and the possible result of that situation.
( ) reflects a realistic possibility.
( ) a main clause and a conditional dependent clause.

2. Complete the text with the verbs in parentheses. Use the appropriate conditional structure.

[...]

Choose the best option: cycling and walking

It's a no-brainer: burning our personal energy rather than **fossil fuels** is the most sustainable way to get around – and good for our health and **hip pockets**, too. But few Australians regularly choose active travel, like walking or cycling to work or study.

Again, the **sheer** size of our country is partly to blame. But if you _____ (live) close to work, active transportation is attractive when the math _____ (be) considered. "Owning and operating a car costs about $225 per week, not including parking," the Bicycle Queensland chief executive, Anne Savage, says. "If you _____ (ride) 10km to and from work regularly, it _____ (save) the average household at least $1,700 per year in transportation costs, and it _____ (reduce) **greenhouse gas** emissions by 1.5 tons annually." If you _____ (ride) a bike to work, it _____ dramatically _____ (modal verb for possibility, lower) the risk of heart disease and cancer, Savage says.

These days, one doesn't even need to own a bike. Sharing schemes such as Reddy Go, oBike, ofo, and mobike all operate via mobile phone apps, while many major cities also offer local sharing systems. And if going up hills _____ (discourage) you, _____ (consider) electric bikes (ideally if you have solar power at home for recharging).

Going carless won't always be possible, but if you _____ (consider) more sustainable modes of transportation, it _____ (modal verb for possibility, make) a big difference.

[...]

Adapted from www.theguardian.com/lifeandstyle/2018/mar/18/car-share-public-transport-and-walking-better-ways-to-get-from-a-to-b.
Accessed on September 20, 2018.

LISTENING COMPREHENSION

1. Listen to a piece of news and check (✓) the alternative that best describes what it is about.
   a. (   ) The advances in self-driving vehicles.
   b. (   ) The investments Uber has been making in self-driving vehicles.
   c. (   ) An accident caused by a self-driving vehicle that made Uber stop using them.
   d. (   ) A few accidents caused by self-driving vehicles that were under trial.

2. Listen again and complete the text with the missing words.

   A self-driving car has killed a pedestrian for the first time ever.

   The _____ car, operated by Uber, struck a pedestrian and killed them in what is thought to be the first death of its kind. The autonomous taxi was operating as part of a trial that Uber hoped would represent the future, but has now been suspended.
   At the time of the accident, the car was driving itself in autonomous mode, Tempe police said. There was a _____ operator behind the wheel, but they weren't in control of the car at the time of the crash.
   […]
   A spokesman for Uber Technologies Inc. said the company was _____ its North American tests.
   People have died in crashes involving vehicles that are driving themselves before. But this is thought to be the first time that a pedestrian has died after being hit by a self-driving vehicle.
   Uber's autonomous taxis, like the self-driving cars made by other companies, use a series of sensors built into the car to spot _____, cyclists, and other cars, feeding that into a computer that is able to steer and accelerate. Until recently, they have required a real person to be sat in the front of the car and ready to take over – but recently California officials approved the testing of such vehicles without humans in the front _____.
   […]
   The cars have also been involved in smaller issues, such as running red lights.

   Adapted from www.independent.co.uk/life-style/gadgets-and-tech/news/uber-self-driving-car-killed-pedestrian-death-tempe-arizona-autonomous-vehicle-a8263921.html.
   Accessed on October 5, 2018.

3. Do you think self-driving cars should be given another try after safety adjustments? In your opinion, how will transportation and traffic change after self-driving vehicles? Discuss your ideas with your classmates and teacher.

›› EXPAND YOUR HORIZONS ››››

Check (✓) the column that best describes your opinion about each statement. Then discuss your answers with your classmates and teacher, justifying your point of view.

	I agree.	I'm not sure.	I disagree.
a. Fast-moving trends have been influencing urban mobility.			
b. Advances in autonomous driving will definitely solve road-safety concerns.			
c. The first truly autonomous cars will probably cost a fortune, so not many people will buy them.			

REVIEW 1

Units 1 and 2

1. Skim the text and identify its target audience. *Skimming to identify target audience*

---

www.oecd.org/brazil/innovation-urban-mobility-brazil.htm

OECD

Business brief: Innovation and urban mobility in Brazil

"What is the city but the people?" asked Shakespeare in *Coriolanus*. All city planning focuses on people and the quality of life. The big cities in Brazil took shape from the 1950s, when the country's population **amounted** to approximately 52 million inhabitants, only 36.2% of whom lived in cities. The development focus during the post-war period, led by the modernist **canons** that guided the conception of Brasília, **spread** across numerous cities where the automobile was the leading actor, and was supported by investments all over the country to build roads and other infrastructure, such as ports, railroads, and electric power plants.

[...]

It is obvious that today's urban population of over 160 million, with the rate of urbanization **standing at** 84.4%, is stimulating massive expansion, with ever-increasing distances and extremely high costs to attend to for public transportation networks. The Brazilian government's policies **remain** quite unclear on this issue, and few of Brazil's cities have effective urban-mobility plans. On the other hand, the automobile industry delivers 200,000 vehicles to the market every month. This perpetuates the car/city combination, while forcing planners to find solutions for sustainable mobility that are compatible with the extending urban space.

[...]

The fundamental starting points for proper integrated city planning, and consequently mobility, are first, a deep familiarity with the clear social and economic profiles of the city's inhabitants (together with their expectations and demands regarding work, education, and health), and second, to know the origin and destination of their journeys. Sustainable planning of mobility depends basically on city planning, and this requires a social, participative approach that reaches beyond how to manage just the city itself.

[...]

Brazil was a pioneer in creating the BRT (Bus Rapid Transport), with exclusive corridors and boarding stations that reduce waiting times for commuters. Based on TOD (Transit-Oriented Development), a worldwide city planning approach that combines walking, cycling, and public transportation spaces with compact, well-serviced, population centers, this medium-size system is far less costly than building subway lines. **Nevertheless**, the BRT systems, which can use sustainable fuels like biodiesel or electric power, still need infrastructure work to guarantee large-scale **viability**.

[...]

Integrated planning, supported by clear public policies, new technologies, and ways to **safeguard** the environment, is the **path** towards sustainable mobility in cities in Brazil, as elsewhere.

Visit http://fgvprojetos.fgv.br/

Sponsored by **FGV PROJETOS**

Adapted from www.oecd.org/brazil/innovation-urban-mobility-brazil.htm. Accessed on July 25, 2018.

---

2. Read the text in activity 1 carefully and check (✓) the correct statements. *Understanding details*

a. ( ) BRT systems first started in Brazil, but they lack the appropriate infrastructure to work efficiently.

b. ( ) City planning and a social, participative approach are extremely important for sustainable mobility in Brazilian cities.

c. ( ) The Brazilian government's policies have worked with well-structured and efficient urban-mobility plans.

3. Using your own words, explain the "car/city combination" mentioned in the second paragraph of the text.

4. In "Nevertheless, the BRT systems, which *can* use sustainable fuels like biodiesel or electric power, still need infrastructure work to guarantee large-scale viability," what does the modal verb in italics indicate?

_____

5. Read an extract that was omitted from the text on page 25 and fill in the blanks with the verbs *increase* and *help* in the present perfect tense.

> "[...]
>
> Meanwhile, the use of technologies to control and oversee transit _____ to improve the quality of city commuting. The centers for monitoring with cameras and GPS localization devices on collective vehicles, as well as collaborative applications that commuters use, such as Waze and Google Maps, on about 7 million smartphones _____ the efficiency of commuting. Not only smartphones, but also vehicles and objects that rely on tiny sensors to provide masses of data, can help make mobility more efficient.
>
> [...]"

Adapted from www.oecd.org/brazil/innovation-urban-mobility-brazil.htm. Accessed on July 26, 2018.

6. Read the comic strip below. Then circle the completed actions or states in the past and underline the past ongoing action.

Grand Avenue by Mike Thompson

Extracted from www.gocomics.com/grand-avenue/2013/12/03. Accessed on July 26, 2018.

7. Answer the questions about the comic strip above.

a. What **did** Grandma **say** she **was doing** in the video?

_____

b. Did Grandma really **want** to post the video?

_____

c. What **did** Gradma **want** to do?

_____

d. Why **did** the kids **say** that they **were getting off** the computer?

_____

8. Talk to a classmate about things you did last weekend. Then write two things that you both did last weekend.

_____
_____

UNIT 3
Generation Z: Conservative or Liberal?

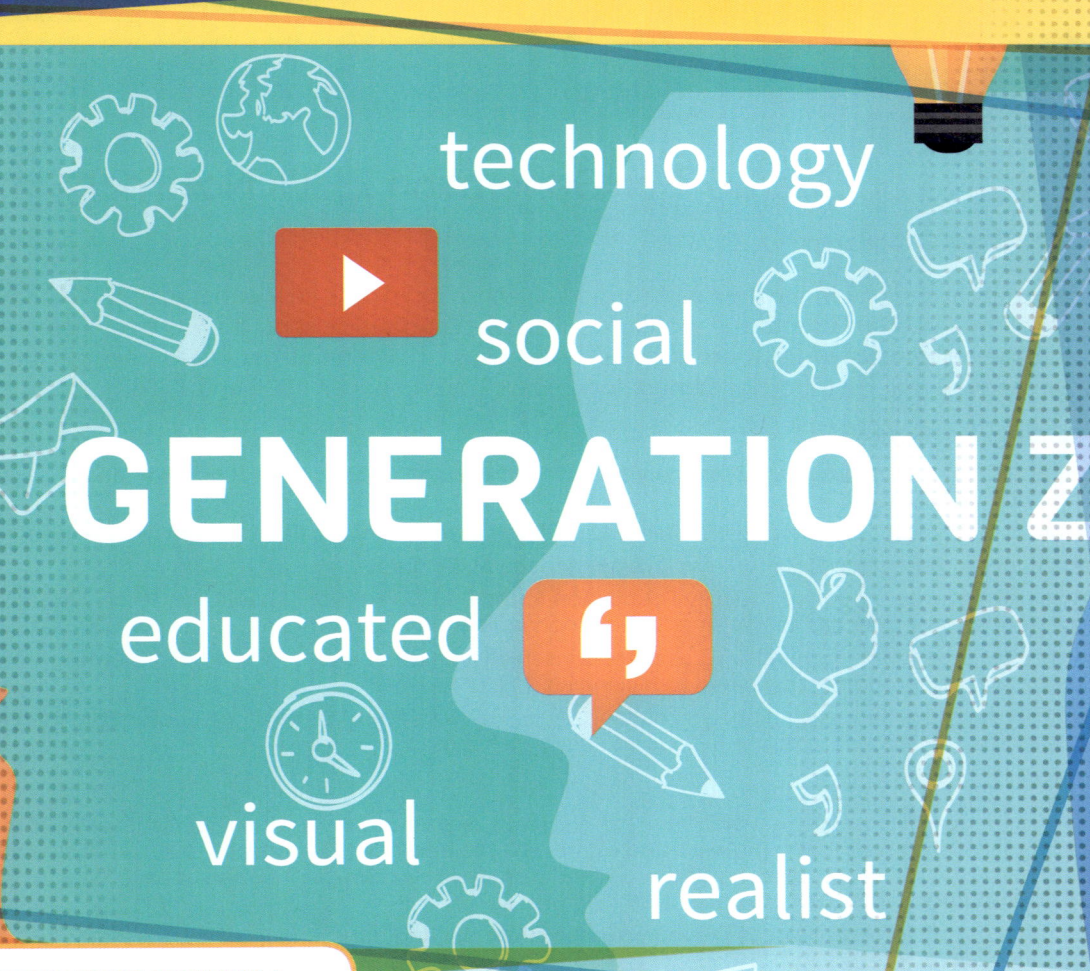

technology

social

GENERATION Z

educated

visual

realist

▶ IN THIS UNIT YOU WILL...
- take part in discussions about Generation Z;
- exchange ideas about what characterizes Generation Z and other generations;
- learn how to use defining relative clauses;
- learn how to use the linking word *so*.

LEAD OFF

- What is the so-called Generation Z or iGeneration?
- What clear differences can you notice between your generation and your parents'?
- What influences the values, styles, and interests of a generation?
- Do you consider yourself conservative or liberal? Why?

READING

» BEFORE READING

Read the title of the text below. List everything that comes to your mind about this theme.   *Brainstorming*

_____

_____

» WHILE READING

Identifying the author's perspective

Read the text and examine how the author feels about the topic she is writing about. What opinions or beliefs are evident?

---

huffingtonpost.com/entry/conservative-or-liberal-its-not-that-simple-with_us_59ea34f7e4b034105edd4e32

Conservative or Liberal? For Generation Z, It's Not That Simple

10/20/2017 01:48 pm ET **Updated** Oct 20, 2017

Anne Loehr, Contributor
Expert in Preparing Leaders for the Workforce of the future

It might be time for the Millennial media obsession to wind down as a new generation inches up in age and takes their first baby steps into the workforce. I'm talking about Generation Z, the next demographic **cohort** after the Millennials. While there is no set consensus on when this generation begins, it is commonly believed that members of Generation Z were born between 1998 and 2001.

Is Generation Z Conservative?

- A 2016 American study found that while only 18% of Millennials attended church, church attendance was 41% among Generation Z.
- **Polls** found eight out of ten members of Gen Z considered themselves "fiscally conservative."
- In certain areas, Generation Z is more risk-averse than the Millennials. [...]
- A 2016 study done by the Annie E. Casey Foundation found that Generation Z had lower teen pregnancy rates, less substance abuse, and higher on-time high school graduation rates compared to Millennials.
- Business Insider describes Generation Z as more conservative, more money-oriented, more **entrepreneurial** and **pragmatic** about money compared to Millennials. [...]
- One British study conducted by global consultancy firm, The Gild, found Generation Z participants ten times more likely than Millennials to dislike tattoos and body piercings.

Is Generation Z Liberal?

- Gen Z is more diverse than any generation. Frank N. Magid estimates that Gen Z is 55% Caucasian, 24% Hispanic, 14% African American, 4% Asian, and 4% mixed race or other. He also states that Gen Z exhibits positive feelings about ethnic diversity in the U.S. and is more likely than older generations to have social circles that include different ethnic groups, races, and religions. [...]
- Generation Z is more liberal in areas like marijuana legalization, and transgender issues, according to a study done by The Gild. [...]
- 75% of Gen Z support same sex marriage. They're more likely to have grown up around same sex parents, and **therefore** don't see this as unusual—or illegal.
- 76% are concerned about global warming. [...]
- It has been reported that Generation Z is, "the least likely to believe that there is such a thing as the American Dream."

[...]

It's Time to Rethink What Divides Us

So, which is it? How do we categorize a generation that presents common ideals of both conservatives and liberals? Maybe we don't. Maybe we need to rethink what it is to be "conservative" and "liberal" and consider that in the future the distinction will be different. This generation just might **disrupt** the huge US bipartisan divide we are experiencing now. And maybe we would be better for it.

Adapted from www.huffingtonpost.com/entry/conservative-or-liberal-its-not-that-simple-with_us_59ea34f7e4b034105edd4e32. Accessed on July 13, 2018.

Unit 3

>> AFTER READING

1. What clause best states the gist of the text? *Understanding main ideas*

   a. ( ) To discredit theories about Generation Z and persuade the reader to believe Generation Z is complicated and pragmatic at the same time when it comes to Americans.

   b. ( ) To summarize the reasons why Generation Z might be considered conservative or liberal and advocate a reconsideration of what it is to be conservative and liberal in the US.

2. Decide whether the excerpts below refer to conservative (C) or liberal (L) concepts, according to the text. *Understanding details*

   a. ( ) "Over a third of Gen Z respondents also strongly agreed that gender did not define a person as much as it used to."

   b. ( ) "In 2013, 66% of teenagers had tried alcohol, down from 82% in 1991."

   c. ( ) "This makes sense considering the amount of environmental disasters they've **witnessed** so far, including the 2013 Colorado forest fires (most destructive wildfires in history,) tornado in Joplin, Missouri in 2011 (single deadliest tornado in U.S. history since the advent of modern weather forecasting), the flooding that devastated the Mississippi river valley (one of largest and most damaging **floods** recorded in the past century) and many more."

   Adapted from www.huffingtonpost.com/entry/conservative-or-liberal-its-not-that-simple-with_us_59ea34f7e4b034105edd4e32. Accessed on July 13, 2018.

3. In your opinion, can we categorize Generation Z as either conservative or liberal? Explain.

EXPAND YOUR VOCABULARY

1. Find the alternative that best explains each word or expression in bold in the excerpts below.

   a. "It might be time for the Millennial media obsession to **wind down** as a new generation inches up in age and takes their first baby steps into the workforce."

   b. "In certain areas, Generation Z is more **risk-averse** than the Millennials."

   c. "One British study conducted by global consultancy firm, The Gild, found Gen Z participants ten times more **likely** than Millennials to dislike tattoos and body piercings."

   d. "Generation Z is more liberal in areas like marijuana legalization, and transgender **issues**, according to a study done by The Gild."

   e. "76% are **concerned about** global warming."

   f. "This generation just might disrupt the huge U.S. **bipartisan** divide we are experiencing now."

   ( ) a subject or problem that is often discussed or argued about, especially a social or political matter that affects the interests of a lot of people

   ( ) involving two political parties, especially parties with opposing views

   ( ) to gradually reduce the work of a business or organization so that it can be closed down completely

   ( ) something that will probably happen or is probably true

   ( ) worried about something

   ( ) not willing to take risks

   Extracted from www.ldoceonline.com. Accessed on July 13, 2018.

2. How does the cartoon below relate to the text on page 28? What are some themes that people from different generations disagree on? What changes in traditional values contribute to a generation gap? Work in pairs and write your answers.

VOCABULARY IN USE

1. Pay attention to another excerpt from the text "Conservative or Liberal? For Generation Z, It's Not That Simple." Observe that the part in bold shows a collocation with the verb *make*. Check (✓) the correct meaning conveyed by that combination.

> This **makes sense** considering members of Generation Z have watched their parents live through the second worst economic decline in American history (starting in 2008), and have witnessed the aftermath of mass layoffs and rampant foreclosures.

a. ( ) find out if something is true or check that something has been done
b. ( ) have a clear meaning and be easy to understand
c. ( ) promise to do something or behave in a particular way

Extracted from www.ldoceonline.com. Accessed on July 13, 2018.

The verb *make* can be confusing in English because its meaning is similar to the meaning of the verb *do*, but they are combined with different words. These combinations are called *collocations*. They refer to words that often go together.

2. Can you figure out new collocations with the verbs *make* and *do*? Complete the chart with the words from the box. Then use one collocation from each column to complete the texts.

a difference	a favor	an effort	an offer
business	friends	good	harm	money
noise	(my) nails	exercise

DO	MAKE

a. **Millennials want job stability, Gen Z wants passion**

[...]

Generation Z is "The Change Generation," because all of the recent global events increase their desire to _____ in their future careers — and it also exacerbates their need for more "mental health support" from their employers, according to Lovell Corp.'s "2017 Change Generation Report: How Millennials and Generation Z Are Redefining Work."

Extracted from www.benefitspro.com/2017/11/21/millennials-want-job-stability-gen-z-wants-passion/?slreturn=20180613095527. Accessed on July 13, 2018.

b. **"iGen" author on how digital devices are slowing the development of today's kids**

[...]

"Anything that's done with a screen: texting, social media, TV, online, computer games — all of those are correlated with lower happiness," Twenge said. "The smartphone's one of the keys in explaining why they [iGen] are so different from Millennials. So, for example, their mental health has really trended downwards starting around 2012."

Despite this correlation, Twenge said up to an hour and a half a day of screen time likely won't _____, but that "two hours and beyond—that's when you start to see a link to these mental health issues."

[...]

Extracted from www.cbsnews.com/news/igen-author-effect-of-digital-devices-on-generation-born-1995-to-2012. Accessed on July 13, 2018.

3. Answer the questions below. Use collocations with *make* and *do* in your answers. Compare your answers with a classmate's and explain your opinions.

a. Some define the super-connected iGens as less happy and more unprepared for adulthood. How would that affect their relationships at all levels?

_____
_____
_____

b. Assuming that today's teens are better behaved than in past generations, what factors contribute to this?

_____
_____
_____

c. In your opinion, what are iGens' worries? What pressures do they suffer? Do you share those same feelings?

_____
_____

LANGUAGE IN USE 1

Unit 3

RELATIVE CLAUSES

1. The excerpt below was extracted from the text on page 28. Read it and answer: what does the relative pronoun in bold refer to? Why was it used?

   > How do we categorize a generation **that** presents common ideals of both conservatives and liberals?

2. Use the words from the box to complete the information about relative clauses.

   > person   possession   relative   which   who

   a. Relative clauses can be defining or non-defining. Defining relative clauses such as the one in activity 1 often begin with a _____ pronoun (*who, that, which, whose, where, when*) and provide specific information to identify or define the _____ or thing we are talking about.

   b. In defining relative clauses, we can use _____ or *that* to talk about people, with no difference in meaning, although *who* is often preferred in more formal contexts.

   c. *That* or _____ are used to talk about things and again *that* is mostly used in more informal contexts. The relative pronouns *where, when,* and *whose* refer to places, time, and _____, respectively.

3. Now read another excerpt from the text on page 28 and check (✓) the correct alternative to complete the sentence that follows.

   > This generation just might disrupt the huge U.S. bipartisan divide we are experiencing now.

   It is possible to reduce or simplify defining relative clauses in various forms, for example, omitting the relative pronoun. In the excerpt above, it is possible to omit the relative pronoun *that* or *which* after the word *divide* because…

   a. (   ) it is the subject of the verb form *are experiencing*.

   b. (   ) it is the object of the verb form *are experiencing*.

4. Match the relative clauses with their corresponding main clauses and learn more about the previous and present generations.

   a. The Greatest Generation (1901–1924) grew up without modern conveniences…
   b. The Silent Generation (1924–1945) was a period…
   c. Baby Boomers (1946–1964) had rock and roll, miniskirts, and Barbie™ dolls. They were the ones…
   d. Generation X (1965–1980) grew up street-smart but lonely because they're the kids…
   e. Generation Y or Millennials (early 1980s—early 2000s) are those from a technological and globalized world…
   f. Generation Z (1995—) has never known a world…

   (   ) **where** price comparisons and product information are common.
   (   ) **when** children had no voice. They were seen, but they were not heard.
   (   ) **whose** parents often divorced or were more worried about their careers.
   (   ) **which** make our lives much easier, such as refrigerators, air conditioning, TV etc.
   (   ) **who** fought the Cold War and pulled the Berlin Wall down.
   (   ) **that** doesn't depend on computers and cell phones.

   Based on http://fourhooks.com/marketing/the-generation-guide-millennials-gen-x-y-z-and-baby-boomers-art5910718593. Accessed on July 14, 2018.

5. Work in pairs. Which generation from the ones listed in activity 4 do you find most interesting? Justify your choice. Then write two new sentences about it. Use relative clauses.

EXPAND YOUR READING

1. Read psychology professor Dr. Jean Twenge's interview about her book on the iGeneration (also known as Generation Z) and relate it to the text on page 28. Then underline the information that matches your reality and aspirations as an iGeneration teen.

> **Move Over, Millennials: How 'iGen' Is Different From Any Other Generation**
> By: Angie Marcos
> 8/22/2017
> [...]
> We sat down to ask Twenge what we should know about the iGen children, teens, and young adults — how they're different, what they care about, and how they'll make their mark on the world.
>
> **Q: How is iGen different from their Millennial predecessors and other generations before them?**
> **Dr. Jean Twenge:** iGen was born between 1995 and 2012, so they are the first generation to spend their entire adolescence with a smartphone; this has had ripple effects across many areas of their lives. As teens especially, they spend their time differently from any generation before them.
> iGen is more practical in their work attitudes than Millennials were at the same age. They are more **willing** to work overtime to do a good job and less likely to have **unrealistically** high expectations.
> However, due to their slow and protected **upbringing**, they are also less independent. iGen arrives at college with less experience with adult situations — including sex and alcohol — thus, they may not know how to handle them. Compared to previous generations, iGen high school seniors are less likely to drive, work, drink alcohol, date, have sex, or go out without their parents. This is part of a broader cultural **trend** toward growing up more slowly and taking longer to become an adult.
>
> **Q: What is the significance of iGen being the first generation to spend their entire adolescence on a smartphone?**
> **Dr. Twenge:** Around 2012, I started to notice big shifts in the large national surveys of the teens and young adults I use in my research. Depression and **loneliness** started to rise sharply and soon reached all-time highs.
> [...]
>
> **Q: According to your book, iGen is more interested in safety and tolerance than any other generation. You also write that they "have no patience for inequality." Where do this generation's values come from?**
> **Dr. Twenge:** iGen was born into a more individualistic culture than previous generations, one that favors the self more and social rules less. [This culture] treats people as individuals instead of as members of groups, and thus promotes equality for all. This is a central tenet of individualism and iGen reflects that.
> [...]
>
> **Q: How does iGen see higher education?**
> **Dr. Twenge:** iGen is more likely than previous generations to go to college to get a good job and less likely to go to get an "education." Although we have to bring students around to the idea of the importance of education for its own sake, we also have to keep their practical goals in mind when reaching out to them and teaching them.
> iGen brings unique experiences to the classroom. As just one example, they have spent much more time online and much less time reading books than previous generations. That alone means we have to think about teaching them differently.

Adapted from www2.calstate.edu/csu-system/news/Pages/Move-Over-Millennials-How-iGen-Is-Different-Than-Any-Other-Generation-.aspx. Accessed on July 13, 2018.

2. Choose the correct alternatives in parentheses to complete the statements about interviews.

a. Interviews are very popular in _____ (the news / museum brochures), but they are also seen in other contexts such as research and entertainment, for instance.

b. They are essentially _____ (a written / an oral) genre. Written interviews often derive from a transcription of an oral interaction.

c. Interviews are organized with _____ (quotations / questions) and answers between one or more interviewers and interviewees.

d. There may be a short passage before the interview to _____ (introduce / criticize) the interviewee and mention his/her credentials.

LANGUAGE IN USE 2

Unit 3

CAUSE AND RESULT — THE USE OF SO

1. Read an excerpt from the interview on page 32 and compare it to two other excerpts from the text on page 28. Which linking word / conjunction do they have in common?

   > iGen was born between 1995 and 2012, so they are the first generation to spend their entire adolescence with a smartphone.

   > It's important to note that generational lines are not based on science, so clear definitions are not always available.

   > So, which is it? How do we categorize a generation that presents common ideals of both conservatives and liberals?

2. What is the word you identified in the excerpts above commonly used for? Underline the correct alternatives.

   a. To introduce clauses of result or decision.
   b. To link contrasting ideas.
   c. To connect sentences and make discourse more coherent.
   d. To introduce a series of examples referring to previously stated ideas.
   e. To express logical relations between ideas.

3. The linking word *so* was omitted once in the text below. Choose the sentence from which it was omitted and rewrite the sentence inserting it.

   > Generation Z Under Academic Pressure
   > […]
   > **(a)** We also learned from both African-American and Hispanic participants that getting a four-year degree has been preached to them as the "only option" to be successful — especially if they are to be the first in their families to graduate from college. **(b)** And at their high schools, tours were being organized to visit four-year degree-conferring colleges but no other options. **(c)** These kids weren't considering community college to hold education costs down nor were they exposed to trade schools. […]
   >
   > Adapted from www.mediapost.com/publications/article/309010/generation-z-under-academic-pressure.html. Accessed on July 15, 2018.

4. Work in pairs. Now read these other sentences, paying attention to the structures in bold. Then answer the questions.

   > Technology is **so essential** to iGens **that** we end up picturing them as the multi-screening and multi-tasking generation.

   > There is **so much** pressure on teenagers nowadays **that** some of them might not be able to just stand, stare, and value simple aspects of their lives.

   a. Does the structure *so + adjective* before the *that-clause* in the first sentence express concession or cause and effect?

   b. What does the structure *so + quantifier (much)* before the *that-clause* in the second sentence indicate?

   c. In this structure, the word *so* can be followed by either an adjective or an adverb. What kind of word is it in the first sentence? How about in the second sentence?

5. Read the excerpt, paying attention to the sentence in italics, to identify cause and effect. In pairs, discuss whether it is true for you and your friends.

   > […] The desire for Gen Z to stay connected constantly has shaped the way they choose to communicate. For Gen Z, communication is fluid and continual, with online communication seamlessly flowing on from any face-to-face interaction and vice versa—there is no real barrier or demarcation between online and offline. *Social media is now so integrated into everyday life that it is no longer considered separate from other forms of interaction*, and many find it easier to communicate online with their peers and social network than they do face to face. […]
   >
   > Adapted from https://clairemadden.com/10-reasons-generation-z-use-social-media-part-1. Accessed on July 15, 2018.

   a. Cause: _____

   b. Effect: _____

LISTENING COMPREHENSION

1. Think of the name of different generations and list characteristics you think they have. Exchange ideas with a classmate.

   _____
   _____
   _____

2. **06** Listen to part of a guide to generations. Are any of the generations you listed in activity 1 mentioned?

   _____

3. **07** Listen again carefully, underline the mistakes in the sentences below, and rewrite them according to the recording.

   a. Generation Z is smarter and more reckless than Gen Y.
   _____
   _____

   b. Gen Z likes to spend their money.
   _____
   _____

   c. Generation Z is described as the second tribe of digital natives.
   _____
   _____

   d. Generation Y, or Millenials, are those born until 1990.
   _____
   _____

   e. Generation X has spent too little of their adulthood sitting around in coffee shops.
   _____
   _____

4. Work with a partner and discuss the questions below. Then share your opinions with your classmates.

   a. Do you think the same generation labeling applies to generations throughout the world, in developed and developing countries, for example? Why (not)?

   b. What can we do to overcome generation gaps in different contexts, such as at home and at school?

   c. If you could record one important message for the generations to come, what would it be? Justify your answer.

›› EXPAND YOUR HORIZONS ››››

Check (✓) the column that best describes your opinion about each statement. Then discuss your answers with your classmates and teacher, justifying your point of view.

	I agree.	I'm not sure.	I disagree.
a. Labeling Generation Z as conservative, liberal, conventional, or modern depends on the perspective of the person doing the analysis.			
b. Generation gaps are inevitable and the reason why they occur is because of differences in psychological and behavioral patterns.			
c. All generations suffer different pressures throughout their lives. What really changes is the way that each generation deals with pressure.			

UNIT 4
What's Going Abroad Like?

IN THIS UNIT YOU WILL...
- exchange ideas about traveling to undiscovered destinations;
- talk about responsible travel;
- understand the difference between *need to* and *have to*;
- learn what tag questions are and how to use them.

LEAD OFF

- How can you relate the picture to the title of the unit?
- What feelings can a teenager in that situation have?
- In your opinion, what makes people leave their countries to go after opportunities overseas?

READING

BEFORE READING

Read the title of the blog post. What do you think the text is about? Exchange ideas with a classmate.

Predicting

WHILE READING

Skim the article to check your predictions. Then read the whole text and do the activities that follow.

Skimming to check predictions

TRAVEL TIPS | ABOUT | BLOG | DESTINATIONS | RESOURCES | COMMUNITY | MEDIA SCHOOL

Undiscovered destinations: Now *that's* what I call off the beaten track

By TOM CHESSYRE
UPDATED: 15:23 GMT, 25 March 2009

Do not expect the Costa del Sol, Florida or the French Riviera when you book a break with **perhaps** the most adventurous of all Britain's tour operators - Undiscovered Destinations.

This company's name does what it says, with no **messing** around. A list of a few of the countries **featured** in its holidays gives a **flavor** of what is offered: Burma, East Timor, Ethiopia, Sierra Leone, Papua New Guinea, Comoros and Sudan. It was set up two years ago by Jim Louth, a former employee of mass-market travel agent Trailfinders, who once lived in Brazil and has traveled to more than 80 countries. 'I wanted to do something a little bit different,' he says, in rather an **understatement**. 'People are incredibly well traveled these days and they're really looking to go off the beaten track.

There are tour operators like Exodus and Explore that offer adventures but, with respect to them, they've become a bit mainstream and are not as challenging as they used to be.' One of his favorite trips is to Angola, on the west coast of southern Africa. Few tourists have visited the country, which was engaged in a bloody 27-year civil war until 2002, when a ceasefire brought an end to the violence and a chance for more than four million refugees to return home.

Undiscovered Destinations regards its 17-day expedition as 'pioneering', as it was the first to offer group holidays in the country. The tour is in four-wheel-drive, off-road vehicles - 'There is no road in most places so it has to be off-road,' says Louth - with most nights spent camping. The country is so unused to tourists that many people have never seen white faces before and visits to local Himba villages have to be spontaneous, as there are few phones to make contact in advance. This is all part of the appeal, says Louth. 'Sure, you can visit Himba tribes in Namibia [directly south of Angola], but everything there is a bit stage-managed. In Angola it's much more real.'

The scenery is a mixture of bush and desert - with the sands of the Skeleton Coast of Namibia extending into Angola. Trips are arranged to local markets, volcanic fissures, coffee-growing regions and **pristine** beaches (where great seafood is served at restaurants or cooked at night on camp fires). A highlight is the journey to Kalandula Falls, one of Africa's largest waterfalls. There is also a drive through Kissama National Park, where guides explain Operation Noah's Ark, a project to relocate elephants from overcrowded parts of Botswana and South Africa to Angola. It can get bumpy - there are 'boneshaking' rides across rugged **terrain**. But it is not exhausting; most of Undiscovered Destinations' customers are aged over 50 and many are retired. Angola, however, is not cheap. This is because there is a shortage of both vehicles and English-speaking guides, according to Louth. The country, a former Portuguese colony that gained independence in 1975, makes most of its money from diamonds and petroleum, not from tourists.

The Foreign Office says it is unsafe to visit the ironically named Democratic Republic of Congo, to the north, where Joseph Conrad set The Heart Of Darkness. But Angola is OK. 'For those who like their travel on the wild side, it has everything,' says Louth.

Adapted from www.dailymail.co.uk/travel/article-1163915/Undiscovered-destinations-Now-thats-I-beaten-track.html. Accessed on November 20, 2018.

>> AFTER READING

1 Check (✓) the statement that best describes the main purpose of the writer.

Determining the author's purpose

a. ( ) To present an unusual travel destination and a company that can take you there.

b. ( ) To discuss differences between travel destinations and how travel agencies feel about it.

2 Read the statements below and write true (T) or false (F) according to the information in the text.

Understanding details

a. ( ) The name of the agency which can take you to unusual destinations is *All Britain's Tour Operators*.

b. ( ) Jim Louth is the man who started *Undiscovered Destinations*.

c. ( ) Jim Louth has visited almost 80 countries.

d. ( ) The civil war in Angola ended in 2002.

e. ( ) Caucasians are very uncommon in Angola.

f. ( ) *Undiscovered Destinations* has only a few customers aged under 50.

g. ( ) There are many English-speaking guides in Angola.

3 Rewrite the false statements from the previous activity making the appropriate corrections.

_____
_____
_____
_____
_____
_____
_____
_____
_____
_____

EXPAND YOUR VOCABULARY

1 Find the words to the definitions below in the article on page 36. Then use two of these words to complete the extracts that follow. Make any necessary changes.

a. _____ : designed to be used on rough ground as well as on roads

b. _____ : to start a company, organization, committee etc.

c. _____ : accepted by or involving most people in a society

d. _____ : designed to be a public event, such as a meeting, in a way that will give you the result that you want – often used to show disapproval

e. _____ : filled with too many people or things

f. _____ : rough and uneven

Adapted from www.ldoceonline.com. Accessed on November 20, 2018.

> " [...] Not all _____ destinations are suitable for off-season travel (Machu Picchu in rainy season? No thanks). And some are far from ports. Going elsewhere, for now, may be the best option. [...] "

Extracted from http://time.com/4915745/crowded-tourist-cities-alternatives/. Accessed on November 20, 2018.

> " Hitting the open road is a distinctly American pastime, and no season calls for it more than summer. But might we suggest a little twist on the idea? We call it the _____ trip, for the folks with four-wheel-drive and a taste for adventure—not to mention dust. [...] "

Extracted from www.roadandtrack.com/car-culture/travel/g6375/america-10-best-off-road-trips-4x4/. Accessed on November 20, 2018.

2 Work in small groups. Answer the questions below and then report your answers to the class. Remember to support your answers.

a. Do you think the author is convincing when he defends Angola as a great tourist destination?

b. What do you think you would like about traveling to Angola? What wouldn't you like?

c. If you had to choose between traveling to a famous destination and to an unusual destination, which one would you choose? Why?

VOCABULARY IN USE

1. Reread this extract from the text on page 36, paying attention to the idiom in bold. Then choose its most appropriate meaning.

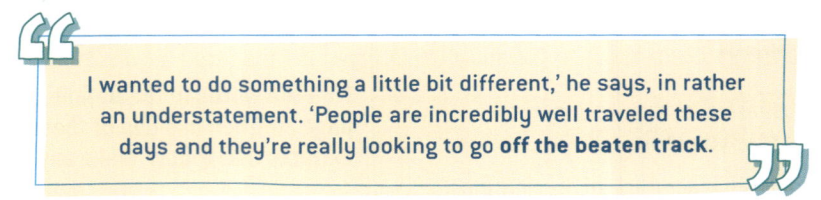

> 'I wanted to do something a little bit different,' he says, in rather an understatement. 'People are incredibly well traveled these days and they're really looking to go **off the beaten track**.'

a. (   ) to approach, confront, or deal with a problem or difficult situation directly and with clear, confident action

b. (   ) a place that is not well known and is far away from the places that people usually visit

Extracted from https://idioms.thefreedictionary.com. Accessed on October 2, 2018.

2. Read the following extracts, paying attention to the underlined idioms. Then match them with their most appropriate meanings.

   a. "Tommy Hamilton's wife told him they would not <u>ride out the storm</u> at their house. He was stubborn at first, 'you don't want to leave your home. You want to stay.' She won the argument, and they rode the storm out at a different location."

   Extracted from www.southeastfarmpress.com/peanuts/storm-takes-homes-rattles-community-and-cripples-foundation. Accessed on October 2, 2018.

   b. "How do you <u>live out of a suitcase</u> for a year? Sounds like a **tall order**. You may think it is impossible. [...]

   To be honest, living out of a **carry-on sized backpack** was **freeing** but came with a few minor inconveniences. For example, when I walked into the luxurious Four Seasons Hotel Lion Palace in St. Petersburg, Russia with my backpack, no one took me seriously until I took out my passports and presented the confirmed reservation for two nights at the hotel. [...]"

   Extracted from www.gocollette.com/en/traveling-well/2017/6/how-to-live-out-of-a-suitcase. Accessed on October 2, 2018.

   c. "[...] So what do you do if you'<u>re all geared up</u> with no one to travel with? Well, you have two options. Don't travel at all or go it alone. If you have a passion for travel and an **itch** to <u>hit the road</u> (or the beach, if it suits you), why not take off on a solo adventure and see the world with a whole new perspective? [...]"

   Extracted from www.uniglobephillipstravel.com/post/view/why-more-and-more-travellers-are-hitting-the-road-alone. Accessed on October 2, 2018.

   (   ) to begin a journey

   (   ) manage to survive a difficult period or situation

   (   ) spend a lot of time traveling

   Adapted from www.ldoceonline.com. Accessed on October 16, 2018.

3. Now read some other idioms and their definitions. Then complete the paragraph with them.

   at the wheel: in control of a vehicle's steering wheel
   the highways and byways: the important and less important parts
   a back seat driver: a passenger in the back of a car who gives unwanted advice to the driver about how to drive

   Adapted from www.ldoceonline.com. Accessed on October 16, 2018.

I enjoy traveling with my cousin. When we travel together, I'm usually the one _____. The only thing I don't like is that he is sort of _____. He keeps telling me when to change lanes, where to turn left... it is so annoying! Anyway, last weekend we decided to travel to England and get to know the surroundings by car. We traveled _____ of Cambridge. That part was awesome! I'm glad we could save enough money to take this trip.

LANGUAGE IN USE 1

Unit 4

HAVE TO and NEED TO

1. The excerpt in A was extracted from "Undiscovered destinations: Now *that's* what I call off the beaten track" on page 36 and the extract in B was extracted from an article called "Why being broke is the best time to travel", by Nomadic Matt. Read them carefully, paying attention to the words in bold, and match them with the meaning conveyed.

a.
> The country is so unused to tourists that many people have never seen white faces before and visits to local Himba villages **have to** be spontaneous, as there are few phones to make contact in advance.

b.
> There's nothing like getting paid to have a conversation in the language you speak every day. These sites are hugely popular – and you **don't need to** be a teacher.

( ) something that's not necessary in order to achieve a goal or make something happen

( ) when there's no other option instead of doing things a certain way. It might be an obligation, something one's committed to, or a situation that cannot be postponed

2. Read the comic strips below and complete with the words from the box. There is an extra option.

> don't have to   have to   need to

a.

[Comic strip 1]
- YOUR BROTHER'S WEDDING WAS GREAT, BUT IT SURE MADE ME REALIZE SOMETHING
- YOU'RE A LOUSY DANCER?
- THAT I'M NOWHERE NEAR READY TO GET MARRIED. THERE ARE SO MANY THINGS I REALLY _____ DO FIRST
- LIKE GET MY DEGREE, TRAVEL THE WORLD, VISIT IMPORTANT MUSEUMS, TOUR HISTORIC SITES, CLIMB THE ALPS...
- RIDE IN A BLIMP, LEARN TO SPEAK FRENCH, TAKE HARP LESSONS...
- FIND A GUY WHO WANTS TO MARRY YOU...

Extracted from www.thecomicstrips.com/store/add.php?iid=152189. Accessed on October 2, 2018.

b.

[Comic strip 2 - AIRPORT SECURITY]
- IT TAKES LONGER GETTING THROUGH SECURITY, BUT BY WEARING ALL MY CLOTHES, I _____ PAY TO CHECK A BAG!

Extracted from www.thecomicstrips.com/store/add.php?iid=64137. Accessed on October 2, 2018.

EXPAND YOUR READING

1. **Read the blog post below and relate it to the one you read on page 14. Which characteristics identified there can you find in this text?**

___

www.nomadicmatt.com/travel-blogs/no-money-go-travel

HOME   WHO WE ARE   BLOG   GET INVOLVED   GO TO AN EVENT   SHOP   MEMBERSHIP

Why the tourism industry has to change and how you can help it do so

October 18, 2016

We talk a lot about ways to enhance the tourism industry and to **spread** our message on responsible travel. Sometimes it's not always easy or clear how we can do that. In this post, Globalhelpswap details
5   their ideas on how we can collectively impact the industry for good and why it's necessary now more than ever.

Hands up if you took a flight last year? The chances are that most of the readers of this blog took a flight
10 at some time in the past year. Last year there were 1.2 billion international tourist arrivals and that **figure** is set to increase to 2 billion people by 2030.

A quarter of the planet's population is visiting new countries, eating different cuisines, and discovering
15 new cultures. Some of those travelers would have witnessed amazing natural phenomena like the Northern Lights, the Great African migration, or the Emperor Penguins of Antarctica. It's exciting, isn't it?

20 Travel breaks down barriers like no other industry and is responsible for 1 in 11 jobs around the world. If you ask most people what they are looking forward to most in the year, their answer will be a well-earned vacation. [...]

Can we change how we travel?

25 The good news is, yes we can. But, and this is a big but, it will take a collective effort from the tourism industry, governments, transportation as well as you and I. [...]

If we are going to redefine tourism, then we all have
30 to put pressure on travel companies to practice sustainable/responsible tourism. We also have to practice what we **preach** by spending our money with the companies that are already practicing sustainable tourism.

35 The amazing thing about sustainable tourism is that when you practice it, your vacation and travels will become more magical.

Helping feed elephants is pretty magical, right? How about sitting with orangutans in their natural
40 environment? What about going on tour where all your money goes to a women's cooperative to help them start businesses? All of these are examples of tours we have done personally with responsible tourism companies.

45 Next time you book a trip somewhere, please book it with a travel company that is practicing sustainable tourism. Let's redefine tourism together and hopefully as Fabien Cousteau said: "*I look forward to the day when there is no sustainable tourism, just
50 tourism*".

How would you redefine tourism? Please leave a comment below.

#RedefineTourism   #LoveYourTravels

This post was done in conjunction with The World Tourism Council.

_{Adapted from www.impacttravelalliance.org/2016/10/18/why-the-tourism-industry-has-to-change-and-how-you-can-help-it-do-so. Accessed on August 28, 2018.}

2. **In small groups, write a comment that answers the question in bold at the end of the text: "How would you redefine tourism?" Share your answer with your classmates.**

LANGUAGE IN USE 2

Unit 4

TAG QUESTIONS

1. Read the excerpt from the text on page 40 again, paying attention to the part in bold. Then circle the pronoun and underline the auxiliary verb.

> A quarter of the planet's population is visiting new countries, eating different cuisines, and discovering new cultures. Some of those travelers would have witnessed amazing natural phenomena like the Northern Lights, the Great African migration, or the Emperor Penguins of Antarctica. It's exciting, **isn't it?**

The part in bold is called *tag question*. Tag questions turn statements into questions. They are often used to check the information we think is true.

2. Now read these statements, paying attention to the parts in bold, and complete the statements that follow with the words from the box.

- You **don't have** a frequent flyer discount, **do you?**
- You **are taking** a road trip with Emma, **aren't you?**
- He **didn't get** on that plane, **did he?**
- They **were coming** home by motorcycle, **weren't they?**
- **Come** to London after your wedding, **will you?**
- **Let's travel** on our next summer vacation, **shall we?**

> negative   tag question   auxiliary
> positive   Let's   main clause   imperative

a. Tag questions are usually made using an _____ verb, such as *be*, *do*, and *did* + a subject pronoun.

b. If the main clause has an auxiliary verb, you use the same verb in the _____.

c. If there is no auxiliary verb in the _____, use *do*, *does*, *did*, just like when you ask a normal question.

d. If the main clause is positive, the tag question is usually _____.

e. If the main clause is negative, the tag question is _____.

f. If there is an _____ in the main clause, the tag question is formed by *will* + the subject pronoun *you*.

g. If the main clause starts with _____, the tag question is formed by *shall* + the subject pronoun *we*.

3. Based on what you studied above, match the main clauses with the appropriate tag questions.

a. Traveling solo is not as difficult as you think,   ( ) will you?
b. Picture yourself in the middle of your ideal trip,   ( ) weren't they?
c. There aren't limitations on when you can go on your trip, ( ) didn't she?
d. But some portions of your trip were spent on your own,   ( ) are there?
e. He was taking a short course overseas at that time,   ( ) is it?
f. She made friends with like-minded people when she visited the country, ( ) shall we?
g. Let's plan a road trip across Latin America,   ( ) wasn't he?

4. Work in pairs. Talk to a classmate about things you know about them, their hobbies, what they did last weekend, and what they will do after class. Use a tag question at the end of your sentences to confirm the information.

41

LISTENING COMPREHENSION

1. **Jason Moore is a frequent traveler who shares his personal experiences about traveling and living abroad on his blog. In one of his podcasts, he interviews Tim Leffel, who talks about the ins and outs of living abroad. Listen to part of the interview and complete the items with the missing information.**

   a. The name of the podcast: _____

   b. The title of Tim Leffel's book: _____

   c. The people interviewed by Tim Leffel were from: _____

   d. The benefit from moving from a really expensive country to a much cheaper country: _____

   e. When people move from an expensive country to a cheap country, they might cut their expenses in: _____

   f. Places where Tim and his wife worked as English teachers: _____

2. **Tim says, "[...] in general, if you move from a more developed country to a less developed country you're just going to be able to cut your expenses in half pretty easily if you do it right." In your opinion, what does "if you do it right" mean in this context? Explain. Then share your ideas with a classmate.**

   _____
   _____
   _____
   _____
   _____

>> EXPAND YOUR HORIZONS >>>

Check (✓) the column that best describes your opinion about each statement. Then discuss your answers with your classmates and teacher, justifying your point of view.

	I agree.	I'm not sure.	I disagree.
a. Picking up and leaving when we are struggling may seem quite scary.			
b. Besides taking us out of our comfort zone, traveling to new destinations usually helps us build self-confidence and be more independent.			
c. We need to change the way we travel and make sure all our choices are sustainable, even when this decision affects our personal goals during a trip.			

REVIEW 2

Units 3 and 4

1. Read the text and examine how the author feels about the topic. What opinions or beliefs are evident? *Identifying the author's perspective*

Generation Z's Rightward Drift

The data is consistent across the board: today's kids are more conservative than their parents were.

By TYLER ARNOLD • February 5, 2018

Blaming "kids these days" for society's shift towards social progressivism and libertinism is common within conservative circles. The right loves to **reminisce** about how previous generations walked uphill both ways to school and romanticize the values with which they grew up. I mean, they did have "Little House on the Prairie" while kids these days just spend all their time on smartphones, right?

5 But is this criticism really fair? Younger generations are actually **embracing** traditional conservative values more than people realize.

[...]

About 40 percent of Generation Z high school seniors disagreed that men should be **breadwinners** and women homemakers, compared to more than 60 percent in the mid-'90s. That study, led by sociologist David Cotter from Union College, shows that younger generations are turning back towards traditional 10 gender roles after a half century of going in the opposite direction.

Business Insider also points out that Gen Z has a stronger entrepreneurial spirit than previous cohorts, and shows signs of being more fiscally responsible. According to one study by a British brand consultancy called The Gild, Gen Z in the UK is exhibiting more socially conservative views than prior generations.

15 On the other hand, a study by Northwestern University shows that Gen Z is about as likely to support gay marriage and government involvement in health care as Millennials, and more likely to support transgender rights. Atheism rises by five percentage points among Gen Z, and despite promising signs of an increase in religiosity, teenagers are taking less traditional **approaches** to Christianity than previous generations, according to researchers at the Barna Group.

20 But while not everything is looking up, decision making and moral behavior definitely are. And while many don't see Millennials as very conservative, they are actually more conservative than Boomers and Gen Xers were when they were growing up. Considering that the latter two generations both got more conservative as they aged, if Millennials and Gen Z do the same, we could see a strong revival of conservative values.

[...]

Extracted from www.theamericanconservative.com/articles/generation-zs-rightward-drift/. Accessed on July 25, 2018.

2. Underline the clause that best explains the gist of the text. *Skimming*

    a. The youngest generations oppose a revival of conservative thoughts and values.

    b. Gen Z society is on an uncontrollable movement towards libertinism and progressivism.

    c. The younger generation is often more cautious and traditional than the previous ones.

3. Check (✓) the alternative that does <u>not</u> correspond to the new generation as described in the text. *Understanding main ideas*

    a. ( ) They are more inclined to approve of transgender rights and gay marriage.

    b. ( ) They follow less conventional approaches to Christianity.

    c. ( ) Most of them don't believe the roles of providers for men and housewives for women should be respected.

4. Read the conclusion of the previous text, paying attention to the verb in bold. What meaning does it convey?

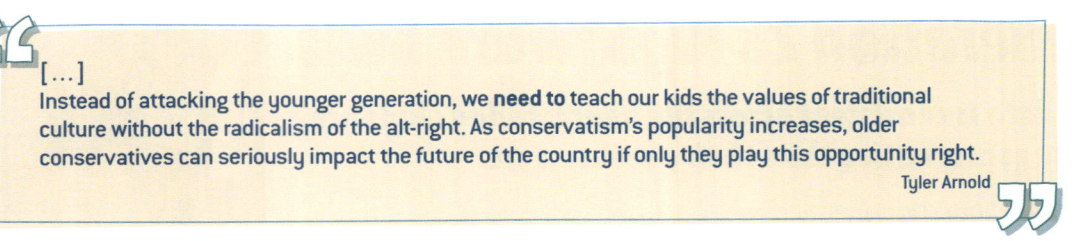

_____

> [...]
> Instead of attacking the younger generation, we **need** to teach our kids the values of traditional culture without the radicalism of the alt-right. As conservatism's popularity increases, older conservatives can seriously impact the future of the country if only they play this opportunity right.
> Tyler Arnold

Extracted from www.theamericanconservative.com/articles/generation-zs-rightward-drift. Accessed on July 25, 2018.

5. Add tag questions to the statements below.
   a. Sustainable tourism requires constant monitoring of social and environmental impacts, _____
   b. Responsible tourism is related to any form of tourism that can be consumed in a more responsible way, _____
   c. Ecotourism trips shouldn't disturb natural areas, _____

6. Read the text and complete the relative clauses with the pronouns *who* or *which*. Then work in pairs. Exchange ideas about the question in the title of the text.

> **Do-gooders on vacation call it voluntourism. But is it doing anyone any good?**
> [...]
> Malawi is a landlocked nation in southern Africa. Its one claim to fame is that Madonna adopted one of its citizens—"Baby David" Banda—in 2006. Other than that, the country is known mainly to people _____ collect statistics on global misery. It's in a three-way tie for seventh place among countries with the lowest per capita income. It also ranks eleventh for overall death rate. By some estimates, the prevalence of HIV/AIDS in Malawi's cities is one person in three.
> One of the few funny things I've heard said about the place was a traveler's joke: "*Malawi*? I thought you said we were going to *Maui*!" It is indeed funny to imagine a tourist, expecting Hamoa Beach, instead being dropped on so-called Devil Street in Malawi's capital, Lilongwe. Not that there aren't any tourist attractions here. Most of the country's eastern edge spills into Lake Malawi, _____ has white-sand beaches and the widest variety of freshwater fish in the world. But the sunburn-and-souvenirs set has generally stayed away. Apparently even bargain destinations have to exceed a **threshold** of human suffering before they're accepted as **believably** fun. [...]
> All of which might suggest that Malawi is **off the beaten track**. Wrong. The place is swarming with visitors, and almost every single one is with an *organization*. They are volunteer tourists—or, if you're a fan of neologisms, *voluntourists*—and they are among the fastest-growing sectors in international adventure travel.[...]

Extracted from www.utne.com/politics/the-dark-side-of-volunteer-tourism-voluntourism. Accessed on July 25, 2018.

7. Rewrite the extract "One of the few funny things I've heard said about the place was a traveler's joke" inserting a relative pronoun where it fits. Then explain why it was omitted.

_____

_____

UNIT 5

What the Future Holds

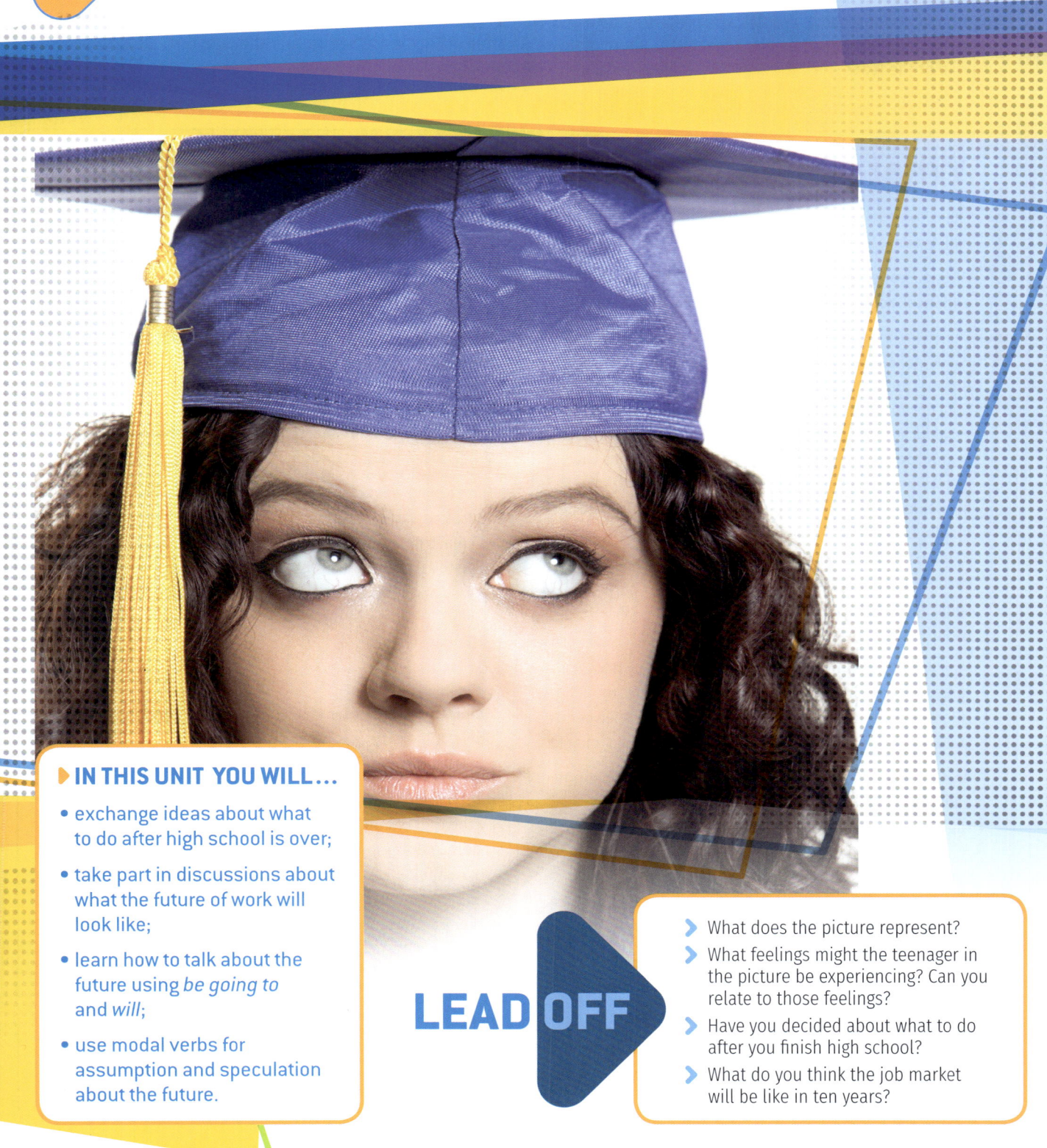

▶ IN THIS UNIT YOU WILL…

- exchange ideas about what to do after high school is over;
- take part in discussions about what the future of work will look like;
- learn how to talk about the future using *be going to* and *will*;
- use modal verbs for assumption and speculation about the future.

LEAD OFF

- What does the picture represent?
- What feelings might the teenager in the picture be experiencing? Can you relate to those feelings?
- Have you decided about what to do after you finish high school?
- What do you think the job market will be like in ten years?

READING

BEFORE READING

Read the title of the text. In your opinion, what is its target audience?

Identifying the target audience

WHILE READING

Read some testimonials by professors presented on a text on the topic "What will universities be like 10 years from now?", presented in the Browne Review, a document about higher education in England. Then answer the question: What's the purpose of the text?

Identifying the main purpose of a text

What will universities be like 10 years from now?

The Browne review suggests drastic changes to the funding of higher education. We ask academics what the effect will be.

Gillian Evans, emeritus professor of medieval theology and intellectual history, University of Cambridge

There will be no more **block grant** for teaching, and the block grant has always provided the infrastructure. So if Browne succeeds in ending funding for all subjects that are not considered priority science and technology subjects, strategically important languages or ones that provide "significant social returns", presumably that means that history, politics, archeology, paleography and English literature will have to move out of the publicly funded buildings and into tents in the car park. Or departments of philosophy may have to go back to the Aristotelian peripatetic method in the streets and stay off-campus. This could widen access to no end. You could have Socratics vs. **hoodies** debates in the shopping mall.

How will library provisions work if in future only books on "priority subjects" may be purchased with public money and the rest put into storage to make space on the shelves? Or **pulped** to save public money being spent on the storage.

And there will be no more buffer body between government and universities. Despite what Browne says about this new Higher Education Council being independent, it is pretty obvious the government is going to decide what the priority subjects are this week. You thought you were studying French? No, sorry, the government's just axed that. It will be Mandarin Chinese.

Danny Dorling, professor of human geography at the University of Sheffield

We have a strange higher education system for historical reasons, and it will become stranger. The Americans will think we are going in the right direction. The Europeans will think we are **fools**.

In 10 years' time, there will be a lot of disappointed moms. Browne moves us away from the trend in the rest of the affluent world, in which a majority go to university and where student numbers are rising. His policy means, at its heart, having no more students than we have at the moment – probably, fewer. How do you get more students if you are charging them more?

[…]

David Colquhoun, research professor of pharmacology, University College London

The existing class divide between who gets to higher education and who doesn't will get wider. Vice-chancellors will make noises about providing **bursaries**, but that won't solve the problem. The problem is partly bursaries, but it's also about perception. Just the big headline fee is **off-putting**. It's like a return to the days of the scholarship boy at grammar school.

[…]

Deian Hopkin, former vice-chancellor of London South Bank University

In 10 years' time, geographically, provision might be **diminished**. The advantage of having a block grant, managed by the Higher Education Funding Council for England, was that it could support institutions in parts of the country where it felt it was appropriate to have them. The market won't necessarily do that. Unless we are careful, we may have larger **patches** of under-provision, or very different provision in different parts of the country. I also fear for the support for subjects that don't have an obvious function in the economy or utilitarian value – such as history. They could find themselves in difficulty, especially outside a small group of institutions, where there will always be demand.

Extracted from www.theguardian.com/education/2010/oct/19/browne-review-university-funding-future. Accessed on January 7, 2019.

AFTER READING

1. Read the sentences below and check (✓) the one that does <u>not</u> relate to the overall content of the text on page 46.

Understanding main ideas

a. ( ) Two of the professors believe that less socially or economically valued subjects, such as history, will stop receiving funds from the government in England.

b. ( ) Even though students are paying less for university tuitions in England, the number of students is still low.

c. ( ) More people won't be able to get higher education in England because of the fees.

d. ( ) Some parts of England may receive fewer provisions for their universities.

2. Write Evans, Dorling, Colquhoun, or Hopkin.

Understanding details

a. _____ says it is necessary to be careful so as to make sure to have provisions in most parts of the country.

b. _____ believes that the problem of higher tuitions can be solved in part by providing scholarships.

c. _____ lists a number of subjects that may stop receiving a fund from the government for being considered less socially important.

d. _____ believes that even some books will be less frequent in libraries to make room for those considered more important for society.

e. _____ claims that students from other wealthy countries in the world enroll in university courses more than students in England.

3. Which of the professors do you think seem to be more concerned about the changes expected for education in England? Refer to the text and underline fragments that support your answer.

4. Work in small groups. What changes do you expect to see in the universities in your country in the next few years? Do you think changes are going to be mostly positive? Why (not)?

EXPAND YOUR VOCABULARY

1. Read the sentences and decide how they are related to the text on page 46.

a. I'm changing my **major** to political science.

b. Many college graduates are paying off huge **loans**.

c. Languages are an essential part of the **school curriculum**.

d. Justice says they should be allowed to attend the **public school**.

Extracted from www.ldoceonline.com. Accessed on January 7, 2019.

2. Now refer back to the text and find other words or expressions about the same topic to complete the chart below.

	amounts of money that you pay to do something or that you pay to a professional person for their work
	areas of knowledge that you study at a school or university
	college or university education as opposed to elementary school or high school
	an amount of money that is given to someone by an educational organization to help pay for their education
	a school in Britain for children over the age of 11 who have to pass a special examination to go there; (AmE) an elementary school
	someone who is responsible for a particular part of some universities in Britain

Adapted from www.ldoceonline.com. Accessed on January 7, 2019.

3. Discuss the following statements in pairs. Use as many words from the previous activities as possible. Then report and justify your opinions to the class.

a. If you plan early in life, paying for college tuitions and fees is easier.

b. Getting a loan to pay for college or university has both positive and negative sides.

c. In Brazil, most high school students know whether they are going to proceed to higher education, enter the job market, or do both.

VOCABULARY IN USE

1. In "His policy means, at its heart, having no more students than we have at the moment - *probably*, fewer." the adverb in italics was formed by adding -*ly* to the adjective *probable*. What function does that adverb have in this context?
   a. ( ) It provides information about the frequency of the activity indicated by the verb.
   b. ( ) It indicates a degree of certainty.

2. Adverbs can modify verbs, adjectives, adverbs, noun phrases, prepositional phrases, and even whole clauses. They can also provide information about the manner, place, time, frequency, certainty, or other circumstances of a verb. Look at the adjectives below and use a dictionary to find the corresponding -*ly* adverbs.

Adjectives	-*ly* Adverbs
a. academic	
b. automatic	
c. especial	
d. financial	
e. hopeful	
f. primary	
g. probable	
h. real	

3. Work in pairs. Choose two adverbs from the chart above and write sentences using them.

4. Look at the painting and read its exhibition label. Then find the -*ly* adverb and indicate its function. Keep in mind that not all words ending in -*ly* are adverbs.

Exhibition Label

Crite thought of himself as an artist-reporter whose assignment was to capture the daily lives of ordinary people. His skill as an acute observer of American life is apparent in *School's Out*, which shows dozens of children leaving the annex of Everett elementary school in Boston's South End at a time when boys and girls were taught separately. Although Crite acknowledged that School's Out may reflect a romanticized view, it also presents a universal statement about community, stability, and the bonds of family life.

African American Art: Harlem Renaissance, Civil Rights Era, and Beyond, 2012

Extracted from americanart.si.edu/artwork/schools-out-5965. Accessed on July 20, 2018.

LANGUAGE IN USE 1

Unit 5

WILL vs. BE GOING TO

1. Read the extracts from the text on page 46 and underline the verb structures used to talk about the future.

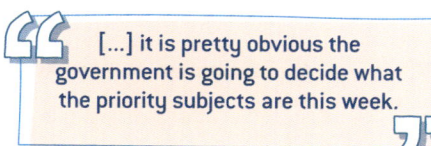

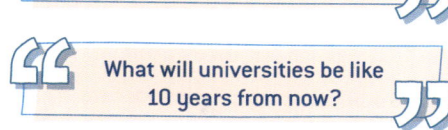

> [...] it is pretty obvious the government is going to decide what the priority subjects are this week.

> What will universities be like 10 years from now?

2. Read the extracts in activity 1 again and check (✓) the correct alternative to complete the paragraph about *will* vs. *be going to*.

We often use *will* and *be going to* to talk about the _____, although it is also possible to use tenses such as the simple present and the present continuous, for example. We use *will* to make _____, to mean *want to* or *be willing to*, to make or talk about offers and _____, and to refer to decisions made at the moment of speaking. *Be going to* is used to talk about _____ and intentions and to say that something is likely to happen, based on real evidence.

a. ( ) future / suggestions / plans / promises
b. ( ) past / requests / arrangements / plans
c. ( ) future / predictions / promises / plans

3. Refer back to the extracts in activity 1, identify the verb usages, and finish the sentences.

a. In the first extract, *be going to* is used because it refers to _____.

b. In the second extract, *will* indicates _____.

4. Use the verbs from the box to complete the text.

> 's going to be   will determine   won't define

Helping Teenagers Find Their Dreams
By Eilene Zimmerman

Some parents are apt to put pressure on their children about choosing a first career, thinking that it _____ the course of their lives. Yet as adults, we often reinvent ourselves more than once, moving among professions. So whatever your children choose now _____ necessarily _____ their future.

"I see many teens who jump on the first career track that someone recommends just to avoid being directionless, only to find themselves miserable a few years later," said Tamar E. Chansky, a child-and-adolescent psychologist in Plymouth Meeting, Pa., and author of "Freeing Your Child From Anxiety. [...]"
You may feel compelled to give career advice because you see particular talents in your child, but parents are more limited by their own experience than they think", said Steve Langerud, director of career services at DePauw University in Greencastle, Ind. As well-meaning as the advice might be, it "doesn't take into account what _____ available to your child in the future," he said.
"The market is changing so fast there may be careers that exist when a student gets out of college that simply didn't exist when they started," he added.

Extracted from www.nytimes.com/2009/10/25/jobs/25career.html. Accessed on July 20, 2018.

5. Answer the questions below. Remember to use *will* or *be going to* in your answers when possible.

a. Why are students often worried and afraid when it comes to choosing their path after high school?

_____
_____

b. What do you think should be taken into consideration when choosing a career?

_____
_____

c. Do you suffer any kind of pressure from family or friends, or even from people at your school, to decide what you want to study at college? Explain.

_____
_____

d. Do you think vocational or career aptitude tests can help teenagers decide on what kind of career they will follow? Explain.

_____
_____

EXPAND YOUR READING

1. You are going to read part of a survey report by PwC entitled "Workforce of the future". What do you think it is about? Read the Foreword fragment and check your predictions.

   Foreword

   We are in the midst of one of the most important periods of change in the workplace that we are likely to see in our lifetime. No one really knows how our world will be shaped by technology, what the future of work will look like, or whether work and employment as we know them will even exist. However, much of this debate focuses on what technology could do, and not around the choices we will have about how we will use it.

   [...]
   Carol Stubbings
   Global Leader,
   People and Organization

   Those with fewer years of formal education are more worried

   One in three of those educated to school leaver level are worried about their future – considerably more than those who are university graduates (13%) or post-graduate educated (11%). What does this mean for employers, governments, and society? We think it means a real need to open up a genuine and fully-
   -inclusive conversation about the future of work.

   [...]

   Key findings

   Excited about the future

   [...]

   73% see a positive future – up from 66% in 2014

   We need an inclusive conversation about jobs

   [...]

   32% educated to school leaver level are worried about their future

   Societal impact is important to people

   [...]

   70% want to work for an organization with a powerful social conscience

   Trading liberties for good jobs

   [...]

   70% would use performance enhancers to improve employment prospects

   Wildly different levels of confidence in skills

   [...]

   74% in India say they have STEM skills – only 33% in UK say the same

   Giving CEOs the soft skills they want

   [...]

   85% say they have problem-solving skills

   Conclusion

   A deeper dive into the survey findings identifies some interesting trends and differences between countries and demographic groups in people's attitudes to the future of work and how it will impact them. PwC highlight some issues which will be of concern to governments. Notably a lack of confidence in skills in some countries and a clear need for an inclusive conversation about jobs to include all educational levels. But also some reasons to be cheerful. Three-quarters of people surveyed are positive about the future and have confidence in their soft skills. These are the skills that businesses will need in the future as human work becomes more collaborative with artificial intelligence. [...]

   Extracted from www.pwc.com/gx/en/services/people-organisation/workforce-of-the-future/workforce-of-future-appendix.pdf. Accessed on July 20, 2018.

2. Underline the only characteristic that <u>doesn't</u> refer to survey reports.
   a. Survey reports present a summary of the data collected in a survey on a given subject.
   b. They present analyses based on the results of the survey, as well as some conclusions.
   c. Data may be summarized using visual representations such as graphics or boxes dividing content.
   d. Survey reports use informal language and never include recommendations.
   e. Statistics are often given by means of proportions and percentages.

3. Read the whole text and decide if the sentences below are true (T) or false (F).
   a. (   ) When people think about how affected their lives will be by the future world of work, most of them feel positive.
   b. (   ) More than 50% of people in the UK believe they have science, technology, engineering, and math skills.
   c. (   ) Less than half of people globally would like to improve their work performances.

LANGUAGE IN USE 2

MODAL VERBS - MAY, MIGHT, COULD

1. Read two extracts from the survey report on page 50 and one extract from the text on page 46 and answer the question that follows.

> However, much of this debate focuses on what technology **could** do, [...]

> PwC expands more on what work **might** look like in 2030 in our report 'Workforce of the future'.

> The market is changing so fast there **may** be careers that exist when a student gets out of college that simply didn't exist when they started.

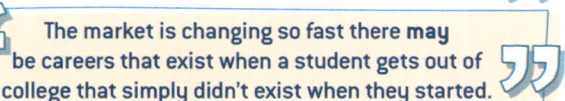

What do the modal verbs in bold have in common in these contexts?

a. ( ) They express ability and permission.
b. ( ) They give advice and indicate a strong belief.
c. ( ) They indicate assumptions or speculations for the future.

2. Match the columns to form complete statements.

a. We can use *may*, *might*, or *could* to say that...
b. *Might not* and *may not*...
c. In this context, *could not* (*couldn't*) is used...

( ) are the forms used for talking about a negative possibility.
( ) to talk about something that is completely impossible.
( ) it is possible that something will happen in the future.

3. The fragments below were extracted from the survey report on page 50. Rewrite them substituting *will* for one of the modals used for assumption or speculation about the future.

a. "These are the skills that businesses will need in the future as human work becomes more collaborative with artificial intelligence."

_____
_____
_____

b. "PwC highlight some issues which will be of concern to governments."

_____
_____
_____

4. Work in pairs. Discuss the skills described by the author as "essential to your future success," come up with 2 others, and describe them on the lines below. Use the modals *may*, *might*, or *could* in your writing.

Top 10 Jobs in 2030: Skills You Need Now to Land the Jobs of the Future
[...]
1. Mental Elasticity and Complex Problem Solving:
[...] Luckily, this skill is highly **developable** and simply takes practice. The more difficult problems you **tackle**, the more **bendy** your brain will get!
2. Critical Thinking:
[...] You'll constantly need to be analyzing various situations, considering multiple solutions, and making decisions **on the fly** through logic and reasoning.
3. Creativity:
Worried about robots **stealing** your job? The more creative you are, the less likely you are to lose your job to a robot! [...]
4. People Skills:
[...] If you want to succeed in the future job market, you'll need to learn how to manage and work with people (and robots), which includes getting in touch with your emotions, having empathy, and listening,
5. STEM:
Even though science, technology, engineering, and math jobs are super hot right now, don't expect them to go away in the future. [...] Also **coding**. Learn how to code.
6. SMAC:
You've heard of STEM, but you probably haven't heard of SMAC (social, mobile, analytics, and cloud). **Catchy**, right? Learning all of these skills/platforms will make you **stand out** in the future job market!
7. Interdisciplinary Knowledge:
Your future career will require you to pull information from many different fields to come up with creative solutions to future problems. This skill's easy to work on as well. Start by reading as much as you can about anything and everything that interests you. [...]

Extracted from https://blog.crimsoneducation.org/blog/jobs-of-the-future. Accessed on July 20, 2018.

_____
_____
_____

LISTENING COMPREHENSION

1. **What is a gap year? Read the word cloud and come up with your own definition for the term.**

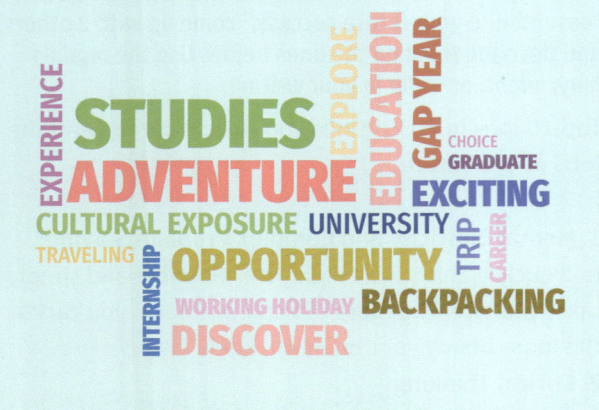

   STUDIES · EXPERIENCE · EXPLORE · EDUCATION · GAP YEAR · CHOICE · ADVENTURE · GRADUATE · EXCITING · CULTURAL EXPOSURE · UNIVERSITY · TRAVELING · OPPORTUNITY · TRIP · CAREER · INTERNSHIP · WORKING HOLIDAY · BACKPACKING · DISCOVER

   _____
   _____
   _____

2. **Listen to the first part of the recording. How does Josh describe a gap year? Is his definition close to yours? Compare your answer to a classmate's.** (09)

   _____
   _____
   _____

3. **Listen to the second part of the recording, read the statements that follow, and decide if they are true (T) or false (F).** (10)

   a. ( ) Josh was 18 when he finished school.
   b. ( ) Josh went away for a year. He worked in a school in England.
   c. ( ) Josh started his gap year teaching computer classes.
   d. ( ) When Josh returned to Macquarie University, he switched his degree into a Bachelor of Arts with the Diploma of Education.
   e. ( ) In Josh's opinion, a gap year is a waste of time and money that should be invested in paying for university.
   f. ( ) Josh felt that he was supported by Macquarie through his gap year.

4. **Listen to the last part of the recording and check (✓) the only thing not mentioned by Josh.** (11)

   a. ( ) It teaches you more about yourself.
   b. ( ) You learn what your strengths are.
   c. ( ) You get homesick.
   d. ( ) You're able to figure out what you want to do with the rest of your life.

5. **Josh says that a gap year "teaches you more about yourself". How do you think a gap year can help you to learn more about yourself?**

6. **Do you think 17- or 18-year-old teens are too young to choose what they want to do for the rest of their lives? Is it common for Brazilian students to take a gap year? Would you like to have such an experience? Justify your answers.**

›› EXPAND YOUR HORIZONS ››››

Check (✓) the column that best describes your opinion about each statement. Then discuss your answers with your classmates and teacher, justifying your point of view.

	I agree.	I'm not sure.	I disagree.
a. Every year, a large number of teenagers graduate from high school without having a clear idea of what they are going to do next.			
b. In a near future, work and employment will be dictated by technology and the ones who lack those skills won't fit.			
c. Most students might benefit from a break right before college so that they can learn how to be responsible for themselves.			

UNIT 6
It's Time We Reforested the Agribusiness

▶ IN THIS UNIT YOU WILL…

- understand the difference between agribusiness and agroforestry;
- talk about the benefits of agroforestry;
- exchange ideas about how farmers can be motivated to plant trees;
- get to know some collocations with the verbs *get* and *set*;
- learn how to use the passive voice;
- distinguish some discourse connectors.

LEAD OFF

- What kind of business can the pictures represent? What do you know about them?
- How can you relate the pictures to the title of the unit?
- "Farmers should use some of their land to plant more trees." Do you agree with this statement?

READING

›› BEFORE READING

Read the statements below. Do you think they are true (T) or false (F)? In small groups, exchange ideas with your classmates.

Activating previous knowledge

a. (   ) It is expected that people will eat less meat in the future.
b. (   ) Small farmers in a large part of the developing world provide most of the food in it.
c. (   ) More than half of the world's land is used for planting.

›› WHILE READING

Read the report below and check your answers to the activity above.   *Scanning*

http://www.fao.org/home/en/

Food and Agriculture Organization of the United Nations

STATISTICS AT FAO

1. FAO (Food and Agriculture Organization) develops methods and **standards** for food and agriculture statistics, provides technical assistance services, and disseminates data for global monitoring. Statistical activities at FAO include the development and implementation of methodologies and standards for data collection, validation, processing and analysis. FAO also **plays** a vital part in the global compilation, processing and dissemination of food and agriculture statistics, and provides essential statistical capacity development to member countries.

2. Statistical activities at FAO cover the areas of agriculture, forestry and fisheries, land and water resources and use, climate, environment, population, gender, nutrition, **poverty**, rural development, education and health as well as many others.

3. Below you can find some recent facts and figures.

FACTS AND FIGURES

4.
- **60-70%** increase in food production is needed to feed more than 9 billion people by 2050.*
- **73%** is the expected increase in the demand for meat by 2050, driven from an emerging global middle class.*
- **80%** of the food consumed in a large part of the developing world is provided by small farmers. ***
- **79%** increase in productivity can be expected if smallholder farmers adopt sustainable agricultural practices.*
- **70%** of the world's freshwater withdrawals are used in agriculture this reaches 95% in developing countries.*
- **38.5%** of the world's land is dedicated to agriculture.*
- **1/4 TO 1/3** of all food produced for human consumption is lost or wasted. **

- **842 MILLION PEOPLE** experienced chronic hunger in 2011–2013.*
- **$3.5 TRILLION** is the cost to the global economy caused by lost productivity related to malnutrition and lack of direct healthcare.*
- **$450 BILLION** is the estimated global demand for small farmer agricultural finance.°
- **100-150 MILLION PEOPLE** could escape hunger if women farmers had the same access to productivity resources as men.*

* Food and Agriculture Organization of the United Nations (FAO)
** FAO and World Resources Institute – World Food Price Watch, February 2014
*** UN Report 2013, Smallholders, food security, and the environment
° Catalyzing Smallholder Agricultural Finance report, published by Dalberg in September 2012

Adapted from www.fao.org/home/en/. Accessed on September 23, 2018.

Unit 6

>> **AFTER READING**

1. Write the number of each part of the text next to what is presented in it. *Understanding main ideas*
   a. ( ) The areas that FAO statistics cover.
   b. ( ) An introduction to the figures presented on food production and consumption.
   c. ( ) An introduction to the organization.
   d. ( ) Data related to food consumption and production.

2. Rewrite these sentences correcting the information that is <u>not</u> true. *Understanding details*
   a. A high increase in the demand for meat is expected in the emerging developing countries.
   _____

   b. The estimated impact of malnutrition on the global economy is higher than US$3.5 trillion.
   _____

   c. By 2050 at least a 70% in food increase will be needed to feed the world's population.
   _____

   d. Women farmers have the same access to productivity resources as men.
   _____

3. Work in small groups. Read the excerpt below and answer: If tree-based farming provides all these benefits, why do you think every farmer isn't planting trees?

> "In communities around the world, agroforestry – which involves growing trees among or around food crops – has been a proven method for farmers to cultivate more diverse, productive, and profitable crops. What's more, it helps protect the environment by preventing soil erosion and reducing reliance on forests.
> As such, agroforestry can make a key contribution to the UN's Zero Hunger Challenge, which aims to end global hunger, eliminate malnutrition, and build sustainable food systems. [...]"
>
> *Extracted from https://forestsnews.cifor.org/55549/agroforestry-why-dont-farmers-plant-more-trees?fnl=en. Accessed on September 25, 2018.*

EXPAND YOUR VOCABULARY

1. Go back to the text and find the words and expressions below. Reread the sentences they are in. Then match them with their meanings.

   a. disseminate
   b. forestry
   c. increase
   d. withdrawal

   ( ) to make something become bigger in amount, number, or degree
   ( ) the science or skill of looking after large areas of trees
   ( ) to spread information or ideas to as many people as possible
   ( ) the removal or stopping of something such as support, an offer, or a service

   Adapted from www.ldoceonline.com/dictionary. Accessed on September 24, 2018.

2. Use one word from activity 1 to complete the excerpt below.

"Agricultural intensification refers to interventions to _____ the outputs per hectare of crops or livestock. **Whilst** intensification can occur through local demand for innovation, it is increasingly imposed through policy interventions in forest-agriculture frontiers."

Extracted from www.espa.ac.uk/projects/ne-p008356-1. Accessed on November 13, 2018.

55

VOCABULARY IN USE

1. Read the excerpts below, paying attention to the parts in bold. They show collocations with the verbs *get* and *set*. Check (✓) the correct meaning conveyed by those combinations.

a. "This includes considering the particular space or **niche** the tree occupies in the farming system, as well as the total number of trees of that species that need to be planted. **Getting** this **right** is important to maximize the ecological and socioeconomic benefits from the tree itself and simultaneously to reduce the potential competition with other components of the system such as annual **crops**. [...]"

Extracted from www.worldagroforestry.org/downloads/Publications/PDFS/B17460.pdf. Accessed on September 25, 2018.

( ) understanding something in the wrong way
( ) understanding something accurately

b. "The current reform of the Common Agricultural Policy (CAP) has **set** new **rules** regarding the eligibility of agroforestry parcels for CAP first **pillar support**. The application of the new Basic Payment Scheme is creating concern for agroforesters, as some of the rules and regulations regarding the presence of trees, **shrubs**, or **hedges** in agricultural land are becoming more restrictive. [...]"

Extracted from www.eurafagroforestry.eu/action/policy/Eligibility_of_agroforestry_parcels_for_CAP_basic_payments. Accessed on September 25, 2018.

( ) established rules
( ) change rules drastically

2. Can you make new collocations with the verbs *get* and *set*? Complete the mind maps with the words and expressions from the box. Then use one collocation from each mind map to write a statement related to the facts and figures showed in the text on page 54.

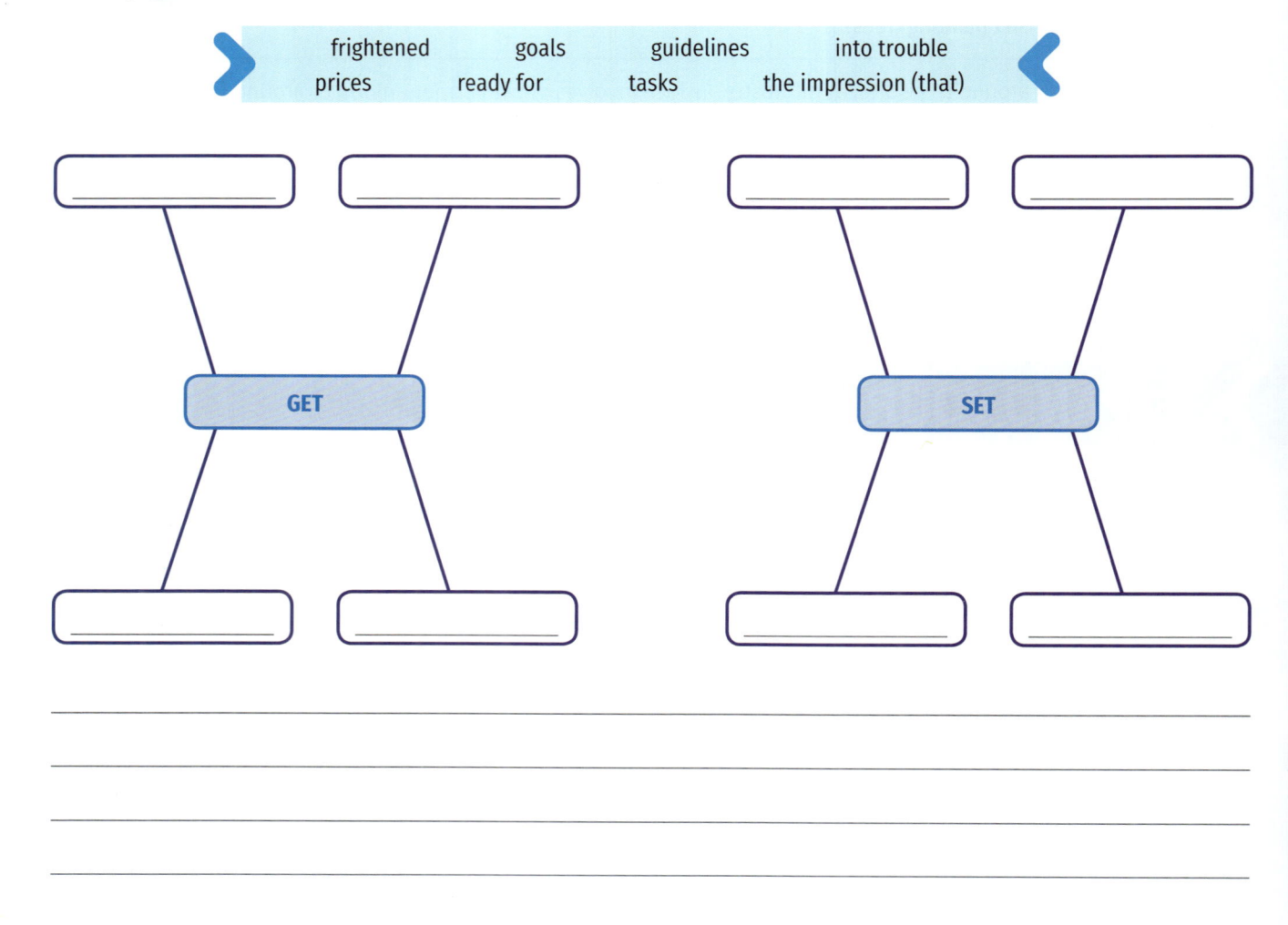

| frightened | goals | guidelines | into trouble |
| prices | ready for | tasks | the impression (that) |

GET

SET

LANGUAGE IN USE 1

Unit 6

PASSIVE VOICE

1. Read these two excerpts from the report on page 54, circle the subjects, and underline all the verb forms. Then decide if the statements are true (T) or false (F) and correct the false one(s).

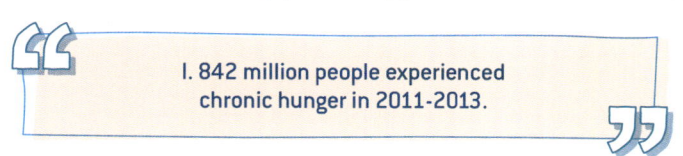

> I. 842 million people experienced chronic hunger in 2011-2013.

> II. 38.5% of the world land is dedicated to agriculture.

a. ( ) The subjects of both extracts I and II are the ones who perform the actions.
_____

b. ( ) In extract II the subject is the one who receives the action.
_____

c. ( ) Extract II focuses on the action itself and not on who or what performs the action. It shows a passive voice structure.
_____

2. Read the statements below carefully and match the columns.

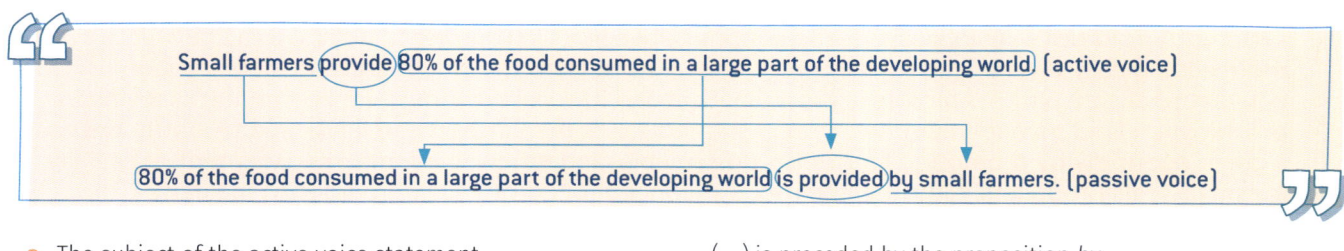

> Small farmers provide 80% of the food consumed in a large part of the developing world. (active voice)
>
> 80% of the food consumed in a large part of the developing world is provided by small farmers. (passive voice)

a. The subject of the active voice statement...
b. The agent of the passive voice statement...
c. The object of the active voice statement...
d. The passive form of the verb has as its basic structure...

( ) is preceded by the preposition *by*.
( ) *be* and a verb in the past participle.
( ) becomes the subject of the active voice statement.
( ) becomes the agent of the passive voice statement.

Keep in mind that:
- in most passive statements, the agent is not mentioned.
- in the passive voice statement, *be* is in the same tense of the main verb of the active voice.

3. Read part of the article "Pesticides Use and Exposure Extensive Worldwide" and complete it with the correct passive form of the verbs from the box.

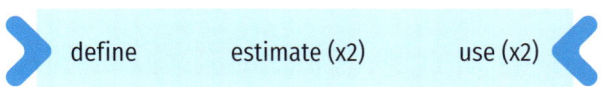

> define   estimate (x2)   use (x2)

"Worldwide it _____ that approximately 1.8 billion people engage in agriculture and most use pesticides to protect the food and commercial products that they produce. Others use pesticides occupationally for public health programs, and in commercial applications, while many others use pesticides for **lawn** and garden applications and in and around the home.

Pesticides _____ as 'chemical substances used to prevent, destroy, repel, or **mitigate** any pest ranging from insects (i.e., insecticides), **rodents** (i.e., rodenticides), and **weeds** (herbicides) to microorganisms (i.e., algicides, fungicides, or bactericides)'.

Over 1 billion pounds of pesticides _____ in the United State (US) each year and approximately 5.6 billion pounds _____ worldwide. In many developing countries programs to control exposures are limited or non-existent. As a consequence, it has been estimated that as many as 25 million agricultural workers worldwide experience unintentional pesticide **poisonings** each year. In a large prospective study of pesticide users in the United States, the Agricultural Health Study, it _____ that 16% of the cohort had at least one pesticide poisoning or an unusually high pesticide exposure episode in their lifetime. […]"

Extracted from www.ncbi.nlm.nih.gov/pmc/articles/PMC2946087/. Accessed on September 26, 2018.

EXPAND YOUR READING

1. Read the encyclopedia entry below. Then refer to the text in activity 3 on page 55 and answer: What other benefits of agroforestry can you learn from this text?

_____
_____
_____

---

www.britannica.com/science/agroforestry

ENCYCLOPEDIA BRITANNICA

Agroforestry

WRITTEN BY: Michael A. Gold (co-editor of an agroforestry newsletter)

Agroforestry, cultivation, and use of trees and shrubs with crops and **livestock** in agricultural systems. Agroforestry **seeks** positive interactions between its components, aiming to achieve a more ecologically diverse and socially productive **output** from the land than is possible through conventional agriculture. Agroforestry is a practical and low-cost means of implementing many forms of integrated land management (which seeks to reduce human impacts on land), and it contributes to a green economy by promoting long-term, sustainable, and renewable forest management, especially for small-scale producers. Although the modern concept of agroforestry emerged in the early 20th century, the use of **woody perennials** in agricultural systems is ancient, with written descriptions of the practice dating back to Roman times. Indeed, integrating trees with crops and animals is a long-standing tradition throughout the world. In 2004 the World Bank estimated that agroforestry practices were being used by 1.2 billion people.

Extracted from www.britannica.com/science/agroforestry. Accessed on September 26, 2018.

---

2. Check (✔) the statements that are true about encyclopedia entries.
   a. (   ) People read encyclopedia entries because they want to go deeper into or learn more about a topic.
   b. (   ) Encyclopedia entries are rarely organized into alphabetical order.
   c. (   ) Encyclopedia entries need to present clearly articulated explanations that can help readers.
   d. (   ) Online and printed encyclopedia entries are always updated once a year or every other year to address changes since the last publication.
   e. (   ) Encyclopedia entries are usually written by experts in a particular field. This lends authority to the encyclopedia and strengthens it as a reference tool.

3. Scan the text and answer the questions that follow.
   a. What is the aim of agroforesty?

   _____

   b. How does it contribute to a green economy?

   _____

   c. When did the modern concept of agroforestry emerge?

   _____

   d. How many people are estimated to be using agroforestry practices?

   _____

LANGUAGE IN USE 2

Unit 6

DISCOURSE MARKERS

1. Read the sentence below, extracted from the encyclopedia entry on page 58, paying attention to the word in bold. Then read the definition and answer the questions that follow.

> **Although** the modern concept of agroforestry emerged in the early 20th century, the use of woody perennials in agricultural systems is ancient.

The word in bold is a discourse marker. Discourse markers, or connectors, are words and phrases that aim at managing the flow of a discourse. They can express various types of relationships, such as addition, contrast, reason, cause and result, order, summary, etc.

a. What does *although* express?

_____

b. Which discourse marker could replace *although* with no significant difference in meaning? Read sentences *a*, *b*, and *c* in activity 2 and choose one of the discourse connectors in bold.

_____

2. What do the discourse markers in bold express in the sentences below? Read, identify, and complete the chart.

a. **Even though** she didn't want to buy products affected by toxic herbicides, she didn't have any other option.

b. She has lived in four other countries **besides** India.

c. **Since** most users canceled their subscriptions, our company has decided to shut down this service.

d. The agricultural expansion and, **consequently**, natural resources degradation can cause a massive impact on the environment.

e. There have been discussions about the exaggerated use of pesticides. **Along with this**, new laws are expected to be created.

f. **Due to** decades of studies and research, scientists are believed to have been able to create herbicides that are harmless to human beings.

g. Most companies say that they are no longer producing and selling toxic herbicides. Some companies, **however**, don't seem to mind the political and social pressures.

h. The pesticides used by farmers were inappropriate for this type of plantation. **For this reason**, crops were severely damaged.

Addition	Cause and result	Contrast	Reason

3. Complete the following statements with your own ideas. Pay attention to the discourse markers used.

a. Besides soil, other important agricultural resources are _____

_____.

b. Although pesticides can cause harm to people and the environment, _____

_____.

c. Many trees are planted every year. Consequently, _____

_____

LISTENING COMPREHENSION

1. You are going to listen to some news about Brazil's position as an agricultural powerhouse. Before you listen, talk to a classmate and guess if the following statements are true (T) or false (F). Then listen and check.

   a. (   ) When the text was published, Brazil was the world's sixth largest economy.

   _____

   b. (   ) Although the agribusiness in Brazil has been growing, the country is not a key player in the international arena yet.

   _____

   c. (   ) At the time the news was published, Brazil had the second largest reserves of farmable and not cultivated land in the world.

   _____

   d. (   ) At the time the news was published, Brazilian bioethanol production was the second largest worldwide.

   _____

   e. (   ) In 2009, agribusiness accounted for more than 3 percent of the labor force.

   _____

2. Listen again and correct the false statements from activity 1.

3. Read the extract below from the audio and answer the question: What does the underlined word mean in this context?

   "Blessed with the world's largest reserves of farmable and not cultivated land, Brazil has carved out its regional and international rank thanks to strong exporting agricultural activities, radical economic reforms, and an <u>aggressive</u> trade and influence policy."

   _____

4. In your opinion, will the agribusiness grow in the next few years in Brazil? Why (not)? How could agroforestry be encouraged in order to occupy some of the land which is not cultivated yet? Exchange your ideas with your classmates.

>> EXPAND YOUR HORIZONS >>>

Check (✓) the column that best describes your opinion about each statement. Then discuss your answers with your classmates and teacher, justifying your point of view.

	I agree.	I'm not sure.	I disagree.
a. Every farmer should be motivated to use part of their land to plant trees.			
b. Agroforestry should not be considered a responsibility of small farmers.			
c. Although pesticides can cause harm to people, they are necessary to protect the food and commercial products.			

REVIEW 3

Units 5 and 6

1. Skim the text and identify its target audience. *Skimming to identify target audience*

---

http://time.com/money/4982643/6-future-jobs/

The 6 Jobs Everyone Will Want in 2040

If you're a new parent, or **prone to** abstract theorizing, you've probably spent some late nights wondering what the future holds for job **seekers**.

In 2040, the babies born today will be at the start of their careers. Will the job market they face look anything like now?

Maybe, maybe not. Automation has already eliminated millions of manufacturing, foodservice, and **retail** jobs, and there's little doubt it will eventually reshape every other industry.

Some good news: Research from Oxford University shows there are hundreds of roles that aren't going anywhere – like occupational therapy, choreography, environmental engineering, and mental health counseling, among others.

Some better news: While some jobs will disappear, **loads** more will be created.

In fact, according to a forecast from the Institute for the Future (IFTF), 85% of the jobs in 2030 haven't even been invented yet. Ten years after that, the workforce may be totally **unrecognizable**.

Here's what the hottest jobs for 2040 could look like:

Virtual Store Manager

More consumers are shopping online, but they still **crave** human connection. […]

Robot Mediator

Sure, robots are **disrupting** some industries. But in others, they're actually just making humans better at their jobs. […]

Robot Trainer

Machine learning, which uses algorithms to train computers to, say, make a Spotify playlist, was once a skill known by an elite few. […]

Drone Traffic Controller

[…] With Amazon and Google testing ways to deliver packages by drone, corporate job openings in this field are an inevitability (future drone pilots are already enrolling at "Unmanned Vehicle" specialty schools). […]

Augmented Reality Designer

Some industries, like marketing and retail, have already tapped AR designers to create interactive experiences for consumers. […]

Micro Gig Agents

As the gig economy expands, independent consultants will work alongside a growing number of independent contractors, says Christie Lindor, a management consultant and host of the MECE Muse Unplugged podcast. […]

Adapted from http://time.com/money/4982643/6-future-jobs/. Accessed on October 12, 2018.

---

2. Check (✓) the statements that are true according to the text. *Understanding details*

   a. ( ) Roles in occupational therapy, choreography, environmental engineering, and mental health counseling, will be extinct in the next 10 years.

   b. ( ) In 2040 the job market will be very different from what it is today.

   c. ( ) Automation will continue to reshape the job market. One example of its impact is the drone delivery service that it is being tested by Google and Amazon.

   d. ( ) Undoubtedly, all industries and businesses are being disrupted by robots.

3. Which extracts from the text correct the false statements from the previous activity? Write them on the lines below. *Understanding details*

_____
_____
_____
_____
_____

4. Read two extracts from the text on page 61, paying attention to the parts in bold, and check (✓) the alternative that states what they indicate.

> In 2040, the babies born today **will be** at the start of their careers.

> Automation has already eliminated millions of manufacturing, foodservice, and retail jobs, and there's little doubt it **will** eventually **reshape** every other industry.

a. ( ) Promises
b. ( ) Plans
c. ( ) Predictions
d. ( ) Decisions made at the moment of speaking

5. Scan the text on page 61 to find passive voice statements and underline them.

6. Change the extracts below into the passive voice.

a. "Sure, robots are disrupting some industries."
_____

b. "Machine learning [...] uses algorithms to train computers."
_____

c. "[...] consumers [...] still crave human connection."
_____

7. Choose the correct alternative to complete the statements below.

a. They were on vacation at the time of the strike, so they _____ be at the factory when it all happened.

b. Due to the advances in technology, by 2040 the job market _____ have as many openings as it does today.

c. Because of technology, companies _____ change the way they hire employees in the future.

( ) may / might not / could
( ) couldn't / might not / may
( ) couldn't / might / may not

8. Read the text and use the connectors from the box to fill in the blanks. There is an extra connector. Then talk to a classmate about the main points of the text.

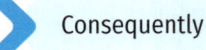

> Consequently   Moreover   Since   Yet

Argentina and Brazil are already agricultural giants. But the best local companies are far more advanced than the rest.

Rising wealth, changing diets, and increased food consumption across the developing world, along with a growing global population, are fueling a steady rise in demand for agricultural commodities such as sugar, soybeans, and meat. _____, the prospects for growers, ranchers, processors, and other agribusinesses are blossoming – and perhaps nowhere more so than in Brazil and to a certain extent in Argentina, already agricultural giants that accounted for $73 billion in exports last year.

The opportunities are considerable. Historically fragmented businesses such as livestock and sugar, for instance, are beginning to consolidate, offering companies the benefits of increased scale. New sources of financing allow players to overcome historically underdeveloped capital markets. Increased demand for affordable and clean energy is creating nontraditional opportunities, such as the production and export of biofuels. (Brazil is already the world's largest producer of ethanol; its exports rose by more than 65 percent in 2006.)

_____ some domestic companies (including local ones and local units of multinationals) aren't benefiting fully, because they aren't as efficient as they could be or aren't getting as much as they could from technology. Smaller enterprises often lack the sophistication to use new financing options to pay for their growth. _____, in some cases, complex or rigid organizational structures promote duplication and inefficiency, which prevent agribusinesses from taking full advantage of a changing commercial environment.

Still, a few companies are moving to address these and related issues and thereby positioning themselves to be leaders in the sector. A look at the practices of these companies – a mix of global powerhouses and smaller players – can show others how to confront some of Latin America's perennial challenges, shed light on the evolution of agribusiness in Argentina and Brazil, and offer insights into the skills and strategies competitors will need in the coming years.
[...]

Adapted from https://industrytoday.com/article/harvesting-latin-americas-agribusiness-opportunity. Accessed on October 12, 2018.

UNIT 7
The Economic Effects of Globalization

IN THIS UNIT YOU WILL...
- talk about how globalization might affect economic growth;
- learn about the rise of new economies;
- use the present perfect tense with *for* and *since*;
- compare the present perfect and the simple past.

LEAD OFF
- What does the picture represent? How does it relate to the title of the unit?
- Have you heard the expression *global village*? If so, what does it mean?
- How might globalization affect the prosperity and economic growth of a country?

READING

BEFORE READING

Look at the text you are about to read. Where was it probably extracted from? *Identifying the source of the text*

a. ( ) An encyclopedia.
b. ( ) An online magazine.
c. ( ) An atlas.

WHILE READING

Read the text and classify the author's tone as mocking, apprehensive, vindictive, or humorous. Underline the fragments that support your answer. *Identifying the author's tone*

The 1914 effect
The globalization counter-reaction
Globalization is a highly disruptive force. It provoked a reaction in the early 20th century. Are we seeing a repeat?

Buttonwood's notebook
Jun 14th, 2017 | by Buttonwood

[...]
Globalization was one of the forces that helped to create the First World War because it has profoundly **destabilizing** effects, effects we are also seeing today. In large part globalization is about the more efficient allocation of resources—labor, capital, even land—and that creates losers. People don't like change, especially when they lose from it. [...]

5   Globalization **disrupted** both international power structures and domestic ones. This rapid change caused a reaction that was often violent. World War I was not inevitable, but it was unsurprising.

So let us move to the current era of globalization, during which the export share of global **GDP** has more than doubled since the 1960s. New economic powers have emerged to challenge American dominance; first, Japan, and now China and potentially India. Imperial **overstretch threatens** America as it did Edwardian Britain. The ability and,
10 more recently, **willingness** of America to act as global sheriff policeman has been **eroded**. [...]

Migration has increased again, not quite to pre-1914 levels but in another direction: from the developing world to the developed. This has led to cultural and economic resentment among voters and imported the **quarrels** of other countries. [...] Economic integration means that financial crises can quickly spread; just as American **subprime mortgages** hit the world in 2008, Chinese bad debt may do so in future.

15 Within the economy two big changes have occurred. Manufacturing capacity has moved from the developed world to Asia. Technology has rewarded skilled workers and **widened pay gaps**. Voters have rebelled by turning to parties that reject globalization. This didn't happen in France, but generally it has made life more difficult for **center-left parties** and turned center-right parties more **nativist**. America's Republicans used to be enthusiasts for **free trade**. Now they have elected Donald Trump.

20 Just as in the first era, globalization has disrupted international and domestic power structures. Thankfully this does not mean that another world war is inevitable. But it is easy to imagine regional conflicts: Iran against Saudi Arabia, or an American attack on North Korea that provokes a Chinese reaction.
[...]
The real danger is that this is a zero-sum game. Governments will appear to **grab** a larger share of global trade for their own countries. In doing so, they will cause trade to **shrink**. That might make voters even angrier. From the early
25 1980s to 2008, most companies could count on a business-friendly political environment in the developed world. But it looks as if that era has ended with the financial crisis. Globalization has caused another counter-reaction.

The best hope is that technology can deliver the economic **growth** and rising prosperity voters want. If that happens, these threats will not disappear, but they will be much reduced. But for all the **hype** about new technology, productivity has been **sluggish**. The **omens** are not great.

Adapted from www.economist.com/buttonwoods-notebook/2017/06/14/the-globalisation-counter-reaction?zid=295&ah=0bca374e65f2354d553956ea65f756e0".
Accessed on July 23, 2018.

AFTER READING

1. What's the main idea of the text? Explain it in your own words. *Stating the main idea of the text*

_____

_____

2. Decide if the sentences are true (T) or false (F). If necessary, go back to the text. *Understanding details*

a. (   ) Globalization has improved domestic and international power structures.

b. (   ) Fortunately, there is some expectation of economic growth and rising prosperity in the face of globalization.

c. (   ) Due to globalization, China and Japan have **come out** as new economic powers that **threaten** American supremacy.

d. (   ) The movement of manufacturing capacity from the developed world to Asia was one of the forces that **triggered** World War I.

e. (   ) Because of the advances in technology, workers are more skilled and payments are quite similar around the world.

3. The author ends the text in a pessimistic tone in "The omens are not great." Do you share the same feeling? Talk to a classmate and justify your opinion relating the author's views to your reality.

EXPAND YOUR VOCABULARY

1. Scan the text on page 64 for the words or expressions from the box and infer their meanings. Then insert them in the headlines that follow.

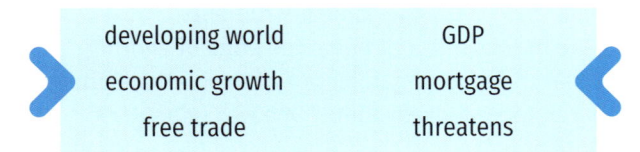

developing world	GDP
economic growth	mortgage
free trade	threatens

a.

The Rise of China and the Fall of the '_____' Myth

By PANKAJ MISHRA FEB. 7, 2018

查看简体中文版 查看繁體中文版

Extracted from www.nytimes.com. Accessed on July 24, 2018.

b.

The circular economy in the _____

BY JEREMY WILLIAMS

September 6, 2016

Extracted from https://makewealthhistory.org. Accessed on July 24, 2018.

c.

BUSINESS

April 25 2018 - 17:04

World Cup Generates All of Russia's _____ – Deputy PM

Extracted from https://themoscowtimes.com. Accessed on July 24, 2018.

d.

Japan's _____ market slammed by higher rates

Consumers shun increased borrowing costs

January 19, 2017 04:07 JST

Extracted from https://asia.nikkei.com. Accessed on July 24, 2018.

e.

TRADE TENSIONSu

Trump's China trade war _____ world economy

Risks grow of dangerous economic divorce despite Beijing's efforts to stop it

Minxin Pei

March 25, 2018 11:00 JST

Extracted from https://asia.nikkei.com. Accessed on July 24, 2018.

f.

Brazil sees one-percent _____ growth in 2017

Source: Xinhua 2018-03-02 06:19:55

Extracted from www.xinhuanet.com/english/2018-03/02/c_137009512.htm. Accessed on July 24, 2018.

2. How does the economic status of a country affect its people's behavior? How does it affect you in particular? Exchange ideas with a partner. Then report your opinions to the class.

Unit 7

VOCABULARY IN USE

1. Reread these excerpts from the text on page 64.

   > So let us move to the current era of **globalization**, during which the **export share** of global GDP has more than doubled since the 1960s.

   > In large part globalization is about the more efficient allocation of **resources**—**labor**, **capital**, even **land**.

   The words in bold are part of a word group about economy. Go back to the text and circle other words or expressions related to the same word group.

2. Below are other words or expressions that belong to the same word group mentioned in activity 1. Match them with their definitions.

   a. inflation
   b. interest rate
   c. budget deficit
   d. bond
   e. recession
   f. capital market
   g. depreciation

   ( ) a market where companies can get capital in the form of shares or bonds, etc.

   ( ) the amount by which what a government spends is more than it receives in taxes or other income, during a particular period of time

   ( ) a continuing increase in prices, or the rate at which prices increase

   ( ) an official document promising that a government or company will pay back money that it has borrowed, often with interest

   ( ) the percentage amount charged by a bank, etc. when you borrow money, or paid to you by a bank when you keep money in an account there

   ( ) a difficult time when there is less trade, business activity, etc. in a country than usual

   ( ) a reduction in the value or price of something

   Extracted from www.ldoceonline.com. Accessed on July 24, 2018.

3. Use the words from the box to complete the text. If necessary, refer back to the definitions in activity 2.

   > bonds   budget deficits   depreciations
   > inflation   interest rates

Is the next global financial crisis brewing?

By Robert J. Samuelson Columnist May 13

The world is not ready for another financial crisis, but another financial crisis may be ready for the world.

[…]

Think Thailand in 1997; a run against the Thai baht ultimately led to crises in South Korea, Indonesia, Russia, and Brazil. Or consider U.S. subprime mortgages; in 2008, they triggered a collapse of global credit markets. Or recall Greece in 2010; its debt threatened the very existence of the euro.

The action these days involves Argentina. It has suffered a sudden loss of confidence. Since mid-April, its currency, the peso, has lost about 12 percent of its value against the dollar. To stem the panic — that is, to persuade investors not to sell pesos for dollars — Argentina's central bank has raised _____ on pesos to 40 percent from 27.25 percent.

[…]

The present president, Mauricio Macri, who took office in late 2015, inherited a doleful legacy of economic mismanagement: high _____, unemployment, and _____ after 12 years of leftist economic policies.

[…]

What is to be feared is the possibility that what's happening to Argentina could happen to other nations. For the past two years or so, international investors have poured money into "emerging market" countries, such as Argentina, Brazil, Mexico, India, China, and Indonesia.

[…]

If these inflows slowed significantly—or stopped altogether—there would be negative consequences for the wider world economy. Countries might have to raise interest rates to defend their currencies against crippling _____. At some point, herd behavior might take over: Investors would buy or sell financial instruments (stocks, _____, currencies, and the like), mainly because they thought that others were going to buy or sell the same instruments.

[…] We may or may not be on the edge of another financial crisis, but regardless of what you think, there's plenty of room for self-doubt. One way or another, Argentina matters.

Extracted from www.washingtonpost.com/opinions/why-the-financial-crisis-in-argentina-matters/2018/05/13/ee84f270-553f-11e8-a551-5b648abe29ef_story.html?utm_term=2a90fdcf29c8. Accessed on July 24, 2018.

4. Work in pairs to answer the question from the title of the text. Use the words and expressions from the previous activities.

LANGUAGE IN USE 1

Unit 7

PRESENT PERFECT — SINCE / FOR

1. **Read an excerpt from the text on page 64 and check (✓) the correct alternative to complete the sentence.**

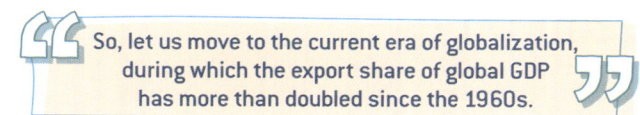

   > So, let us move to the current era of globalization, during which the export share of global GDP has more than doubled since the 1960s.

   The expression "since the 1960s" refers to…
   a. (   ) a period of time.
   b. (   ) a starting point.

2. **Now read the quote and check (✓) the correct alternative to complete the statement about it.**

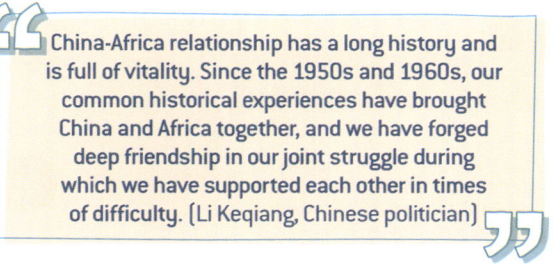

   > China-Africa relationship has a long history and is full of vitality. Since the 1950s and 1960s, our common historical experiences have brought China and Africa together, and we have forged deep friendship in our joint struggle during which we have supported each other in times of difficulty. (Li Keqiang, Chinese politician)

   Extracted from www.brainyquote.com/quotes/li_keqiang_690958. Accessed on July 24, 2018.

   According to Li Keqiang, China and Africa have had friendship bonds for…
   a. (   ) the 1950s and 1960s.
   b. (   ) more than 60 years.

3. **The present perfect is often used with time expressions preceded by *for* and *since*. Use those words to complete the sentences below.**
   a. We use _____ to talk about the time when an action started.
   b. We use _____ to talk about the duration of an action.

4. **Why is the present perfect tense used in the sentences in activities 1 and 2?**

   _____

5. **Read the texts and fill in the blanks with the verbs from the box in the present perfect tense, as well as *for* or *since* when needed. Then exchange ideas about the texts in small groups.**

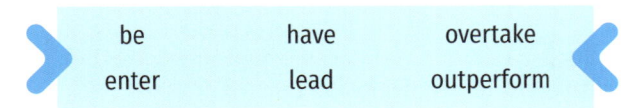

be	have	overtake
enter	lead	outperform

   a. China shines a bright light on the **path** ahead

   […]

   In his keynote address to a high-level meeting on July 26, Xi Jinping, general secretary of the Central Committee of the Communist Party of China, said socialism with Chinese characteristics _____ a new development stage _____ the 18th National Congress of the CPC.

   […]

   Extracted from www.telegraph.co.uk/news/world/china-watch/politics/china-socialism-new-dawn. Accessed on July 24, 2018.

   b. China vs. United States: A Tale of Two Economies

   […]

   The United States _____ the world's largest economy _____ about 140 years, and it **roughly** accounts for 22% of global GDP. However, in recent times China _____ the U.S. by at least one measure of total economic strength, which is GDP based on purchasing power parity (PPP).

   Either way you slice it, the economies are the two strongest globally in absolute terms.

   […]

   Extracted from www.visualcapitalist.com/china-vs-united-states-a-tale-of-two-economies. Accessed on July 24, 2018.

   c. The Next Global Financial Crisis is Inevitable (Pt 1/2)

   July 22, 2018

   It _____ ten years _____ the last major financial crisis. With systemic **deregulation undoing** the safeguards, we are due for another crisis very soon. Thomas Hanna, research director of the Democracy Collaborative's Next System Project, says it is almost guaranteed.

   […]

   Adapted from https://therealnews.com/stories/the-next-global-financial-crisis-is-inevitable-pt-1-2. Accessed on July 24, 2018.

   d. China is the world's new science and technology powerhouse

   […]

   While the U.S. _____ the world in the production of scientific knowledge for decades, in terms of both quantity and quality, and the EU as a bloc (still including the UK) _____ the US in numbers of scientific publications _____ 1994, China now publishes more than any other country apart from the U.S. China's scientific priorities are shown by a particularly big increase in its share of published papers in the fields of computer sciences and engineering. While China—for now—is making modest **inroads** into the top-quality segment of publications, it is already on par with Japan.

   Extracted from http://bruegel.org/2017/08/china-is-the-worlds-new-science-and-technology-powerhouse. Accessed on July 24, 2018.

67

EXPAND YOUR READING

1. Skim the text and answer: What's the purpose of this infographic?

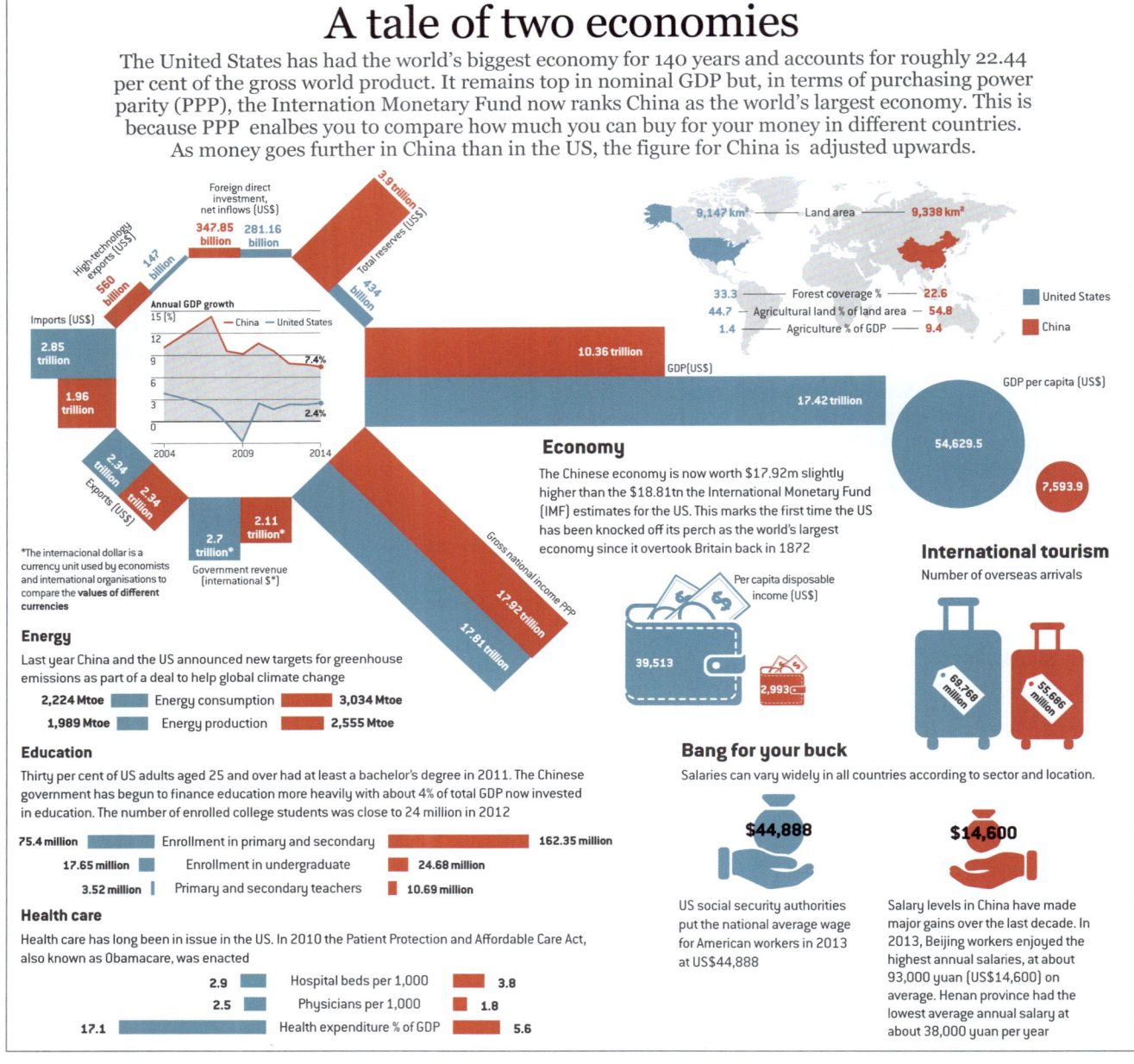

   _____

A tale of two economies

The United States has had the world's biggest economy for 140 years and accounts for roughly 22.44 per cent of the gross world product. It remains top in nominal GDP but, in terms of purchasing power parity (PPP), the Internation Monetary Fund now ranks China as the world's largest economy. This is because PPP enalbes you to compare how much you can buy for your money in different countries. As money goes further in China than in the US, the figure for China is adjusted upwards.

High-technology exports (US$): 147 billion / 560 billion
Foreign direct investment, net inflows (US$): 347.85 billion / 281.16 billion
Total reserves (US$): 3.9 trillion / 434 billion
Imports (US$): 2.85 trillion / 1.96 trillion
Exports (US$): 2.34 trillion / 2.34 trillion
Government revenue (international $*): 2.7 trillion* / 2.11 trillion*
Gross national income PPP: 17.81 trillion / 17.92 trillion
GDP (US$): 17.42 trillion / 10.36 trillion
GDP per capita (US$): 54,629.5 / 7,593.9

Annual GDP growth: China 7.4% / United States 2.4% (2004–2014)

Land area: 9,147 km² / 9,338 km²
Forest coverage %: 33.3 / 22.6
Agricultural land % of land area: 44.7 / 54.8
Agriculture % of GDP: 1.4 / 9.4

*The internacional dollar is a currency unit used by economists and international organisations to compare the **values of different currencies**

Economy
The Chinese economy is now worth $17.92m slightly higher than the $18.81tn the International Monetary Fund (IMF) estimates for the US. This marks the first time the US has been knocked off its perch as the world's largest economy since it overtook Britain back in 1872

Per capita disposable income (US$): 39,513 / 2,993

International tourism
Number of overseas arrivals: 69,768 million / 55,686 million

Energy
Last year China and the US announced new targets for greenhouse emissions as part of a deal to help global climate change
- Energy consumption: 2,224 Mtoe / 3,034 Mtoe
- Energy production: 1,989 Mtoe / 2,555 Mtoe

Education
Thirty per cent of US adults aged 25 and over had at least a bachelor's degree in 2011. The Chinese government has begun to finance education more heavily with about 4% of total GDP now invested in education. The number of enrolled college students was close to 24 million in 2012
- Enrollment in primary and secondary: 75.4 million / 162.35 million
- Enrollment in undergraduate: 17.65 million / 24.68 million
- Primary and secondary teachers: 3.52 million / 10.69 million

Bang for your buck
Salaries can vary widely in all countries according to sector and location.
$44,888 / **$14,600**

US social security authorities put the national average wage for American workers in 2013 at US$44,888

Salary levels in China have made major gains over the last decade. In 2013, Beijing workers enjoyed the highest annual salaries, at about 93,000 yuan (US$14,600) on average. Henan province had the lowest average annual salary at about 38,000 yuan per year

Health care
Health care has long been in issue in the US. In 2010 the Patient Protection and Affordable Care Act, also known as Obamacare, was enacted
- Hospital beds per 1,000: 2.9 / 3.8
- Physicians per 1,000: 2.5 / 1.8
- Health expenditure % of GDP: 17.1 / 5.6

Adapted from www.visualcapitalist.com/wp-content/uploads/2015/10/tale-of-two-economies2.html. Accessed on May 26, 2018.

2. Read the infographic and check (✓) the correct alternative about its content.
   a. ( ) A larger amount of money from other countries is invested in the USA, when compared to China.
   b. ( ) Both the USA and China have developed policies that address global warming and its effects.

3. Underline the only statement that is not true about infographics.
   a. They are visual representations of complex information.
   b. They present often brightly colored messages with small, clearly-displayed chunks of information.
   c. They are divided into acts and scenes and the use of direct speech is predominant.
   d. Their format includes timelines, flow charts, annotated maps, graphs, Venn diagrams, etc.

LANGUAGE IN USE 2

Unit 7

PRESENT PERFECT vs. SIMPLE PAST

1. Below you will find some extracts from the infographic on page 68. Read them, paying attention to the verb forms in bold, and then use these to complete the chart.

> Salary levels in China **have made** major gains over the last decade. In 2013, Beijing workers **enjoyed** the highest annual salaries, at about 93,000 yuan (US$14,600) on average.

> Thirty per cent of U.S. adults aged 25 and over **had** at least a bachelor's degree in 2011. The Chinese government **has begun** to finance education more heavily with about 4% of the total GDP now invested in education.

Actions or events that started and finished at a specified time in the past	Actions or events that started in the past and continue in the present

2. Go back to the infographic on page 68 and look for another extract that contrasts the use of the present perfect and the simple past. Write it on the lines below, highlighting the verb tenses.

_____
_____
_____
_____

3. Now, based on activities 1 and 2, complete the following explanations with present perfect or simple past.

  a. We use the _____ for actions or events that happened at unspecific times in the past and for actions that started in the past and continue in the present or have consequences in the present.

  b. We use the _____ for actions or events that happened at definite times in the past, actions or events that started and finished in the past, and actions or events that are part of a list of complete actions in the past.

  c. We use expressions such as *yet*, *since*, and *for* with the _____ and expressions such as *yesterday*, *two months ago*, and *last week* with the _____.

4. Complete the following text with the verbs in parentheses. Use the present perfect or the simple past.

> New Economy
> […]
> Are We in the New Economy?
> The question ever since the bursting of the tech bubble is, of course, whether or not the new economy is here or still on the horizon. Since the tech boom of the 90s, we _____ (see) the growth of many new and exciting subsectors in tech. These include the sharing economy, the streaming economy, the **gig** economy, cloud computing, big data, and artificial intelligence. The companies involved in tech, particularly Google, Facebook, and Apple, _____ (overtake) most companies in the world in terms of **market cap**. More and more of the traditional manufacturing economy is being automated using innovations coming out of the tech sector. Of course, we still buy and sell products, but the service economy – again enabled by technology – is becoming an ever growing part of the global economy.
>
> So, we are definitely living in an economy that is qualitatively different from the one in the 1980s. Less people are employed in direct manufacturing, we are more anxious about being replaced by a machine than outsourced and data _____ (become) a currency of its own. Now that the new economy is here, we're not as confident that it _____ (be) the one we _____ (want) after all.

Adapted from www.investopedia.com/terms/n/neweconomy.asp#ixzz5MGNDNcwj. Accessed on July 25, 2018.

5. Use your own words to explain the two economies mentioned in the infographic on page 68. Contrast the present perfect and the simple past in your answer.

_____
_____
_____
_____
_____

6. Talk to a classmate about what you know regarding economic changes of your country. Use the present perfect and the simple past.

LISTENING COMPREHENSION

1. **Answer in small groups:** What's a financial crisis? Are we due for another one soon? Explain your views.

2. **Listen to Sharmini Peries, from *The Real News Network*, and check (✓) the correct alternatives to complete the sentences.**

   1. According to a report issued by the Next Systems Project, another major financial crisis is...
      - a. ( ) certain.
      - b. ( ) doubtful.

   2. The report is entitled...
      - a. ( ) "Will there be another financial crisis, or even another great recession like that of 2007 and 2008?"
      - b. ( ) "The Crisis Next Time: Planning for public ownership as an alternative to corporate bank bailouts."

   3. The report estimates that the next financial crisis could be...
      - a. ( ) less severe than the last one we experienced.
      - b. ( ) worse than the last one we experienced.

   4. The report recommends the creation of a public banking sector...
      - a. ( ) to cope with the next crisis and prevent future crises.
      - b. ( ) to banish upcoming crisis for good.

3. **Listen to Thomas Hanna and Sharmini Peries in the second part of the recording and choose the correct segments from the box to complete the transcript. Note that there are three extra alternatives.**

10 years	corporate bank bailouts	neoliberal period
70 years	deregulation	taxpayer-funded rescue
addressing or changing	financial crisis	
average	Great Depression	

THOMAS HANNA: Thank you very much for having me.
SHARMINI PERIES: Thank you for joining us here. […] Let's start with the first issue, which is you went back _____, and you took a look at the history of crises. And so, based on that, tell us why there's another crisis pending.
THOMAS HANNA: Well, I think the first thing that we need to understand is that we are exactly _____ from the last major financial crisis, which was essentially the biggest financial crisis in this country in 70 years, since the _____. And if you look at history in the post-1970 period, what we call the _____, crises happen on _____ about once every 10 years. So, 10 years from the financial crisis, we're looking at a time when there should, or probably would be, another _____ just based on history alone. That's not taking into account what has happened in the intervening 10 years since the financial crisis. And essentially what has happened is nothing. We've had very little movement on _____ any of the underlying basis of the financial sector that caused the crisis.
[…]

Extracted from https://therealnews.com/stories/the-next-global-financial-crisis-is-inevitable-pt-1-2. Accessed on May 20, 2018.

4. **Work with a partner to answer the questions:** In what ways would Brazil be affected if a new financial crisis erupted in the USA? In your opinion, what's the best way out of a crisis? How could growing economic inequality be addressed in middle-income countries like Brazil, for example? Report your opinions to the class.

>> EXPAND YOUR HORIZONS >>>

Check (✓) the column that best describes your opinion about each statement. Then discuss your answers with your classmates and teacher, justifying your point of view.

	I agree.	I'm not sure.	I disagree.
a. Globalization is beneficial to the world economy because it allows countries to interact and cooperate, enables the development of new technologies, and improves citizens' lives.			
b. China has become a leading manufacturer of goods without being ready to take over so much and at such low costs.			
c. Everyone should prepare for the worst financial crisis since the 2008 crisis that started in the United States and spread across the world.			

UNIT 8

Spotting Fake News among the Real Stories

FACTS
FAKE NEWS

▶ IN THIS UNIT YOU WILL…

- talk about the importance of distinguishing fake from real stories;
- understand what can be done to check if news is fake or not;
- review some verb tenses;
- learn what embedded questions are and how they are formed.

LEAD OFF

- What does the image mean to you?
- How can you relate the image to the title of the unit?
- In your opinion, why do people fabricate fake news?

READING

BEFORE READING

Check (✓) the statements that are true about you. *Thinking about personal experience*

a. ( ) I get my news from print newspapers.
b. ( ) I listen to the news on the radio.
c. ( ) I watch the news on TV.
d. ( ) I read the news online.

WHILE READING

Read the news article below and find the answer to the following question: Why does Facebook have a fake news "war room"? *Scanning*

---

www.theguardian.com/technology/2018/oct/18/facebook-war-room-social-media-fake-news-politics

Facebook has a fake news "war room" — but is it really working?

Corporation shows off room of engineers, data scientists and other experts but offers reporters few new specifics

Facebook is promoting a new "war room" as a part of its solution to election interference, unveiling a team of specialists working to stop the spread of *misinformation* and propaganda.

It's unclear how well it's working.

The Silicon Valley company, which has faced intensifying *scrutiny* over its role in amplifying malicious
5 political content, opened its doors to reporters to tour a new workspace at its Menlo Park **headquarters** on Wednesday. Engineers, data scientists, **threat** investigators and other Facebook experts from 20 teams recently began collaborating inside the so-called "war room", a term that political campaigns typically use to describe operation centers.

The press **briefing** provided minimal new information about Facebook's specific strategies and impacts
10 when it comes to combatting foreign interference and false news. The corporation has been **eager** to publicly demonstrate that it is taking abuses on its platforms seriously *amid* an avalanche of scandals. That includes a vast data **breach**, government *inquiries* across the globe, new ad fraud allegations, and the continuing stream of viral fake content and hate speech.

[…] WhatsApp, the Facebook-owned messaging service, has also been linked to widespread false news stories
15 that have led to violence and mob lynchings in India. The platform has further struggled to mitigate harms it is causing in Myanmar, where an explosion of social media hate speech has contributed to violence and genocide. American hate groups and far-right activists have also weaponized the site.

On Wednesday morning, a group of journalists **crowded** outside a windowless room, *snapping* iPhone photos of a closed door with a small sign stuck to it that said "WAR ROOM" in red letters. Inside, digital
20 dashboards displayed real-time information about activity on the platform. CNN played in the background, and the wall displayed a large American flag and motivational posters saying "Focus on impact" and "Bring the world closer together".

Some screens were "off the record" and could not be photographed, Facebook communications representatives said. The names of employees inside the room could not be published.

[…]

25 Samidh Chakrabarti, Facebook's director of elections and civic engagement, said WhatsApp had been "doing quite a bit of work to try to stay ahead of any sort of emerging issues", adding: "They've been **cracking down** on *spamming* accounts on WhatsApp – and they've removed hundreds of thousands."

Facebook […] noted that it has a fact-checking partnership with the Associated Press in all 50 states for the midterms. The continuing collaborations with **third-party** factcheckers, however, have been controversial, with
30 some partner journalists expressing frustration over the **seemingly** minimal impact.

Asked how Facebook has been measuring the success of the factchecking and if the company had new data on its effectiveness, Harbath told the Guardian that it was "one piece of the puzzle" and cited "automated work" to reduce the reach of "clickbait" and "ad farms".

[…]

Adapted from www.theguardian.com/technology/2018/oct/18/facebook-war-room-social-media-fake-news-politics Accessed on November 20, 2018.

AFTER READING

1. Read the text and complete the chart below with the information presented in it. *Understanding details*

a. What Facebook is trying to combat together with the press:	
b. The name of the operation center Facebook uses to meet with journalists:	
c. Characteristics of the war room:	
d. Kind of partnership that Facebook has with Associated Press:	
e. Examples of abuses taking place on the Facebook platform:	

2. Read the statements below and check (✔) the one that describes the main purpose of the text. *Identify the main purpose of a text*

  a. ( ) To present the main companies involved in spreading false news.

  b. ( ) To present Facebook and what kind of false news it may spread.

  c. ( ) To inform readers about the existence and the meaning of a term used to describe the fighting of false news.

  d. ( ) To inform readers about an action Facebook is taking in order to avoid the spread of false news.

3. Read the questions below and discuss them with a classmate. Then share your ideas with the rest of the class.

  a. What negative effects can you think of regarding the spread of fake news?

  b. Do you think that social media companies have an obligation to prevent people from being exposed to fake news?

  c. What do you think makes some fake news go viral? Do you think that people are aware of the fact that some pieces of news are false when they share them? Justify your answer.

  d. Do you think that fake news is more likely to be spread by bots (web robots) than by people? Justify your answer.

EXPAND YOUR VOCABULARY

Refer to the text on page 72 and find the words in italics that correspond to the definitions below.

  a. _____ : careful and thorough examination of someone or something

  b. _____ : while noisy, busy, or confused events are happening – used in writing or news reports

  c. _____ : incorrect information, especially when deliberately intended to deceive people

  d. _____ : questions you ask in order to get information

  e. _____ : taking a photograph

  f. _____ : email accounts that send the same message to many different people, usually as a way of advertising something – used to show disapproval

Adapted from www.ldoceonline.com. Accessed on November 20, 2018.

VOCABULARY IN USE

1. Read a fragment extracted from the article on page 72 and choose the most appropriate explanation for "clickbait."

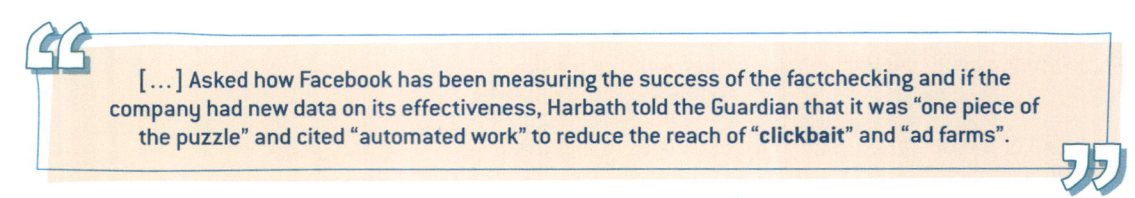

   > [...] Asked how Facebook has been measuring the success of the factchecking and if the company had new data on its effectiveness, Harbath told the Guardian that it was "one piece of the puzzle" and cited "automated work" to reduce the reach of "**clickbait**" and "ad farms".

   a. ( ) Online tool developed to keep users online for the longest time possible in order to make them interact with people from different locations without displaying their identity.

   b. ( ) Social media tool that allows people to create content on the web and spread it as fake news.

   c. ( ) Online content intended to attract users and encourage them to click on a link to access a certain webpage.

2. The following words are commonly used when talking about fake news. In pairs, match them with their meanings.

   a. sham
   b. slander
   c. hoax
   d. bot
   e. web crawler

   ( ) a false warning about something dangerous

   ( ) a computer program that finds information on the Internet, especially so that this information can be used by a search engine

   ( ) a false spoken statement about someone, intended to damage the good opinion that people have of that person

   ( ) someone or something that is not what they are claimed to be – used to show disapproval

   ( ) a computer program that continuously performs the same operation, such as searching for specific information online

   Extracted from https://www.ldoceonline.com/. Accessed on October 05, 2018.

3. Still in pairs, read the following extract and decide which word from the previous activity it refers to.

   _____

   > In 2011, Katie Holmes settled a lawsuit against celebrity gossip rag, *The Star*, for $50 million. The suit was over an article that claimed that Holmes was a drug addict. The magazine issued an apology and even said that they would donate a "substantial donation" to one of Holmes's favorite non-profits. [...]

   Extracted from www.ranker.com/list/celebrities-who-sued-for-defamation/jacob-shelton. Accessed on October 7, 2018.

4. How is it possible to tell a fake from a real story? Are you able to identify a fake story? How important is this? Work in small groups and figure out which of the statements below are real and which are fake. Then exchange ideas with your classmates.

   a. (_____) There are more tigers in captivity in the U.S. than in the wild worldwide.

   b. (_____) Queen Elizabeth II removed Barack and Michelle Obama from royal wedding guest list.

   c. (_____) Between 2011 and 2013, China used more cement in three years than the U.S. did in the entire 20th century.

   d. (_____) A woman named Violet Jessop survived the sinking of both the Titanic and its sister ship, the Britannic.

   e. (_____) Scientists who work with cockroaches often become addicted to pre-ground coffee.

   f. (_____) England intends to forbid Canadians to use expressions created by Shakespeare.

LANGUAGE IN USE 1

Unit 8

VERB TENSE REVIEW

1. Work in pairs. Read the fragments below, extracted from the article on page 72, paying attention to the underlined parts. Then match them with what they express.

> a. The corporation has been eager to publicly demonstrate that it is taking abuses on its platforms seriously amid an avalanche of scandals.

> b. The Silicon Valley company, which has faced intensifying scrutiny over its role in amplifying malicious political content, opened its doors to reporters to tour a new workspace at its Menlo Park headquarters on Wednesday.

> c. Facebook is promoting a new "war room" as a part of its solution to election interference, unveiling a team of specialists working to stop the spread of misinformation and propaganda.

> d. [...] "war room", a term that political campaigns typically use to describe operation centers

( ) a finished action in the past
( ) an action in progress at the moment
( ) an action that started at an indefinite time in the past and is still true in the present
( ) a fact

2. Use *will* or *be going to* and the verbs from the box to complete the extracts below.

> end up   happen   miss

a. "That is, if we take the current culturally liberal consensus of what is fake news as our decider, then we _____ entirely _____ that news which is speaking truth to the power of that consensus, aren't we? Which is rather to miss the point of the speaking truth part."

b. "Any system which suppresses the news _____ also _____ enforcing, not challenging, current misconceptions that are widely believed."

Extracted from www.washingtonexaminer.com/opinion/youtube-is-going-to-fight-fake-news-but-how-do-you-define-fake-news. Accessed on October 8, 2018.

c. "Throughout the history of the 20th century, whether in Soviet-era Russia or Nazi Germany, regimes based on lies have ultimately collapsed because reality catches up with them. In today's more open societies, this reality check _____ more quickly."

Extracted from www.ft.com/content/a352f9a6-99f4-11e8-ab77-f854c65a4465. Accessed on October 8, 2018.

EXPAND YOUR READING

1. Read the title of the following essay and answer: What kind of information do you expect to find in the text?
___
___
___

EXPERIENCE: I WRITE FAKE NEWS
by AMLE - Association for Middle Level Education

I've been writing articles for far-right websites in the US for a year now. I didn't set out to do this; it started in October 2016, when I was finishing my PhD in London. My funding ran out, and I
5 started writing content to pay the rent. I found clients through websites that allow potential writers to bid for work, and then build a portfolio of reviews from clients. There is an enormous amount of work available – everything from
10 writing product copy to ghost-writing novels.

The first jobs I got were pretty shady. I was writing fake Amazon reviews and descriptions of perfume that had yet to be produced. A reliable client put me in touch with a colleague
15 who runs a number of websites, one of which focuses on news about, and reviews of, guns. I have never seen a gun, let alone used one, but I took the job. The site carries reviews of handgun accessories, and for each product there is a link
20 to Amazon. My client gets paid for every click-through he generates through Amazon's affiliate scheme. There are vast numbers of such sites: I've written fake reviews of amplifiers, baby products, printers, […].

[…]

25 Recently, we've tried to boost the site up the Google rankings. This involves writing for other sites that are visited by gun enthusiasts, a lot of them pretty extreme, and sneaking in a link to our own site. This is against their rules, so you
30 have to hide the link deep in the middle of a dense paragraph, so no one notices.

[…]

But I don't have a moral problem with it. I wish I had some snappy argument about why what I'm doing is not wrong. I'm furthering ignorance,
35 certainly, and perhaps contributing to an atmosphere of hatred. But I don't think people have died as a result of my work. […]

I have never made up a statistic, invented a story, or been racist. I think I would refuse to do so. I
40 see my role as providing an extreme right-wing interpretation of breaking news. Though I do not believe the stories I write, I don't count this as lying.

I suppose the articles I write would be regarded as fake news. Though that has got a lot of
45 attention recently, I think it is merely a new term for an old phenomenon. This type of ideologically driven journalism pre-dates the Internet and perhaps even the printing press. […]

My friends know what I do for a living, and
50 find it amusing. There is an absurd humor in a young(ish), left(ish), British arts student pretending to be a far-right, middle-aged, American gun enthusiast. They recognize that my earnings give me the freedom to live and
55 work where I want.

I'll continue to work for this client for at least another six months, by which time I will have finished my PhD and saved enough to go traveling. Then I'll get my first proper job in five
60 years. If my rate continues to increase, though, I'll continue to write for this client. It's easy money.

Adapted from www.theguardian.com/lifeandstyle/2018/jan/26/experience-i-write-fake-news. Accessed on October 8, 2018.

2. Were your guesses in activity 1 correct? Why or why not? Talk to your classmates.

3. What kind of essay is this? Check (✓). Then justify your choice.
   a. ( ) exposition
   b. ( ) description
   c. ( ) argument
   d. ( ) narrative

LANGUAGE IN USE 2

Unit 8

EMBEDDED QUESTIONS

1. Read the sentences below, paying attention to the parts in bold, and check (✓) the appropriate alternatives.

   > **Can you tell** which news story is real and which one is fake?
   > (Which news story is real and which one is fake?)

   > **I wonder if** fake news might actually be a good thing for real journalism.
   > (Might fake news actually be a good thing for real journalism?)

   > **Do you know** how to spot fact from fiction?
   > (How do you spot fact from fiction?)

   > **We need to find out** whether he is a victim of fake news or not.
   > (Is he a victim of fake news or not?)

   a. ( ) The sentences above are questions, but they are not direct questions. They are inside another question or statement.

   b. ( ) The parts in bold are introductory phrases to these questions.

   c. ( ) The structure of these questions is the same as the one used in direct questions.

   In English, a question that appears in a declarative statement or in another question is called an *embedded question*.

   Embedded questions are used when we don't want to be too direct. Below you'll find some other common introductory phrases used in embedded questions:

   > Could you tell me…?   The question is…
   > I wanted to know…   Who knows…?

2. Transform the direct questions below into embedded questions. Use the introductory phrases from the box. Make sure you do not repeat them in two different questions.

   > I wonder…
   > I can't understand…
   > What I need to know is…
   > Would you mind telling…
   > We need to find out…
   > I'd like to know…

   a. Where does she live?

   _____
   _____

   b. Why do people post fake content on social media?

   _____
   _____

   c. Is this post real or fake?

   _____
   _____

   d. What does this news report mean?

   _____
   _____

   e. Where do her friends live?

   _____
   _____

   f. Did she order this package online?

   _____
   _____

LISTENING COMPREHENSION

1. **You are going to listen to a teacher talk about what he does to help students identify real news. Listen and answer the following questions.**
   a. In how many steps can real news be confirmed?
   _____
   b. What are these steps?
   _____
   _____

2. **Match the columns according to what the teacher says about each step. Then listen again and check.**
   a. argument   c. language
   b. evidence   d. reliability

   (   ) "determine if a source is trustworthy"
   (   ) "check sources, citations, and facts"
   (   ) "identify the two sides in every story"
   (   ) "show how words and tone matter"

3. **Read the extracts from the text and identify which step from activity 2 each of them corresponds to.**
   a. _____ "The final step of identifying real news is to evaluate the tone and level of sensationalism of an article. Incorporate analysis of word choice in evaluating the reliability of a news source."

   b. _____ "As students learn to discern real from fake news, it is important to remember that there is a difference between fake news and inaccurate information. Reliable news sources will include links to professional sources, fact-based evidence, and will present multiple sides of an issue. Train students to check the evidence within the article they are reading."

   c. _____ "We now know that there are intentional efforts to widely disseminate false content on social media channels, blogs, and other websites. Making sure students know how to measure the reliability of a source is a critical first step to helping them spot fake news."

   d. _____ "This step can be tricky, as even the most factual news outlets can still have a bias or unique perspective on a topic. A biased article does not inherently imply that it's fake news; rather, it's part of the overall formula (along with reliability and evidence) that can help students. A well-written article is balanced, representing many sides of a story. Recognizing that there are, more often than not, multiple perspectives of an event or a political issue, can lead students to better understand their community and the world as a whole."

4. **Do you usually follow these four steps to check if the news is true? Why or why not? Are you going to follow them from now on? Justify.**

>> EXPAND YOUR HORIZONS >>>>

Check (✓) the column that best describes your opinion about each quote below. Then discuss your answers with your classmates and teacher, justifying your point of view.

	I agree.	I'm not sure.	I disagree.
a. The source of information might affect its credibility and authenticity; that's why it's always important to check our sources and references.			
b. Trends demonstrate that people are changing the way they access the news or access information. In a few years, TV will not be as relevant as it is today.			
c. The rise of fake news has brought a new set of worries to the spotlight. We are now subject to many threats when surfing the web, and it's our responsibility to make sure we spread only relevant and real content.			

REVIEW 4

Units 7 and 8

1. Look at the text below. Where do you think it is from? *Identifying the source of the text*

   a. (   ) An online encyclopedia   **b.** (   ) A print newspaper   **c.** (   ) A news website

---

Are people becoming less reliant on Facebook for their news?

Paul Chadwick

Two new surveys suggest the public still values traditional news publishers

When you try to imagine a media diet consisting only of retweets, random blogs or the Facebook posts of family and friends, you grasp the value of journalism created by professional media organizations. Traditional news organizations aren't perfect, but they are not fake. Nor are they as readily manipulated as we know social media can be. Professional journalism's longstanding skills of access to sources, verification, presentation and dependable distribution remain an essential element of what **nourishes** democratic societies.

That insight, sharply conveyed in images accompanying this column, informs a new campaign to promote the well-regarded Columbia Journalism Review (CJR), a not-for-profit magazine based at the graduate school of journalism at Columbia University, New York. The campaign's assertion of the importance to a healthy democracy of the public sphere – alongside the private, of course – coincides with two new reports that, in different ways, affirm the same. However, the emerging picture is not clear yet.

"Americans and the news media: what they do – and don't – understand about each other" **broadly** finds that journalists and the public have similar aims, but that to maintain trust journalists have to better explain what they do. The American Press Institute and the Associated Press-Norc Center for Public Affairs Research at the University of Chicago surveyed 2,019 adult Americans and 1,127 journalists, and analyzed their expectations. Both groups strongly valued accuracy and fairness. Journalists rated their role as watchdogs who scrutinize the powerful far more highly (93%) than did the public (54%). Both groups saw transparency and trust as linked. The CJR has been casting a critical eye over journalism for almost 60 years, and its editor and publisher, Kyle Pope, told me demands on CJR from the public have been growing as US media organizations dispense with their public editors, who are in-house but independent contacts/critics known elsewhere as news **ombudsmen** or readers' editors.

[…]

Looking beyond the US, the 2018 digital news report of the UK-based Reuters Institute for the study of journalism tends to support the notion that the public understands that "real journalism matters", although the authors' optimism is cautious. Reliance on Facebook for news is falling, they report, and **willingness** to pay for professionally produced journalism seems to be increasing. But a majority prefer "side-door access" to news through search and social media, rather than going direct to the traditional news publishers. Use of messaging apps is rising "as news consumers look for more private (and less confrontational) spaces to communicate", the report says.

Adapted from www.theguardian.com/commentisfree/2018/jun/17/facebook-news-publishers-accuracy Accessed on November 20, 2018.

---

2. Find what each of these numbers refer to in the text and match them with the alternatives. *Understanding details*

   a. 1,127   **b.** 93   **c.** 54

   (   ) the percentage of journalists who value accuracy and fairness in news
   (   ) the number of journalists interviewed in the survey
   (   ) the percentage of random people who value accuracy and fairness in news

3. From your point of view, does "real journalism" matter? Is most news on Facebook and other social media reliable? Justify your answer.

_____

_____

4. Read the text and fill in the blanks with the verbs from the box.

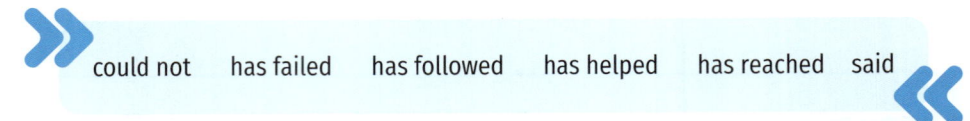

> could not   has failed   has followed   has helped   has reached   said

[…]
China faces certain social challenges, and creative measures are needed to overcome them.
[…]
Two key words, transcendence and rejuvenation, best describe this new era. Here transcendence means going beyond the two preceding stages. Mr. Xi _____ a major conclusion — that the two previous stages _____ negate each other. The new stage will help deepen reform and opening-up under the socialist system. […]
Transcendence also means going beyond the Western mode of development, which _____ only a small number of countries with a cumulative population of about 1 billion to lead comfortable lives but _____ to realize common prosperity. […]
China _____ its own path of economic development and become the largest and fastest-growing developing country. As Mr. Xi _____, socialism with Chinese characteristics has widened the path of modernization for developing countries […].

Adapted from www.telegraph.co.uk/news/world/china-watch/politics/china-socialism-new-dawn. Accessed on October 14, 2018.

5. Read the extracts from the previous text and write whether the verb forms in bold indicate a prediction for the future, an action that started in the past and continues up to the moment, or a fact.

a. "China **faces** certain social challenges":
_____

b. "The new stage **will help** deepen reform and opening-up under the socialist system":
_____

c. "As Mr. Xi said, socialism with Chinese characteristics **has widened** the path of modernization for developing countries":
_____

6 Check (✓) the text that contains an embedded question. Then underline that question.

a.
( ) **Will Facebook Decide Which News Is Fake?** 
Facebook, a site from which a substantial number of people acquire their daily news, has decided that pages that post fake stories will be banned from advertising. That's a perfectly fine decision, but it raises a bigger and more profound question: Who decides which news is fake? Mark Zuckerberg?
Read more

b.
( ) **Apparently, CNBC Is Now A PR Firm** 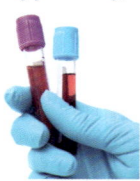
Wonder why "fake news" is taking hold as a concept and a description? Look no further than a recent CNBC article and its accompanying video, showcasing a new blood collection product.
Read more

c.
( ) **An Object Lesson In Fake 'News' Sites** 
"Fake news" has become a meme — and it's all over the Internet. For example, take a look at a site that claims to provide real evidence that aspartame is carcinogenic in humans. Not only does it cite old data, it has picked a study whose authors don't agree with them. Can you get much more fake than that?
Read more

Extracted from www.acsh.org/tags/fake-news. Accessed on October 14, 2018.

GRAMMAR OVERVIEW

Verb tenses

Tense	Use(s)	Example(s) – affirmative	Example(s) – negative	Example(s) – interrogative
Simple past	• Completed action in the past. When used with the past continuous, refers to an action that interrupts an action in progress in the past.	She was sleeping when I **arrived** home.	When their boss **came** in, everything was a mess.	Were you studying when she **called** you?
Past continuous	• An action in progress in the past.	While the students **were doing** the activities, the teacher **was correcting** their tests.	Debbie **was not / wasn't talking**, so I **was not / wasn't talking** either.	What **were** you **doing** while I **was doing** my homework?
Present perfect	• Past experiences when time is not mentioned; • Actions that started in the past and are still going on in the present; • Finished actions that influenced the present; • When someone has gone to a place and returned (been); • When someone has gone to a place and has not returned yet (gone).	I **have / 've lived** in Canada since 2009. She **has started** a new job. Sue is tired. She **has studied** hard all day. I **have / 've been** to Spain once. The kids **have gone** to the beach and they will be back by Sunday.	She **has not / hasn't lost** her tickets. He **has not / hasn't finished** his homework yet. I'm hopeless. I **have not / haven't done** my chores lately. I **have / 've never been** to China. Dad **has not / hasn't returned** from France.	**Have** you **met** the new neighbor? **Have** you **started** planning your trip? You look exhausted. **Have** you **worked** hard today? **Have** you ever **been** to Greece? Where is Grace? **Has** she **returned** from work?
Present perfect (adverbs) Just Already Always Since For Never Yet	• *just*: an action that happened very recently; • *already*: an action that is not a new experience; • *always*: something that has been true for a lifetime; • *since*: a previous point in time; • *for*: indicates how long something lasts; • *never*: something that has not ever happened; • *yet*: an activity that has not happened, but is expected to happen soon;	I've **just** finished work. He has **already** bought the tickets. We have **always** loved this house. I've lived in NY **since** 2015. We've been traveling **for** two weeks. They have **never** been to China.	I haven't met him **yet**.	Have you read this book **yet**?

Modal verbs

Modal verb	Use(s)	Example(s) – affirmative	Example(s) – negative	Example(s) – interrogative
Can	• Ability; • Permission; • Possibility; • Requests; • Offers; • General truths; • Prohibition (can't).	I **can drive** your car. You **can come** here anytime you'd like.	I **cannot / can't read** without my glasses. You **cannot / can't** dive in this pool.	**Can** you play the drums? **Can** you give me some information, please?
Could	• Ability in the past; • Formal requests; • Suggestions; • Possibility.	He **could go** camping.	Susan **could not / couldn't run** that fast before; now she's beating everyone in the race.	**Could** I **take** your order?
Be able to*	• Ability (in all tenses); • To use the infinitive.	He **was able to** pay for his own food. I would love to **be able to** travel to Greece.	He**'s not able to** drive at this age. I **won't be able to** finish this game today.	**Are** you **able to** walk that far? Do you think he **would be able to** take me home after school?

* It is not a modal verb, but sometimes it replaces *can* and *could*.

GRAMMAR OVERVIEW

Need to vs. Have to

Verb	Use(s)	Example(s) – affirmative	Example(s) – negative	Example(s) – interrogative
Need to	• To talk about something that is / isn't necessary for someone to do.	She **needs to pick up** her luggage before she checks out.	I **don't need to worry** about her.	**Do** I **need to dress up** for the party?
Have to	• To express obligation; something we are committed to; • Something that cannot be postponed; • To express no obligation or necessity to do something (*not have to*).	Flight attendants **have to wear** uniforms. You can't miss this plane. You **have to be** on time for your next flight.	They **don't have to worry** about it anymore.	**Do** you **have to tell** him our secret?

Phrasal verbs

Kind of phrasal verb	Use	Examples
Separable	• With the object between the verb and the particle.	I have to **take back** the book I lent you. I have to **take** it **back**.
Inseparable	• Cannot separate the verb from the particle.	I just **came across** this new app. It's awesome!

Conditional sentences

Conditional	Use	Form	Examples
Zero	• To talk about things that are always true; • To talk about general habits.	If + simple present, → simple present	**If** you **add** one and one, you **get** two. **If** you **exercise** daily, you **stay** in shape.
First	• To talk about results that are likely to happen in the future.	If + simple present, → future with *will*	**If** I **study** hard, I **will** pass the test.

Tag questions

Verb tense	Examples – affirmative	Examples – negative
Simple present	I am coming with you, **aren't I**? You have some news for us, **don't you?**	You are never late, **are you**? There are no leftovers from lunch, **are there**?
Simple past	He was late again, **wasn't he**?	They weren't very nice to us, **were they**?
Present perfect	You have traveled to Europe many times, **haven't you**?	Mary has never been to England, **has she**?

Make vs. do

Verb	Common collocations	Examples
Do	do research	The teacher told us to **do** some **research** on sea animals.
Do	do the shopping	Mom is responsible for **doing the shopping** on Saturdays.
Make	make plans	I would like us to **make plans** for the summer.
Make	make a reservation	Don't forget to **make a reservation** at the Plaza.

Relative clauses

Relative pronoun	Use	Example(s)
Who	• People (Defining and non-defining)	I don't know the girl **who** called you yesterday.
Which	• Animals and things (Defining and non-defining)	This is the rarest species **which** can only be found in Africa.
That	• People, animals, and things; • Informal situations. (Defining only)	The man **that** spoke at the meeting was very wise.
Whom	• Formal style or written form; as the object of the relative clause. (Defining and non-defining)	There was only one person to **whom** the boy spoke frequently.
Whose	• People and animals; • Possessive situations. (Defining and non-defining)	I have a friend **whose** brother is annoying.
Where	• Places (Defining and non-defining)	I want to live in a place **where** there are plenty of trees.
No pronoun	• When the object of the clause is defined by the relative pronoun. (Defining only)	I'm sorry, but that is all (**that**) I have to say. The people (**who / whom / that**) we talked to were very happy.

Set vs. get

Verb	Common collocations	Examples
Set	set a tone	Her speech today **set the tone** for the group meeting.
Get	get a call	I didn't **get a call** from anyone.

Word categories

Category	Use	Examples
Idioms related to technology	• To talk about technology.	Being part of a **well-oiled machine** makes things work smoothly! His new car has all the **bells and whistles** he could dream of.
Expressions about travel	• To talk about different and modern ways of traveling.	We often go **couchsurfing** on our vacation. Ann goes **glamping** every year with her boyfriend in beautiful nature and modern luxury. I can't wait to read the chronicles of a **solivagant** journey through Asia.
-ly adverbs	• To show us how someone does something. Adverbs can modify verbs, adjectives, or other adverbs. They occur in different types such as: manner, time, frequency, degree, focusing, and evaluative.	George spoke **softly** to his wife. We watch the news **daily**. I come to this coffee shop **regularly**. This class starts at **precisely** 8 o'clock. **Honestly**, I could watch another episode. Exceptions: Look, it's raining **hard**! They are running very **fast**.
Terms related to fake news	• To talk about fake news.	The **anonymous group** was asked to apologize for spreading **fake news**. Salespeople often use **confirmation bias** to state only the positive aspects of their product. They used digital **misinformation** to turn the public against the president.

GRAMMAR OVERVIEW

Passive voice

Verb tense	Form	Examples
Simple present	am / is / are + past participle	The housework **is done** by everyone at home.
Present continuous	am / is / are + being + past participle	A poem **is being written** by a famous poet.
Simple past	was / were + past participle	A very nice song **was sung** by the group.
Modal verbs: can, must, will, should, may, might, could.	modal verb + be + past participle	Pancakes **can be made** here in the kitchen. Employees **must be paid** in the first week of the month. The contract **will be signed** by the manager. This car **should be repaired** by Friday. The book **may be read** by the teacher.

Discourse markers

Use	Discourse markers	Examples
Addition	furthermore	The boys were cold and tired, and, **furthermore**, they were starving.
Cause / reaction / effect	therefore	It's raining. **Therefore**, they need their umbrellas.
Comparison	unlike	**Unlike** her brother, she cannot swim.
Consequence / result	so	**So**, we'll see you at the party, Michael.
Contrast	however	They are lost. **However**, we still have hope.
Emphasis	as a matter of fact	I'm not a child. **As a matter of fact**, I'm sixteen years old.
Condition	as long as	You will pass the test **as long as** you study.
Illustrating	for instance	What would you do, **for instance**, if you found some money in the train?
Ordering	now	**Now**, let's welcome Kate to our show!
Purpose	in order (not) to	We never forget the homework **in order not to** upset the teacher.

Embedded / Indirect questions

Use	Common beginnings	Example(s)
A question that is included inside another question or statement in order to sound more polite. The word order in the main question doesn't change.	Can you remember...? Can you tell / show me...? Do you have any idea...? Do you know...? I wonder if you would mind telling / showing me...? Let's ask... We need to find out... Would you mind explaining...? Would you mind telling / showing me...?	**Can you remember** what he said? **Can you tell me** if we are almost there? **Do you have any idea** if he is the doctor? **I wonder if you would mind telling** me what to do? **Let's ask** what time the bus arrives. **We need to find out** where we should go next. **Would you mind explaining** why she decided not to come? **Would you mind telling me** where he is?

LANGUAGE REFERENCE

UNIT 1

PRESENT PERFECT

Usage Notes

The present perfect is often used to refer to:

- our past experiences.

    Have you ever **tried** Thai food?

- actions that started at an unspecific time in the past and continue up to the present.

    They **have started** making their honeymoon plans.

- actions that happened in the past but are important at the time of speaking.

    I'm exhausted. I**'ve worked** hard all day long.

    We**'ve missed** the bus. Let's take a cab.

- actions that refer to a time that is not yet finished.

    Has she **been** to the club **this week**?

    We **haven't had** time to talk **today**.

- When someone has gone to a place and returned, we use the present perfect of the verb *be*.

    A: **Have** you ever **been** to the new mall by the bay?

    B: No, I haven't. Is it nice?

- When someone has gone to a place but has not returned, we use the present perfect of the verb *go*.

    A: Where's Grandma? She hasn't visited us lately.

    B: She**'s gone** to your aunt's farm and won't be back until the end of the month.

PAST CONTINUOUS – SIMPLE PAST

Usage Notes

- The past continuous is used to talk about actions in progress in the past.

    I **was working** in the morning.

- In general, the action described by the simple past interrupts the situation described by the past continuous.

    Leo **was taking** a shower when the lights **went out**.

    Where **were you going** when I **called** you?

- Use only the past continuous for multiple actions happening at the same time in the past.

    While Claire **was getting dressed** for work, her brother **was doing the dishes**.

    What **were you doing** while I **was having** lunch?

- The conjunctions *when* and *while* are used to indicate "during the time that" and to connect two situations happening at the same time.

    They took lots of pictures **when** they were traveling.

    While he was watching his favorite TV show, he preferred to remain silent.

SEPARABLE AND INSEPARABLE PHRASAL VERBS

Many phrasal verbs are transitive, which means that they take an object, while others are intransitive and don't take an object.

Transitive phrasal verbs can be used in different ways: in some the verb and the particle can be separated (these are called **separable phrasal verbs**) and the object can be positioned in the middle, between the verb and the particle, or at the end; while in others the object must come at the end because the verb and the particle can't be separated (these are called **inseparable phrasal verbs**).

When **separable phrasal verbs** are used with a pronoun, the pronoun must be placed between the verb and the particle.

Can you repeat that old saying? I want to **write it down**.

I want to **write down** that old saying. Can you repeat it?

Here are some separable and inseparable phrasal verbs.

Separable phrasal verbs	Inseparable phrasal verbs
throw away	catch up
turn on / off	check in
look up	come across
call off	drop by
figure out	grow up
make up	put up with
pick up	run into
put on	look after
turn down	run out of
get on / off*	write down

*can be both separable and inseparable depending on the context of the sentence.

LANGUAGE REFERENCE

IDIOMS

Idiom	Meaning	Example
a well-oiled machine	something that works very smoothly and effectively	If you're trained correctly you become like **a well-oiled machine**.
bells and whistles	extra things that are offered with a product or system to make it more attractive to buyers	The basic rule about computer memory is this: Buy as much as you can afford, even if it means sacrificing other **bells and whistles**.
get your wires crossed	to become confused about what someone is saying because you think they are talking about something else	We **got our wires crossed** and I waited for an hour in the wrong place.
leading edge	the area of activity where the most modern and advanced equipment and methods are used	Software companies are on the **leading edge** of technology in very competitive markets.
press / push the panic button	to do something quickly without thinking enough about it, because something unexpected or dangerous has suddenly happened	Why haven't governments in the region **pushed the panic button?**
silver surfer	an old person who uses the Internet	Many **silver surfers** use the Internet to keep in touch with their grandchildren.

Extracted from www.ldoceonline.com/dictionary. Accessed on August 2, 2018.

UNIT 2

CAN vs. COULD
BE ABLE TO

Usage Notes

We sometimes use *be able to* instead of *can* and *could*. Although *be able to* sometimes replaces *can* and *could*, it is not a modal verb. The expression consists of the verb *be* followed by the adjective *able* and a verb in the infinitive form.

- *Be able to* replaces *can* and *could* to express ability.

    I **am** not **able** to drive.

    Are you **able** to read without your glasses?

- We can use *be able to* for abilities in all tenses, while *can* and *could* are used for present and past abilities, respectively.

    They **will be able to** swim backstroke if they practice hard.

    She **has been able to** speak Spanish fluently since she was 14.

- As *can* and *could* have no infinitive form, we use *be able to* when we want to use the infinitive.

    I **would like to be able to** windsurf.

    Do you think you **would be able to** hand in the report by Monday?

ZERO AND FIRST CONDITIONALS

Usage Notes

Conditions are expressed mainly by the word *if* in English. To make a condition, two clauses are necessary: an <u>*if* clause</u>, in which <u>the condition is stated</u>, and a <u>main clause</u>, which <u>states the results of the successful completion of the condition</u>.

You can make a condition about a situation or a fact in the present, in the past, or in the future (a hypothetical situation), and that condition can have its result in the past, in the present, or in the future. In order to identify the time in which your condition and results are going to be in, you need to observe the verb tense of the clauses.

	Idea	*If* clause	Main clause
Zero Conditional	The result always happens if the condition is met.	present	present
		If you leave ice cream out of the freezer for too long,	it melts.
First Conditional	The result is likely to happen in the future because of a condition in the present	present	will
		If you meet Claire on your way home,	she will ask you for a ride.

- Note that in the zero conditional, *if* can be replaced with *whenever*.

    Whenever you leave ice cream out of the freezer for too long, it melts.

    Whenever red and blue are mixed, you get purple.

- In the first conditional, it is possible to use *can*, *may*, *might*, or *could* instead of *will* to indicate that something is a possible consequence, and not a certainty, in the future.

    If it is rainy, I **may** stay indoors on the weekend.

    If they beat their next opponent, they **might** win the championship.

    Could she flunk math if she doesn't take the finals?

- It's sometimes possible to vary the tenses in conditionals. In the first conditional, for example, the present continuous or the present perfect might be used, depending on the context.

    If she **is working**, I won't disturb her.

    If you **have called** a cab, you will have to wait right here.

- The imperative can also be used in the result clause in the first conditional to indicate an instruction.

    If you finish your assignment, **turn** to page 20 for the reading passage.

    Ask me for help if you think you can't do the activity by yourself.

UNIT 3
RELATIVE CLAUSES

Relative clauses can be either defining or non-defining. Defining relative clauses add important information and non-defining relative clauses provide additional information.

   The man **whose** son was awarded the first prize is a famous chef.

   The movie **that I watched last week** was nominated for the Oscar.

In non-defining relative clauses, the relative pronoun can't be omitted and *that* can never be used. Non-defining clauses are more frequent in written English and they are separated by commas.

   Lucy, **who is a sports fan**, was invited to host the prom dance.

   My dog, **which is a bull terrier**, is 3 years old.

Usage Notes

- In relative clauses, we can use the relative pronoun *whom* instead of *who* when it's the object of the verb or the object of a preposition in the dependent clause, preferably in formal styles and in writing.

    The cashier **whom** I gave my credit card to warned me it had expired.

    The girl with **whom** I spoke at the party was very polite.

- Relative clauses can be reduced to shorter forms if the relative clause modifies the subject of a sentence. They might be reduced to an adjective phrase, a prepositional phrase, a past participle phrase, a past participle, and a present participle.

    Full: The people **who were tall** had to sit at the back of the auditorium.

    Reduced: The **tall people** had to sit at the back auditorium.

    Full: The children, **who seemed to be afraid of the animals**, were accompanied by their parents.

    Reduced: The children, **afraid of the animals**, were accompanied by their parents.

    Full: The worker **who was promoted** is very well-known.

    Reduced: The **promoted worker** is very well-known.

    Full: The man **who was elected** was very popular.

    Reduced: The **elected man** was very popular.

    Full: The lady **who lives near my store** takes the subway every day.

    Reduced: The lady **living near my store** takes the subway every day.

SO
Usage Notes

In sentences showing cause and effect, *so* is used to show the effect while *as, since, because,* and other connectors may be used to show the cause.

   Most guests have arrived, **so** we will start serving dinner.

   As most guests have arrived, we will start serving dinner.

   Since most guests have arrived, we will start serving dinner.

   Because most guests have arrived, we will start serving dinner.

COLLOCATIONS WITH *DO* AND *MAKE*

Collocation	Example
do a course	I decided to **do a course** in gardening this summer.
do homework	I never go out before **doing** my **homework**.
do one's best	Kelly **did her best** but it wasn't enough to get a good grade.

LANGUAGE REFERENCE

do research	You should **do** some **research** before you buy a new car.
do the housework	He spent all day **doing the housework**.
do the laundry	We **did the laundry** and hung it out to dry early in the morning.
do the shopping	I prefer to **do the shopping** on weekdays.
make a joke	The **jokes** he **makes** aren't funny at all.
make a mess	They **made a mess** of their lives. But it's never too late to start all over.
make a mistake	I can't **make** such **a mistake** in my calculations!
make a reservation	At that restaurant, you should **make** table **reservations** in advance.
make plans	Have you **made** any **plans** for the weekend?
make time	The doctor told me to **make time** for exercise in my life.
make sure	He just called to **make sure** I was all right.

UNIT 4

NEED TO / DON'T NEED TO / HAVE TO / DON'T HAVE TO

Usage Notes

- We use *need to* or the negative form *don't / doesn't need to* when we want to talk about something that is / isn't necessary for someone to do. In this context, we often mention who is going to do it.

  We **need to** go over our notes before the test.

  (It's necessary for us to go over our notes before the test.)

  I **don't need to** reread the text to answer the questions.

  (It's not necessary for me to reread the text to answer the questions.)

  We use *have* to express an obligation, something we are committed to, or a situation that can't be postponed.

  Do students **have to** wear a uniform in your school?

  Lydia can't answer phone calls because she **has to** keep her phone in her bag when she's teaching.

- We use *don't have to* when there is no obligation or necessity to do something.

  You **didn't have to** take care of your little brother last night because his babysitter was here.

  She **doesn't have to** call me every time there's something to be resolved at the office! She can make her own decisions.

- Unlike *don't have to*, *must not* is used when we want to say that something is not allowed.

  You **must** not use your cellphones if you're attending classes in my school.

  You **must not** turn right on Oak Avenue. Look at the prohibition sign!

TAG QUESTIONS

Tag questions are often used as confirmation questions at the end of a sentence.

Usage Notes

- For question tags with "I am", the question tag "aren't I" is used.

  I'm your best friend, **aren't I**?

  I'm calling the right phone number, **aren't I**?

- When we use the *there be* structure, it is reflected in the question tag.

  There's a little sugar left, **isn't there**?

  There weren't other alternatives to choose from, **were there**?

- When *nothing, nobody, somebody, something*, or other similar compounds are the subject in the statement, we use *it* in the question tag to refer to *something* or *nothing* and *they* in the question tag to refer to *someone* or *nobody*.

  Something should be done to solve the problem, shouldn't **it**?

  No one agreed to work late on Fridays, did **they**?

- When we want to express surprise or some particular interest, we can use a positive question tag with a positive statement.

  So you're celebrating your promotion, **are you**? Congratulations!

  Oh, you've passed the finals, **have you**? Great news!

MODERN WORDS / EXPRESSIONS ABOUT TRAVEL

Word / Expression	Meaning
couchsurfing	the practice of moving from one friend's house to the other, often sleeping on the couch or floor while you are temporarily of no fixed abode

staycation	a vacation that is spent at home enjoying time to relax and exploring your local area
flashpacker	not to be confused with a naked backpacker, flashpackers are usually a little bit older than the standard beer-swilling, party hostel staying backpacker
ratpacker	their priority is usually drinking copious amounts of beer or buckets full of the local alcohol
mancation	a vacation for men only, where women are banned and the guys do some sort of "manly" activity like go spear fishing, play poker in Vegas, or head to a rowdy sports game final
glamping	camping in luxury and can be in house-like tents or something creative like a yurt
grey nomad	a mature aged traveler with a keen sense of adventure who travels around a country staying in a campervan, caravan, or tent for a reasonably long time
solivagant	solitary wanderer
wayfarer	a person who travels from place to place, usually on foot
fernweh	a German word that means a craving for travel or distant places

Extracted from www.huffingtonpost.com/shanti-burton/10-modern-travel-words_b_9001326.html. Accessed on October 15, 2018.

UNIT 5

WILL VS. BE GOING TO
MODAL VERBS: MAY, MIGHT, COULD

Usage Notes

- We often use *will* for prediction with the following verbs and phrases: *be sure, be afraid, believe, expect, hope, think, wonder,* etc.

  I'm sure my classmates **will get** good grades.
  I'm afraid I **won't be** able to help you this time.
  He hopes she **will** never **leave** her job.
  Do you think we **will make** it to the top?

- We often use *will* (and not *be going* to) with adverbs of certainty such as *certainly, perhaps,* and *probably*.

  Jennifer **will certainly run** for class representative this year.
  Perhaps Claude **will invite** you to join him at the party tonight.
  We **will probably travel** together again next time.

- In question tags after imperatives, we use *will* (and not *be going to*).

  Take those heavy boxes upstairs, **will** you?
  Don't pretend you forgot to sign the list, **will** you?

- For threats, we also use *will*.

  Pay what you owe me, or I **won't** lend you any more money.
  Listen carefully or you **will** miss important details.

OTHER COMMON EXPRESSIONS USED TO TALK ABOUT THE FUTURE

- *Be about to*: to talk about things that we expect to happen very soon.

  Hurry up! Our bus **is about to** leave.

- *Be due to*: to refer to things that are scheduled.

  My guests **are due to** arrive after 10 P.M.

- *Be to*: to refer to obligations and commands or instructions.

  Helen **is to** visit Grandma tomorrow.
  You **are to** hand in your tests by 11:30 A.M.

- *May, might,* and *could* can be used to talk about future possibility:

  She **may** come to the party, but she depends on a ride.
  We **might** travel abroad, but we haven't decided yet.

TYPES OF -LY ADVERBS

Depending on the aspects of modification, -ly adverbs have different types such as manner, time, frequency, degree, focusing, evaluative, etc.

- <u>Manner adverbs</u> indicate the way something happens or is done.
- <u>Time adverbs</u> indicate when something happens.
- <u>Frequency adverbs</u> indicate how often or how many times something occurs.
- <u>Degree adverbs</u> indicate the degrees of qualities, properties, states, conditions, and relations.
- <u>Focusing adverbs</u> point to something.
- <u>Evaluative adverbs</u> comment or give an opinion about something.

Manner	Time	Frequency	Degree	Focusing	Evaluative
cautiously	lately	usually	completely	especially	surprisingly
quickly	recently	frequently	slightly	mainly	obviously
professionally	early	occasionally	absolutely	particularly	frankly
anxiously	finally	generally	totally	largely	hopefully

LANGUAGE REFERENCE

UNIT 6

PASSIVE VOICE

Usage Notes

The passive voice is used when we are more interested in the action than in the agent (or doer of the action), when we are more interested in the receiver of the action than in the agent, or when the agent is not important, not known, or obvious.

Formation chart

Passive forms are composed of an appropriate form of the verb *be* followed by the past participle form of the main verb.

Verb Tense	Passive Voice
Simple present	*am / is / are* + past participle
Present continuous	*am / is / are* + *being* + past participle
Simple past	*was / were* + past participle
Modal verbs (present)	*can / must / should / could / may / might* + *be* + past participle

Usage Notes

- In non-standard English, *get* is sometimes used instead of *be* in passives.

  Henry **got promoted** last week.

  Sandra **got stood up** this morning. She was waiting for the guy, but he never showed up.

- When verbs have two objects, a direct and an indirect object, we can use two different formations.

  (Active voice) The students **gave** a present to the teacher.

  (Passive voice) A present **was given** to the teacher (by the students).

  (Passive voice) The teacher **was given** a present (by the students).

DISCOURSE MARKERS

Discourse markers (or connectors) have distinct functions such as showing turns, joining ideas, changing a topic, adding information, contrasting information, ordering speech, expressing reason and effect, concluding, etc.

Some common discourse markers are listed in the following chart.

Addition	Cause, Reason, or Effect	Comparison	Consequence or Result	Contrast
and	because	like	consequently	but
moreover	for	as	as a result	however
furthermore	as	unlike	so	even though
in addition	since	similarly	thus	nevertheless
also	therefore	in the same way	hence	yet
besides	given that	just as	in conclusion	whereas
along with this	due to	in comparison	because (of)	on the contrary

Emphasis	Condition	Illustrating	Ordering	Purpose
in fact	if	for example	first	so that
as a matter of fact	whether	for instance	second	to
indeed	as long as	in some cases	then	not to
actually	provided that	such as	next	in order to
in reality	assuming that	like	now	in order not to
essentially	unless	let's say	continuing	so as to
fortunately	now that	be it	finally	so as not to

COLLOCATIONS WITH *GET* AND *SET*

Collocation	Example
get dressed	It takes her half an hour to **get dressed** in the morning.
get drunk	Lisa **got drunk** last night and had to take a taxi home
get lost	Without your help, I would **get lost**. Thank you!
get sick	Gosh, this is the second time I've **gotten sick** this month!
set a precedent	What you have done will **set a** legal **precedent**.
set an example	Parents and teachers should **set an example**.
set the date and time	Have you **set the date and time** for Jason's farewell party?
set the table	She hasn't **set the table** yet. How can I serve dinner?

UNIT 7
PRESENT PERFECT – ADVERBS

Some adverbs are often used with the present perfect tense.

Example	Form	Meaning
He's **just left** for work.	subject + have/has + **just** + past participle	*Just* indicates the fact that the activity has been completed very recently.
I **have already made** up my mind about college.	subject + have/has + **already** + past participle	*Already* indicates the fact that the activity is not a new experience.
They **have always liked** the country.	subject + have/has + **always** + past participle	*Always* indicates something that has been true for a lifetime.
She**'s lived** in LA **since** 2010.	subject + have/has + past participle + **since** + time phrase	*Since* indicates a previous point in time.
We**'ve been** here **for** 15 minutes.	subject + have/has + past participle + **for** + time phrase	*For* indicates how long something lasts.
We**'ve never been** friends.	subject + have/has + **never** + past participle	*Never* indicates a situation that has not happened ever.
You **haven't had** lunch **yet**.	subject + have/has + not + past participle + object + **yet**	*Yet* indicates an activity that has not happened but will hopefully happen soon.
Have you **been** to the new Italian restaurant **yet**?	have / has + subject + past participle + object + **yet**	*Yet* indicates an activity that we expected to be completed but we are still waiting for it to be done.
Have you **ever bought** any pieces of clothes and never worn them? This is the best pizza I **have ever eaten**!	have / has + subject + **ever** + past participle	*Ever* is used in questions to indicate "at any time" or "at all times". It is commonly used in interrogative forms or superlative sentences.

PHRASAL VERBS RELATED TO BUSINESS AND ECONOMY

Phrasal Verb	Meaning
cash in	to make a profit from a situation in a way that other people think is wrong or unfair
contract out	to arrange to have a job done by a person or company outside your own organization
draw up	to prepare a written document, such as a list or contract
hire out	to allow someone to borrow something for a short time in exchange for money
lay off	to stop employing someone because there is no work for them to do
pencil in	to make an arrangement for a meeting or other event, knowing that it might have to be changed later
put back	delay or postpone
rip off	to charge someone too much money for something, or sell someone a product that is faulty
sell out	to sell your business or your share in a business
set up	to start a company, organization, committee etc
stock up	to buy a lot of something in order to keep it for when you need to use it later
take over	to take control of something
write off	to write a letter to a company or organization asking them to send you goods or information

Extracted from www.ldoceonline.com/dictionary/. Accessed on August 05, 2018.

LANGUAGE REFERENCE

UNIT 8
EMBEDDED QUESTIONS

Embedded or indirect questions are more formal than regular questions and they don't need a change in word order in the main question. With embedded questions, we make our requests or questions in a softer and more polite way.

Usage Notes

- Embedded questions can be used as part of other questions or as part of statements.

  (Regular question) — Where does he live?

  (Embedded question as part of a question) — Could you tell me where he lives?

  (Embedded question as part of a statement) — I don't know where he lives.

- Other common introductory phrases used in embedded questions are:

  Can you remember…?

  Can you tell / show me…?

  Do you have any idea…?

  Do you know…?

  I wonder if you would mind telling / showing me…?

  Let's ask…

  We need to find out…

  Would you mind explaining…?

  Would you mind telling / showing me…?

TERMS RELATED TO FAKE NEWS

Term	Meaning
anonymous	of unknown authorship; not revealing one's identity
bogus	false; counterfeit; fake; fraudulent
confirmation bias	the tendency to seek information that supports one's decisions and beliefs while ignoring information that does not match one's decisions and beliefs.
distortion	an exaggeration or stretching of the truth to achieve a desired effect.
fabricated	made up; false; made to deceive
falsehood	a lie
gatekeeper	media executives, news editors, and prominent reporters who decide what news to present and how it will be presented
legitimate	lawful; authentic; genuine
misinformation	creation of fictitious (fake) memories by providing misleading information about an event after it takes place
partisan	biased; one-sided; committed to one group
rumor	a piece of information or a story passed from one person to another without any proof that it is true
reputable	respectable; well thought of considered to be honest and to provide a good service
vetting	checking or investigating. In journalism, internally double- or triple-checking everything in a news report for accuracy, fairness and context.

Extracted from https://quizlet.com/200280714/fake-news-vocabulary-flash-cards/. Accessed on October 15, 2018.

READING STRATEGIES

Ao longo da coleção, estamos sinalizando algumas estratégias de leitura voltadas à melhora na compreensão de textos. O principal objetivo dessas estratégias é fazer com que você, aluno, torne-se um aprendiz mais eficaz e alcance resultados positivos nos exames e vestibulares a serem realizados ao final do Ensino Médio.

A seguir você encontrará uma breve explicação sobre as estratégias mais comumente abordadas antes e durante a leitura dos textos.

Activating or using previous knowledge – Esta estratégia consiste em acionar, quando preciso, o conhecimento que você tem guardado em sua mente. Quando falamos em conhecimento prévio na leitura, estamos nos referindo às informações que você precisa ter para ler um texto sem muita dificuldade para compreendê-lo.

Brainstorming – O termo foi criado a partir da junção das palavras *brain* (cérebro) e *storm* (tempestade), portanto, significa "tempestade cerebral" ou "tempestade de ideias". A estratégia propõe que você e seus colegas de sala explorem sua capacidade criativa, na medida em que trocam ideias a respeito do assunto que será abordado no texto.

Bridging – O termo vem da palavra *bridge*, que significa "ponte". A estratégia consiste, então, em "fazer uma ponte", isto é, em estabelecer uma relação entre o seu conhecimento prévio sobre o assunto que será explorado no texto e o texto propriamente.

Finding organizational patterns or understanding text structure – A estrutura de um texto diz respeito à forma como as informações estão nele organizadas. Artigos, por exemplo, contam com uma introdução, um desenvolvimento e uma conclusão; as informações nas biografias são, em geral, organizadas em sequência cronológica; as receitas, na maioria das vezes, são divididas em duas partes – ingredientes e modo de preparo. Assim, estar atento aos padrões de organização de um texto ajuda-o a identificar seu gênero e, consequentemente, sua função social.

Predicting – A palavra *predict* significa "prever". Ao lermos o título de um texto ou observarmos as imagens que o acompanham, por exemplo, podemos prever ou deduzir seu conteúdo. Quanto mais conhecimento geral você tiver, mais facilmente vai prever o assunto de um texto. Em algumas atividades, você é convidado especificamente a prever o tema e o gênero do texto (*predicting the theme and the genre*).

Recognizing or identifying – Reconhecer significa identificar algo que se conhece. Portanto, reconhecer ou identificar o tipo textual (*textual type*), a voz, ou seja, quem está falando no texto (*voice in a text*), a perspectiva do autor (*the author's perspective*), a fonte do texto (*the source of the text*), o público ao qual o texto se destina (*the target audience*), o propósito principal do texto (*the main purpose*) etc. ajuda-o a antecipar o que está por vir no texto a ser lido.

Skimming – Consiste em observar o texto rapidamente para detectar o assunto geral ou o seu propósito geral (*skimming to identify the main purpose*), por exemplo. Nesse momento, não há nenhuma preocupação em se atentar aos detalhes. É importante que você observe o *layout* do texto, seu título e sub-títulos, cognatos, primeiras e últimas linhas de cada parágrafo, bem como as imagens, gráficos e tabelas que o acompanham.

Scanning - É uma técnica de leitura que consiste em correr rapidamente os olhos pelo texto até localizar a informação específica desejada. O *scanning* é prática rotineira na vida das pessoas. Alguns exemplos típicos são o uso do dicionário para obter informação sobre o significado de palavras ou a utilização do índice de um livro para encontrar um artigo ou capítulo de interesse.

Há, também, estratégias que são trabalhadas após a leitura dos textos. Observe:

Making inferences or inferring – A estratégia de inferência tem como objetivo fazê-lo capturar aquilo que não está dito no texto de forma explícita. Essas adivinhações podem ter como base as pistas dadas pelo próprio texto ou o seu próprio conhecimento. Trata-se de uma estratégia de leitura extremamente importante, pois um texto só terá sentido se você puder estabelecer relações entre as partes, ou seja, entre as palavras, frases, parágrafos etc.

Selecting a good title – Muitas vezes o título de um texto resume sua ideia central. Para selecionar o título mais apropriado para o texto que você acabou de ler, leia-o novamente e anote os pontos que mais chamaram sua atenção. O mesmo se aplica para quando você tiver que afirmar ou declarar a ideia ou o propósito principal do texto lido (*stating the main idea or the main purpose of the text*).

Understanding details – Para entender os detalhes de um texto é preciso fazer uma leitura lenta e concentrar-se durante essa leitura, isto é, ficar longe de qualquer coisa que possa distraí-lo. Recorrer a um dicionário para consultar as palavras e expressões desconhecidas e anotar seu significado, bem como fazer paráfrases durante a leitura, são algumas das ações que contribuem para a compreensão detalhada do texto. Podem contribuir, também, para as atividades que pedem que você resuma o texto lido (*summarizing*).

Understanding main ideas – Para realizar atividades que têm esta estratégia sinalizada, não é necessário fazer uma leitura tão detalhada, nem mesmo procurar todas as palavras desconhecidas em um dicionário. Basta fazer uma leitura geral do texto com atenção e compreender sua mensagem principal.

IRREGULAR VERBS

Base form	Past form	Past participle	Translation
awake	awoke	awoken	acordar
be	was, were	been	ser, estar
become	became	become	tornar-se
begin	began	begun	começar
bend	bent	bent	dobrar
bet	bet	bet	apostar
bite	bit	bitten	morder
blow	blew	blown	soprar
break	broke	broken	quebrar
bring	brought	brought	trazer
build	built	built	construir
burn	burnt/burned	burnt/burned	queimar
buy	bought	bought	comprar
catch	caught	caught	pegar
choose	chose	chosen	escolher
come	came	come	vir
cut	cut	cut	cortar
do	did	done	fazer
draw	drew	drawn	desenhar
dream	dreamed/dreamt	dreamed/dreamt	sonhar
drink	drank	drunk	beber
drive	drove	driven	dirigir
eat	ate	eaten	comer
fall	fell	fallen	cair
feed	fed	fed	alimentar
feel	felt	felt	sentir
fight	fought	fought	lutar
find	found	found	achar
fly	flew	flown	voar
forget	forgot	forgotten	esquecer
forgive	forgave	forgiven	perdoar
get	got	got/gotten	conseguir
get up	got up	got up/gotten up	levantar-se
give	gave	given	dar
go	went	gone	ir
grow	grew	grown	crescer
hang out	hung out	hung out	passar tempo
have	had	had	ter
hear	heard	heard	ouvir
hide	hid	hidden	esconder
hit	hit	hit	atingir
hold	held	held	segurar
hurt	hurt	hurt	machucar
keep	kept	kept	manter

Base form	Past form	Past participle	Translation
know	knew	known	saber, conhecer
lean	leant/leaned	leant/leaned	inclinar-se
learn	learnt/learned	learnt/learned	aprender
leave	left	left	deixar, sair
lend	lent	lent	emprestar
let	let	let	deixar
lose	lost	lost	perder
make	made	made	fazer
mean	meant	meant	significar
meet	met	met	encontrar, conhecer
overcome	overcame	overcome	superar
pay	paid	paid	pagar
put	put	put	colocar
read	read	read	ler
ride	rode	ridden	andar de
ring	rang	rung	tocar
rise	rose	risen	subir, aumentar
run	ran	run	correr
say	said	said	dizer
see	saw	seen	ver
sell	sold	sold	vender
send	sent	sent	enviar
set	set	set	estabelecer
show	showed	shown	mostrar
sing	sang	sung	cantar
sit	sat	sat	sentar
sleep	slept	slept	dormir
speak	spoke	spoken	falar
spell	spelled/spelt	spelled/spelt	soletrar
spend	spent	spent	gastar, passar tempo
split	split	split	dividir
stand up	stood up	stood up	ficar de pé
steal	stole	stolen	roubar
swim	swam	swum	nadar
take	took	taken	pegar, tomar
teach	taught	taught	ensinar
tell	told	told	contar
think	thought	thought	pensar
throw	threw	thrown	jogar
understand	understood	understood	entender
wake up	woke up	woken up	acordar
wear	wore	worn	vestir
win	won	won	ganhar
write	wrote	written	escrever

COMMON MISTAKES

Speakers of Portuguese are more likely to make certain mistakes in English because of interference from Portuguese. Let's take a look at some common mistakes:

TOPIC	COMMON MISTAKE	RIGHT FORM	SOME EXPLANATION
USING PAST TIME EXPRESSIONS WITH PRESENT PERFECT	I have been to the supermarket ~~yesterday~~, that's why the fridge is full.	I have been to the supermarket, that's why the fridge is full. OR I went to the supermarket yesterday, that's why the fridge is full.	In Portuguese, a past form is usually used to indicate that something happened in a recent or unknown past, and therefore, we can use past time expressions. However, in English you can only use time expressions such as *since*, *for*, or *today* with the present perfect.
ASKING QUESTIONS WITH *DID*	Did she work~~ed~~ last weekend?	Did she work last weekend?	When asking a question with the auxiliary *did* or making a negative statement with *did not* or *didn't*, the main verb is in the infinitive form.
NON-ACTION VERBS	I ~~am not seeing~~ you. Are you here in the party, too?	I can't see you. Are you at the party, too? OR I don't see you. Are you at the party, too?	Non-action verbs, such as *see*, *be*, *know*, and *like* can't be used in the continuous tenses.
TALKING ABOUT FUTURE ABILITY OR POSSIBILITY	He will ~~can~~ buy a motorcycle after he gets a job.	He will be able to buy a motorcycle after he gets a job. OR He can buy a motorcycle after he gets a job.	The modal verb *can* refers to present and future, but it can't be used with any other modal verbs (e.g. *will*, *should*, *must*, etc.). When using another modal verb or a perfect tense, we use *be able to* instead of *can*.
USING *THAT* AS A RELATIVE PRONOUN IN NON-DEFINING RELATIVE CLAUSES	The cake, ~~that~~ I made all by myself, was a success at the party.	The cake, which I made all by myself, was a success at the party.	The pronoun *that* cannot be used in non-defining relative clauses (when the information is not essential, and is separated from the rest of the sentence by commas). Beware! *That* can only be used in defining relative clauses in the place of *who* and *which*.
HAVE TO IN NEGATIVE STATEMENTS AND QUESTIONS	We ~~haven't~~ to pay. It's free! AND ~~Have~~ we to pay?	We don't have to pay. It's free! AND Do we have to pay?	Although *have to* performs the function of a modal verb, it is a verb phrase that needs an auxiliary verb in negative statements and questions.
TAG QUESTIONS WITH *I AM*	I'm a good student, ~~am not I?~~	I'm a good student, aren't I?	There are some exceptions to form tag questions, such as using the tag *aren't I?* when the affirmative statement starts with *I am* OR the use of *shall we?* when the statement starts with *Let's*.

TOPIC	COMMON MISTAKE	RIGHT FORM	SOME EXPLANATION
ELLIPSIS OF THE VERB AFTER *WILL*	I will go to your house and she too.	I will go to your house, and she will [go] too.	The modal verb *will* in Portuguese can be translated as "*vou (fazer algo)*" or "*vai (fazer algo)*", depending on the context. However, it is necessary to use *go* when we want to say, for example: "*Eu irei para a sua casa.*" *Will* can come without another verb in short answers or ellipsis.
THE FORM OF THE VERB AFTER MODAL VERBS	I may ~~to~~ see a movie tonight.	I may see a movie tonight.	The verb that follows a modal verb is never conjugated, nor is it an infinitive with *to*. With modal verbs, we use the infinitive <u>without</u> *to*.
ADDING AN AGENT TO A SENTENCE IN THE PASSIVE VOICE	This house was built ~~for~~ my great-grandfather.	This house was built by my great-grandfather.	When referring to the agent of a passive sentence, the preposition we use to mean "*por*" is *by*. We would use *for* if we wanted to say "*Esta casa foi construída <u>para</u> meu bisavô.*"
GET VS. *STAY*	I don't go to class when I ~~stay~~ sick.	I don't go to class when I get sick.	Both *get* and *stay* can be translated into "*ficar*". However, *stay* conveys the idea of "*permanecer*" while *get* refers to starting having a feeling or an idea.
ALREADY VS. *EVER* IN QUESTIONS	Have you ~~already~~ been to Canada?	Have you ever been to Canada?	Both words can mean "*já*". The use of the adverb *ever* refers to a question about an experience in someone's life, while *already* refers to something that we expect to happen or have happened and we want to ask about its conclusion up to the time of speaking.
USING OBJECT PRONOUNS WITH SEPARABLE PHRASAL VERBS	Is the heater working? Let's turn on ~~it~~!	Is the heater working? Let's turn it on!	When using separable phrasal verbs, such as *turn on / off, pick up*, and *give up* with an object pronoun, the pronoun must come between the verb and the particle. If there is a noun instead of a pronoun, it can go both between the verb and the particle and after the particle (e.g. *turn the TV off / turn off the TV*).
REMOVAL OF *DO / DOES / DID* IN THE FORMATION OF EMBEDDED QUESTIONS	She asked Marco where ~~did~~ he ~~go~~ on Saturdays.	She asked Marco where he went on Saturdays.	When forming an embedded question, it is important to remember that the structure changes. We can't keep the question structure, so the auxiliaries *do*, *does*, and *did* aren't used anymore and the main verb is conjugated.

FALSE FRIENDS

False friends are similar-sounding words with different meanings. When we look at the word *actually*, for example, we immediately associate it with the Portuguese word "atualmente", because of its similarity. However, *actually* means "*na realidade*" as in "It **actually** costs three thousand dollars, not three hundred." Let's take a look at some other examples.

English	Portuguese translation	Example	Don't get confused with…	Which in English is…
alias	pseudônimo, nome falso	He used to work under an **alias**.	aliás	by the way
anthem	hino	Are you able to sing the American national **anthem**?	antena	antenna
appoint	nomear	Tom Leary was **appointed** to a new position.	apontar	point
assist	ajudar	Who is going to **assist** the new judge?	assistir (a um programa)	watch
college	faculdade	I can't believe you are not excited about going to **college**!	colégio	school
comprehensive	abrangente, amplo	It was a very **comprehensive** report.	compreensível	understandable
convict	condenado(a)	The **convict** had to be handcuffed.	convicto(a)	certain
costume	fantasia	How much is the vampire **costume**?	costume	habit
data	dados	We have gathered a lot of **data** on the subject.	data	date
exit	saída	Where is the **exit** door?	êxito	success
fabric	tecido	Silk is a very expensive **fabric**.	fábrica	factory
hazard	risco	This medicine presents no **hazard** to your health.	azar	bad luck
inhabited	habitado(a)	It is an **inhabited** island.	inabitado(a)	uninhabited
journal	revista especializada, diário	Tom is the editor of a very important medical **journal**.	jornal	newspaper
lecture	palestra	The **lecture** had a very young audience.	leitura	reading
legend	lenda	Have you heard of the **legend** of Billy Jack?	legenda	subtitle
library	biblioteca	Is there a **library** around here where I can borrow some comics?	livraria	bookstore
novel	romance	*My Brilliant Friend* is a **novel** written by Elena Ferrante, a mysterious Italian writer.	novela	soap opera
notice	notar, observar	Have you **noticed** the new furniture in the Study Hall?	notícia	news
parents	pais	My **parents** got married in the early nineties.	parentes	relatives
physician	médico	He is a respected **physician** who is looking after the president's health.	físico	physicist
prejudice	preconceito	We must always fight against all kinds of **prejudice**.	prejuízo	harm
pretend	fingir	Stop **pretending**! I know you are not telling the truth.	pretender	intend
realize	perceber	Have you **realized** how far we are from our goal?	realizar	accomplish
resume	recomeçar	After a long break they **resumed** the session.	resumir	summarize
sensible	sensato(a)	Choosing to cross the river in such a small boat is not a **sensible** option.	sensível	sensitive
support	apoiar	The homeless shelter is **supported** by a group of volunteers.	suportar	bear

GLOSSARY

Unit 1

acronym – acrônimo, abreviatura
angst – angústia
diehard – persistente
glazed – olhou fixo (infinitivo: *glaze*)
go cold turkey – parar um hábito de maneira abrupta
hindsight – em retrospecto
landscapes – paisagens
lead to – levar a
littered – repleto(a) (conotação negativa)
omertà – código de honra
pundits – especialistas
refrain – abster-se
remarks – comentários
shorthand – forma curta
somehow – de alguma forma
supposedly – supostamente

Unit 2

acquired – adquiriu (infinitivo: *acquire*)
ameliorate – aperfeiçoar, melhorar
beyond – além de
commutes – deslocamentos
core – principal
currently – atualmente
fill up – encher
fossil fuels – combustíveis fósseis
garbage – lixo
greenhouse gas – gás de efeito estufa
hip pockets – bolsos traseiros (termo financeiro)
income – renda
lavish – extravagante
missing – perder (infinitivo: *miss*)
narrowed – estreitado (infinitivo: *narrow*)
near-miss – quase (acidente)
peer-to-peer – entre pares
P.E.I. – Prince Edward Island, província canadense
poisoning – envenenando (infinitivo: *poison*)
rather – um tanto
ride-hailing – chama-carona
seek – buscar
sheer – completo
slewing – deslizando (infinitivo: *slew*)
stakeholders – investidores
tailored – customizado (infinitivo: *tailor*)
through – através
transitioning – transitando

Review 1

amounted – somou (infinitivo: *amount*)
canons – cânones, padrões aceitos
oversee – supervisionar
path – caminho
remain – permanecer
safeguard – proteger
spread – espalhado(a)
standing at – posicionando-se em (infinitivo: *stand*)
tiny – pequenino
viability – viabilidade

Unit 3

cohort – tropa
disrupt – perturbar
do harm – prejudicar
entrepreneurial – empreendedor
floods – inundações
instead – ao invés disso

GLOSSARY

loneliness – solidão

polls – pesquisas (de opinião)

pragmatic – pragmático, prático

shelf-life – vida útil

short-term – a curto prazo

therefore – portanto

trend – tendência

unrealistically – de modo não realístico

upbringing – criação (de pessoa)

willing – disposto

witnessed – testemunhou (infinitivo: *witness*)

Unit 4

're (are) all geared up – estamos todos preparados (infinitivo: *be geared up*)

carry-on sized backpack – mochila de tamanho pequeno, possível de carregar

Commonwealth – com políticas e economia em comum

daunting – assustador(a)

facet – faceta

featured – destacado(a)

figure – número(s)

flavor – sabor

flocks – rebanhos

freeing – libertador

gap-year – ano sabático

intrepid – intrépido, sem medo

issued – emitido(a) (infinitivo: *issue*)

itch – comichão

laborers – trabalhadores

lesser known – menos conhecido(a)

look forward to – esperar ansiosamente

perhaps – talvez

preach – pregar

pristine – limpo(a)

rookie – novato

spread – espalhar

tailor-made trip – viagem feita sob encomenda com uma agência

tall order – exigência absurda

tempting – tentador

terrain – terreno

understatement – narração incompleta

whetted – aguçado(a) (infinitivo: *whet*)

Review 2

approaches – abordagens

believably – crivelmente

breadwinners – ganha-pão

embracing – acolhendo (infinitivo: *embrace*)

off the beaten track – fora da área turística

reminisce – relembrar

threshold – limite

Unit 5

available – disponível

bendy – flexível

block grant – concessão

bursaries – bolsas de estudos

catchy – cativante

CEO – *Chief Executive Officer*, diretor(a) executivo(a)

cheerful – animado(a)

coding – codificação

crackpot – excêntrico, ruim

developable – possível de desenvolver

diminished – diminuiu (infinitivo: *diminish*)

dive – mergulho

enhancers – potenciadores

fiend – monstro

fools – bobos(as)

future-proof – preparar para o futuro

hoodies – jovens vestidos de moletom (usado para mostrar desaprovação)

midst – meio

misled – enganado(a) (infinitivo: *mislead*)

off-putting – desagradável

on the fly – com pressa

patches – remendos

pigeon – pombo

pulped – destruído (infinitivo: *pulp*)

relieving – aliviando (infinitivo: *relieve*)

school leaver – alguém que para de estudar após a educação básica

stand out – destacar-se

stealing – roubar (infinitivo: *steal*)

STEM skills – habilidades STEM (ciência, tecnologia, engenharia e matemática)

tackle – resolver, lidar com

trading – trocando (infinitivo: *trade*)

whether – se

Unit 6

amid – no meio de

bleak – desanimador(a)

buffer – amortecer

carried out – conduziu (infinitivo: *carry out*)

crops – colheitas

damage – dano

deaths – mortes

droughts – períodos de seca

hedges – cercas vivas

intractable – intratável

lack of – falta de

laid out – disposto(a)

landscape – paisagem

lawn – gramado

livestock – criação

mitigate – atenuar

mitigation – suavização

niche – nicho

output – saída

overworked – sobrecarregado(a)

partnerships – parcerias

pillar support – apoio

plot – terreno

poisonings – envenenamentos

rather than – ao invés de

reap – colher

rodents – roedores

seeks – busca (infinitivo: *seek*)

showcased – apresentado(a)

shrubs – arbustos

the latter – o último

timber – madeira

toughest – mais difícil

waste – lixo

water tables – lençóis freáticos

weeds – ervas daninhas

whilst – enquanto

woody perennials – arbustos lenhosos

yields – produções

Review 3

augmented – aumentado(a)

crave – ansiar

disrupting – perturbando (infinitivo: *disrupt*)

loads – muitos

prone to – inclinado(a) a

retail – varejo

seekers – buscadores

unrecognizable – irreconhecível

Unit 7

center-left parties – partidos de centro-esquerda

come out – surgir

counter-reaction – reações adversas

deregulation – desregulamentação

GLOSSARY

destabilizing – desestabilizador
disruptive – desordeiro(a)
eroded – desgastado(a) (infinitivo: *erode*)
free trade – comércio livre
GDP – *Gross Domestic Product,* Produto Interno Bruto
gig – bico, trabalho informal
grab – apanhar
growth – crescimento
hype – propaganda
inroads – invasões
market cap – valor de mercado
nativist – nativista
omens – presságios
outweighed – superado(a) (infinitivo: *outweigh*)
overstretch – alongamento demasiado
path – caminho
pay gaps – brechas de pagamento
plank – princípio
quarrels – discussões
roughly – aproximadamente
shrink – diminuir
sluggish – lento(a)
subprime mortgages – hipotecas de segunda categoria
survey – pesquisa
threat – ameaça
threatens – ameaça (infinitivo: *threaten*)
triggered – provocou (infinitivo: *trigger*)
undoing – desfazendo (infinitivo: *undo*)
unemployment – desemprego
widened – amplificado(a)
willingness – vontade

Unit 8

abiding commitment – comprometimento duradouro
amusing – divertido
bid – fazer um lance
boost (the site) up – alavancar
breach – violação
briefing – resumo
cracking down – fechando o cerco (infinitivo: *crack down*)
crowded – amontoaram-se (infinitivo: *crowd*)
eager – ansioso(a)
earnings – ganhos
far-right – extrema direita
forefront – frente
funding – fundo
groundbreaking – revolucionário
hatred – ódio
headquarters – sede principal
held – realizado(a) (infinitivo: *hold*)
provide – fornecer
pursuing – buscando (infinitivo: *pursue*)
ran out – acabou (infinitivo: *run out*)
reach – alcance
reliable – confiável
right-wing – de direita
seemingly – aparente
set out – pretender
shady – sombrio(a)
snappy – rápido(a)
sneaking in – esgueirando-se (infinitivo: *sneak in*)
third-party – terceirizado(a)
tough – duro(a)
threat – ameaça
weaponization – armamento

Review 4

broadly – amplamente
enhances – acentua (infinitivo: *enhance*)
fairness – justiça
flaws – falhas
nourishes – nutri (infinitivo: *nourish*)
ombudsmen – mediadores
willingness – desejo

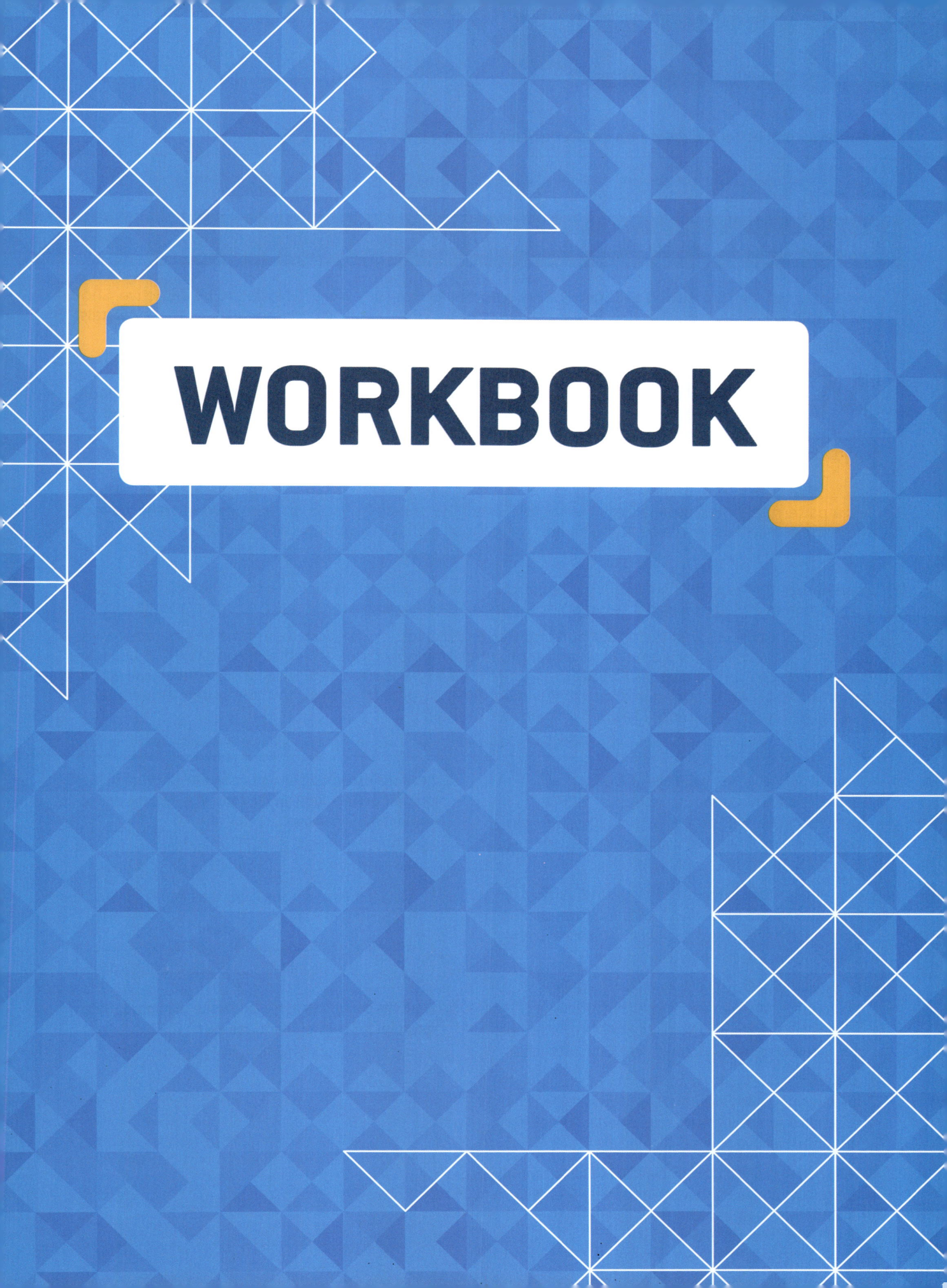

WORKBOOK

Unit 1   **Hooked on Social Media**

1. Read the excerpt below and choose the extract that best summarizes it.   *Skimming*

---

www.theguardian.com/media/2018/jan/23/never-get-high-on-your-own-supply-why-social-media-bosses-dont-use-social-media

WHY SOCIAL MEDIA BOSSES DON'T USE SOCIAL MEDIA

Developers of platforms such as Facebook have admitted that they were designed to be addictive. Should we be following the executives' example and **go cold turkey** – and is it even possible for mere mortals?

by Alex Hern

Mark Zuckerberg doesn't use Facebook like you or me. The chief executive has a team of 12 moderators dedicated to deleting comments and spam from his page, according to Bloomberg. He has a "handful" of employees who help him write his posts and speeches and a number of professional photographers who take perfectly stage-managed pictures of him meeting veterans in Kentucky, small-business owners in Missouri, or cheesesteak vendors in Philadelphia.

[...]

It is a pattern that holds true across the sector. For all the industry's focus on "eating your own dog food", the most **diehard** users of social media are rarely those sitting in a position of power.

[...]

Sean Parker, the founding president of Facebook, broke the **omertà** in October last year, telling a conference in Philadelphia that he was "something of a conscientious objector" to social media.

"The thought process that went into building these applications, Facebook being the first of them, was all about: 'How do we consume as much of your time and conscious attention as possible?' That means that we need to sort of give you a little dopamine hit every once in a while, because someone liked or commented on a photo or a post or whatever. And that's going to get you to contribute more content and that's going to get you more likes and comments," he said.

Adapted from www.theguardian.com/media/2018/jan/23/never-get-high-on-your-own-supply-why-social-media-bosses-dont-use-social-media. Accessed on July 18, 2018.

---

a. Since social media was intentionally developed to be addictive and time consuming, developers of these platforms recommend people not to use it regularly and only occasionally check the amount of likes and comments they get on their posts.

b. The author suggests that social media users should not be worried about social media executives' behavior, since it has never been proved that social media may have negative effects on people's lives.

c. Social media developers never meant to design a platform for their own amusement, but they were looking for alternatives to intentionally take as much of our time as they possibly could. And they succeeded.

d. Sean Parker, the founding president of Facebook, is also an advocate for social media relevance when he admits to building something that would entertain people for the longest amount of time possible.

e. Sean Parker claims that social media is able to control the amount of dopamine a person can experience in one day by sharing or withholding comments directed to them on their social media profile.

2. Read the excerpt again and underline the verb in the present perfect form. In the context given, the use of the present perfect shows...

   a. something that happened in a non-specific moment in the past, but is still relevant at the present time.

   b. a situation that started in the past and is still happening in the present.

   c. something that happened in a specific moment in the past and has no influence on events taking place now.

3. Read the sentences below and write the appropriate question for each of them. Use *ever*.

   a. Yes, I have already been to the USA.

   _____

   _____

   b. No, Chloe has never seen any of the Star Wars movies.

   _____

   _____

Unit 1

4. Complete the sentences below using the present perfect form of the verbs given.

a. Although I have already seen your brother, I _____ (never talk) to him in person.

b. Shonda _____ (live) in Atlanta for over a decade now. The last time I saw her we had a farewell party.

c. My sister started looking for a new job months ago. She _____ (apply) to a lot of positions on LinkedIn, but she _____ (not hear) from any headhunters yet.

d. I _____ (live) in this house since my parents moved to Chicago.

e. _____ you _____ (ever spend) more than five hours in a row on social media?

5. Read the sentences and say if they are in the simple past (SP), past continuous (PC), or present perfect (PP).

a. (   ) Jason has already traveled to the Hamptons with his girlfriend.

b. (   ) My father didn't go to the west coast with us last year.

c. (   ) We haven't spoken in years. What have you done lately?

d. (   ) Did you apply for the Mandarin class like I told you to?

e. (   ) She wasn't calling you, she was texting you.

6. Read the sentences in activity 5 again and identify whether the verbs used in the sentences are regular or irregular.

a. _____

b. _____

c. _____

d. _____

e. _____

7. Read the statements below and complete them with the simple past or past continuous form of the verbs in parentheses.

a. I _____ (not go) to the movies yesterday. I _____ (stay) home with my father.

b. Alicia _____ (do) the dishes when Peter _____ (call).

c. Marcus _____ (visit) his girlfriend yesterday. That's why he _____ (not come) to your house.

d. _____ you _____ (invite) my sister to your party?

e. Sorry, but I _____ (not feel) very well.

f. I _____ (not check) my Instagram again. I _____ just _____ (send) my friend a message.

g. Diana _____ (create) a new email account when Carlton _____ (arrive).

105

8. Read the excerpt below and underline the phrasal verb in it.

Livia Weinstein didn't know what to expect when she created a Facebook account almost 10 years ago. The now 79-year-old from Washington, D.C., said her reason for joining the online world was due to her desire to keep up with the times, more than it was a means for socialization. For the former school counselor, nothing could replace the value of face-to-face communication with all its inflections and tones, a characteristic absent from instant messaging and texting. [...] Older adults across the United States are adjusting to a world of advancing technology. Not only are they accepting the changes, but some, like Weinstein, are actively implementing technology in their daily lives.

Adapted from www.deseretnews.com/article/865685302/How-social-media-and-technology-are-changing-the-lives-of-the-elderly.html. Accessed on July 21, 2017.

9. Use the phrasal verbs in the box to fill in the blanks.

> log on   come up with   run out of   filter out   sign up

a. Morgan hasn't _____ an idea for her new book yet. She has no idea what to write about.

b. If you want more privacy, you must _____ the unwanted contacts from your social media profile.

c. I think my account has been hacked. I keep getting an error message every time I try to _____.

d. If you want to get our weekly newsletter, _____ at the end of this article.

e. We need to go to the supermarket. I have totally _____ paper towels.

10. Read the excerpt from activity 8 again and circle the adjective followed by the preposition *to*. Then complete the sentences with the adjectives from the box and the preposition *to*.

> committed   generous   engaged   dedicated   accustomed

a. She's _____ a certain lifestyle and she doesn't want to lower her standards.

b. Peter is _____ Taylor, but he hasn't told his parents about their engagement yet.

c. Teachers are _____ helping students get ready for the exams.

d. This project is _____ supporting small businesses survive competition.

e. Your mother has been _____ me whenever I need her.

11. Read the following statement. Which alternative best completes it?

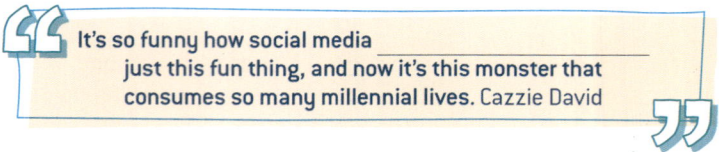

> " It's so funny how social media _____ just this fun thing, and now it's this monster that consumes so many millennial lives. Cazzie David "

Extracted from www.brainyquote.com/topics/social_media. Accessed on January 15, 2019.

a. was

b. was being

c. has been

Unit 1

12. Rewrite the sentences below in the simple past, adding a time expression at the end. Follow the example.

My friends don't have English class.
My friends didn't have English class (yesterday).

a. My mother cooks chicken and pasta.
_____

b. Do you play soccer?
_____

c. Steve doesn't swim, and he doesn't play video games.
_____

d. Miranda speaks English and Spanish fluently.
_____

e. Does William drive automatic cars?
_____

AN EYE ON ENEM

ENEM 2015 – Prova Rosa
Questão 92

> WELL, HERE IT IS. – THE SEASON THAT I HATE.
>
> COME ON, ANNE! THE KIDS ARE IN SCHOOL, THE AIR'S COOL, THE LEAVES ARE TURNING...
>
> I'M NOT TALKING ABOUT AUTUMN, DUMMY!
>
> I'M TALKING ABOUT FOOTBALL.

Na tira da série *For better or for worse*, a comunicação entre as personagens fica comprometida em um determinado momento porque

a. as duas amigas divergem de opinião sobre futebol.
b. uma das amigas desconsidera as preferências da outra.
c. uma das amigas ignora que o outono é temporada de futebol.
d. uma das amigas desconhece a razão pela qual a outra a maltrata.
e. as duas amigas atribuem sentidos diferentes à palavra *season*.

Unit 2 — The Rocky Road of Good Urban Transportation

1. Read part of a news report and check (✓) the correct statement. *Identifying the purpose of a text*

  a. ( ) The news report aims to present research on the effects of commuting on people's time for breakfast in Britain.

  b. ( ) The news report aims to discuss the unhealthy content of breakfasts around Britain.

  c. ( ) The news report provides a detailed report on breakfasts in Britain.

---

www.dailymail.co.uk/news/article-2207637/One-busy-commuting-doing-school-run-eat-breakfast.html

One in three of us is too busy commuting or doing the school run to eat breakfast

- Survey of 2,000 adults was commissioned by electrical goods firm Philips
- Dutch firm claim breakfast takes an average eight and a half minutes to eat

By BEN SPENCER FOR THE DAILY MAIL
PUBLISHED: 00:04 GMT, 24 September 2012 | UPDATED: 22:14 GMT, 24 September 2012

It is, the old saying goes, the most important meal of the day. But it seems millions of Britons are far too busy for breakfast (and old sayings) these days.
One in three adults never eats breakfast at all, research suggests, with the school run and daily commute forcing us to **fill up** on unhealthy snacks later in the day. Another 30 percent of Britons said they ate their food during their commute. Researchers also found that the majority of families – 70 percent – never sit down together to eat breakfast.
The survey of 2,000 adults was commissioned by electrical goods firm Philips. The results said it takes an average eight and a half minutes to make and eat breakfast.
[…]
The survey revealed the people in Birmingham were the best beakfasters, with 73 per cent regularly sitting down for a morning meal. London was ninth on the list, with 63 percent eating breakfast regularly.
Dr. Ollie Hart, a family GP in Meersbrook, Sheffield, said: 'The danger with **missing** breakfast is that you get low blood sugar midway **through** the morning and then you snack.
'If people have breakfast they tend to eat slow-release food such as toast or cereal, which sustains them. But if people miss that meal and get hungry they will probably eat **garbage**.'

Adapted from www.dailymail.co.uk/news/article-2207637/One-busy-commuting-doing-school-run-eat-breakfast.html. Accessed on November 20, 2018.

---

2. Find the following information in the article. *Scanning*

  a. Number of adults who never eat breakfast at all. _____

  b. Percentage of British families who never have breakfast together. _____

  c. Percentage of Britons who eat their breakfast while they are going to work or school. _____

  d. City in Britain where people most eat breakfast regularly. _____

  e. City in Britain which was the ninth best breakfast eaters. _____

3. Read the text again and underline all the statements that are implied by the author. *Understanding main ideas*

  a. Britons don't give importance to breakfast, but they find old sayings important.

  b. It is worrying that so few Britons eat breakfast regularly.

  c. Not having breakfast leads people to eating unhealthy snacks.

  d. The time it takes to make and eat breakfast is considerably long.

  e. Dr. Ollie is concerned about what people end up eating if they skip breakfast.

Unit 2

4. Read the article again. Identify and underline two sentences using a conditional structure. Then read the statements below and circle the correct alternatives.

  a. One sentence shows an example of zero conditional and the other shows an example of first conditional.
  b. The first conditional is used when a situation is generally true, and both verb forms are supposed to be the same.
  c. The zero conditional is used when a situation is generally true, and both verb forms are supposed to be the same.
  d. In the first conditional, the result is likely to happen in the future, but it always depends on a situation that must happen in the present.
  e. A good example of first conditional is: "Whenever my children come home early from school, they do their homework before dinner."
  f. In the zero conditional, the result is likely to happen in the future, but it always depends on a situation that must happen in the present.

5. Use the prompts to write sentences in the first or the zero conditional.

  a. it / rain / we / take an umbrella (first conditional)
  _____

  b. my parents / come over / we / take them to the mall (zero conditional)
  _____

  c. we / work overtime / we / come home late (zero conditional)
  _____

  d. I / go to France / I / need a translation app (first conditional)
  _____

  e. she / need to take two trains / she / not come to the meeting (first conditional)
  _____

  f. he / arrive at the company earlier / I / let you know (first conditional)
  _____

6. Read an extract about commuting in New York and underline the correct alternative.

> "Carson Tate, a productivity consultant who heads Working Simply, a Charlotte, NC-based firm, observes that New Yorkers, despite their long commutes, '**can** take trains or subways and actually get some work done or **recharge**.'"
>
> Extracted from www.nypost.com/2017/11/04/new-yorkers-have-one-of-the-worst-commutes-survey-says.
> Accessed on July 24, 2018.

  a. The modal verb *can* in the statement conveys the idea of...
    a. having an obligation.
    b. being able to (ability).
    c. possibility.
    d. willing to.
    e. enjoying.
    f. suggesting.

  b. The verb *recharge* is formed with the prefix *re-* followed by the verb *charge*. What does the prefix *re-* mean?
    a. not
    b. again or back to a former state
    c. do something with someone else
    d. without
    e. more
    f. less

7. Read the sentences below and check (✓) the statement that best describes each of them according to the use of the modal verbs *can* and *could*.

a. I can't remember where I put my keys.
( ) inability in the present
( ) inability in the past

b. Before she had her second baby, Monica could cycle 10 miles to work.
( ) possibility in the past
( ) ability in the past

c. My mother says that I can't go out with you guys until she has arrived from work.
( ) impossibility in the present
( ) prohibition in the present

d. OK, Lily. You can drive my car to school, but be back by 10!
( ) permission in the present
( ) ability in the present

e. Sorry I couldn't come earlier. I had an important meeting at work.
( ) impossibility in the past
( ) prohibition in the past

f. I can't go by bus because I have no cash with me.
( ) impossibility in the past
( ) impossibility in the present

8. Complete the sentences with *can*, *can't*, *could*, or *couldn't*.

a. Patrick _____ walk to school because he lives too far!

b. When she was younger, Molly _____ speak Spanish very well. Nowadays, not only is she fluent in Spanish, but she _____ also speak French, German, and Portuguese.

c. Sorry, I _____ hear you. Please speak louder.

d. When I was younger I _____ run 5 miles in 40 minutes.

e. My sister _____ play the piano. She's practiced it for years! She has a concert next Wednesday.

f. Do you want to go to a restaurant nearby? If so, you _____ take Sarah to *La Pasta*.

9. Read the following statement and underline the words with prefixes. What do the prefixes in these words mean?

> "Problems involving traffic jams and lack of parking spaces are making it impossible to drive in big cities. More and more people are shifting to public transportation encouraged by the possibility of reaching destinations faster and safer."

_____
_____

10. Read the explanations about prefixes in the box on page 20 of your Student's Book. Then use the words in the box to fill in the blanks adding the appropriate prefix to each of them.

> legal   gain   wanted   experienced   responsible

a. He is very _____. We can't keep him in our company anymore.

b. After losing his job, he had to _____ control of his life.

c. Although she's a wonderful cook, she's _____ in running a restaurant.

d. You can donate your _____ presents to charity.

e. Some countries believe that _____ immigration leads to higher levels of unemployment, crime rates, and poverty.

11. Read the quotes below and underline the words with prefixes. What do the words mean? Complete the chart.

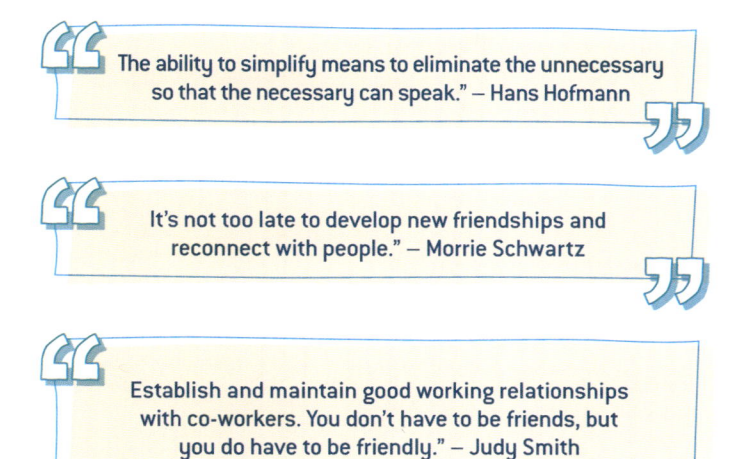

> "The ability to simplify means to eliminate the unnecessary so that the necessary can speak." – Hans Hofmann

> "It's not too late to develop new friendships and reconnect with people." – Morrie Schwartz

> "Establish and maintain good working relationships with co-workers. You don't have to be friends, but you do have to be friendly." – Judy Smith

word with prefix	meaning

Extracted from www.brainyquote.com. Accessed on August 2, 2018.

AN EYE ON VESTIBULAR

UNICAMP 2017 – Provas Q e Y
Questão 87

Ranking Universities by 'Greenness'

Universities these days are working hard to improve their sustainability credentials, with efforts that include wind power, organic food and competitions to save energy. They are also adding courses related to sustainability and energy. But which university is the greenest?

Several ranking systems have emerged to offer their take. The Princeton Review recently came out with its second annual green ratings. Fifteen colleges earned the highest possible score — including Harvard, Yale and the University of California, Berkeley.

Another group, the Sustainable Endowment Institute's GreenReportCard.org, rates colleges on several different areas of green compliance, such as recycling, student involvement and green building. Its top grade for overall excellence, an A-, was earned by 15 schools.

(Adaptado de http://green.blogs.nytimes.com/2009/08/20/ranking-universities-bygreenness/?_r=0. Acessado em 31/08/2016.)

Conforme o texto, universidades norte-americanas estão se empenhando para
a. oferecer mais cursos sobre ecologia.
b. melhorar sua posição em um ranking que define as instituições mais "verdes".
c. oferecer os melhores cursos sobre preservação ambiental.
d. participar de uma competição que define os *campi* com maior área verde.

Unit 3 — Generation Z: Conservative or Liberal?

1. Read part of an online article and mark the statements true (T) or false (F). *Understanding details*

> [...] The labor market of modern society has greatly changed. [...] The modern labor market is more exciting, vibrant, diverse, and personal, welcoming Millennials and their talents.
>
> **Short-term jobs**
> [...] Millennials no longer commit to a single job for the rest of their lives, but are always looking for something better, more exciting, and promising. [...] Millennials are turning to freelancing and **short-term** projects rather than traditional employment. Not only does this provide them with more job opportunities, but it also gives them more flexibility both in terms of job responsibilities and working hours.
>
> **Value and purpose before money**
> Millennials are well aware of their personal worth and do expect to be paid accordingly, but they don't mind putting other perks of a job, such as opportunities for job advancement, personal growth, and fun working environment, before compensation.
>
> **Organizations with personalities**
> Millennials don't want to work for a company where they would be just another face in the crowd. This is why they are looking for positions in organizations with a clear personality. [...]
>
> **Dynamic workplace**
> Millennials don't want to work in cubicles isolated from the rest of their colleagues. **Instead**, they are looking for a fun and informal workplace where their creativity will be valued and encouraged. [...]
>
> Adapted from www.chelseakrost.com/millennials-changing-job-market. Accessed on July 30, 2018.

Inside This Issue
What are Millenials' greatest talents?
The Job Market then and now.
Who are the so called Millennials?

a. ( ) Millennials value long term jobs, that will get them recognition and provide them with opportunities to advance in their careers the fastest way possible.

b. ( ) The difference between Millennials and past generations has changed the way the labor market deals with career and professional priorities.

c. ( ) Millennials are likely to have several jobs throughout their lives and that's because they are always looking for better opportunities and they are not afraid of change.

d. ( ) Millennials really care about their compensation package. So, recruiters need to be aware that, besides demanding high salaries, Millennials are also looking for fun and informal workplaces.

e. ( ) When choosing their jobs, Millennials take into account the company's position in the job market. They want to work at a place where they'll be noticed, in a company with personality.

f. ( ) Being able to express their creativity is not so relevant for Millennials. They are willing to give up working in groups if they feel their creativity is encouraged by the company.

2. Read the titles below and choose the one that best fits the article in activity 1. *Skimming*

a. Job Market: Baby Boomers and Millennials being confronted

b. Are the changes in the job market affecting the new generations?

c. How Millennials are changing the job market

d. Dynamic workplaces: how Millennials deal with careers and the job market

e. Four reasons why Millennials won't go to work

3. Using your previous knowledge and the information provided in the article and on page 28 of your Student's Book, write some similarities we can notice between Millennials and the Generation Z.

_____

_____

4. Read the following statement extracted from the article and complete the tasks that follow:

"Millennials don't want to work for a company **where** they would be just another face in the crowd."

a. The author used the relative pronoun _____ in the sentence above to provide specific information about the kind of place Millennials wouldn't like to work at.

b. What's the name of the structure used in this sentence? _____.

c. The subject pronoun *they* refers to _____.

d. The relative pronoun *where* refers to _____.

5. Match the clauses using one of the relative pronouns given. Then write the sentences you come up with.

She lives in a neighborhood	whose	showed up at my house yesterday
I'm not sure if I know the boy	where	boss refuses to pay double for overtime
Here at our company, we use a computer program	when	explains how the job market is impacted by Millennials
We are the employees	which	we must come together to fight prejudice
This is a time	that	people barely know each other
HR executives are looking for research	who	detects and blocks spyware

a. _____

b. _____

c. _____

d. _____

e. _____

f. _____

6. Fill in the blanks with the relative pronouns in the box. Then underline the three sentences where the relative pronoun can be omitted.

> when   where   whose   which   who

a. Not a day goes by _____ I don't think about moving to Canada.

b. Caleb usually travels to the same place _____ he first met his wife.

c. These are the pictures _____ Louise took during her trip to Morocco.

d. I have a friend _____ parents moved to an island in the Pacific.

e. Tania was the first person _____ I met when I joined this company.

7. Read the comic strip below and complete the tasks that follow.

Extracted from www.garfield.com/comic/2018/05/18. Accessed on July 28, 2018.

a. Which word best fills in the blank in the conversation, *do* or *make*?

b. Read the statements below and check (✓) the ones that are correct about the use of *do* and *make*. Then rewrite the incorrect ones.

( ) With phrases such as *the homework* and *a favor*, we use *do*.
_____

( ) With phrases such as *a phone call* and *lunch*, we use *make*.
_____

( ) With phrases such as *the homework* and *a favor*, we use *make*.
_____

( ) With phrases such as *the bed* and *an offer*, we use *do*.
_____

8. Read the sentences below and write *make* or *do* in the correct form to complete the collocations in bold.

a. She's been so thoughtful to me. It really _____ **a difference** when someone shows their support through hard times.

b. After several interviews and a formal presentation, the company has finally _____ me **an offer**.

c. Would you please _____ me **a favor**? I need you to pick up the kids from school this afternoon.

d. Louise was really sorry to have hurt your feelings. I'm convinced she never meant to _____ you **harm**.

e. She's trying to _____ some **money** and pay for her trip herself. She doesn't want her parents to pay for anything.

f. I love going out to parties. It's a nice opportunity to have a great time and _____ new **friends**.

g. She needs to _____ **well** on the exams if she wants to pass.

9. Complete the sentences with *so... that...* and a word from the box.

> little   cool   handsome   many   happy   big   much   high

a. Prices were _____ clients refused to buy their products.

b. There is _____ to be decided _____ we'll work overtime until we have everything figured out.

c. Their house is _____ they won't have it renovated in time for the holidays.

d. They looked _____ in that picture _____ you wouldn't believe the problems they were dealing with.

e. There was just _____ space in the room _____ most of the people had to wait outside.

f. He looked _____ in that suit _____ no one recognized him.

g. We had _____ friends over to our party _____ we had to pay extra for the catering service.

h. The movie Andrew and I watched yesterday was _____ we ended up getting tickets to watch it again next Wednesday evening. Do you want to come with us?

10. Write sentences connecting the clauses in the two columns with the conjunction *so*.

a. Sonja called in sick,
b. We decided to stay home tonight,
c. The local farmer's market has been shut down,
d. Mark's on a diet,
e. I had to ask my mom to move her head,
f. The criminal didn't want to leave the house,
g. Alex was in a hurry when he left,

now we have to drive to the city whenever we need to buy groceries.

she won't come to work today.

we could watch the season finale of our favorite show.

I could see the TV screen better.

he needs to stop eating chocolate.

the police had to call for backup.

he didn't realize he'd left his suitcase at home.

a. _____
b. _____
c. _____
d. _____
e. _____
f. _____
g. _____

AN EYE ON ENEM

ENEM 2011 – Prova Rosa
Questão 93

Na fase escolar, é prática comum que os professores passem atividades extraclasse e marquem uma data para que as mesmas sejam entregues para correção. No caso da cena da charge, a professora ouve uma estudante apresentando argumentos para:

a. discutir sobre o conteúdo do seu trabalho já entregue.
b. elogiar o tema proposto para o relatório solicitado.
c. sugerir temas para novas pesquisas e relatórios.
d. reclamar do curto prazo de entrega do trabalho.
e. convencer de que fez o relatório solicitado.

REPORTS DUE TODAY!

"My report is about how important it is to save paper, electricity, and other resources. I'll send it to you telepathically."

Unit 4 — What's going abroad like?

1. **Read the fragment below, extracted from the blog post "How to find work overseas: 15 ways to earn money when you travel," and find the information that follows.** *Understanding details*

   ### Under 30? Get a working holiday visa!

   Working holiday schemes allow people under the age of 30 to work abroad. These programs tend to be used mostly by **gap-year** travelers, students, or young adult backpackers. Most of the countries that offer these programs are English-speaking **Commonwealth** countries such as Canada, England, New Zealand, and Australia (under 35 now). The visa application process is pretty simple, and the visas are usually **issued** for one year. Typically, the visa comes with the stipulation that you can't work in one place for more than six months.

   Most of the working holiday jobs you can find are typically service or low-wage office jobs. Most people become office assistants, **laborers**, bartenders, or waiters. The pay is not always great, but it's enough to live off of and usually will give you a little extra money to save for traveling.

   For these jobs, you'll need to bite the bullet, fly to these countries, and look for work when you land. While sites like Gumtree have some listings, you'll find the majority of work when you land. Many companies specialize in placing travelers. And hostels usually have job boards and can offer a lot of assistance in finding work!

   Extracted from www.nomadicmatt.com/travel-blogs/working-overseas. Accessed on August 19, 2018.

   a. the types of work offered to people under 30 in the circumstances described: _____
   b. the country that accepts people older than 30 years old: _____
   c. how difficult it is to apply for this type of visa: _____
   d. the maximum amount of time people can spend in the country with this type of visa: _____
   e. places where job boards are available: _____

2. **Read the extract again and circle the correct alternatives.** *Understanding main ideas*
   a. You **have to** / **don't have to** be on a gap year to apply for these jobs.
   b. You **have to** / **don't have to** be under 30 to apply for these jobs in England.
   c. You **need to** / **don't need to** be under 30 to apply for these jobs in Australia.
   d. You **will have to** / **won't have to** fly to these countries and look for work when you land.
   e. Visas usually stipulate that you **can** / **can't** work for one place for more than six months.

3. **According to the text, certain jobs are more popular among travelers. If you were moving to a foreign country, which of those jobs would you choose? Justify your answer.**

   _____
   _____
   _____

4. Look at the words in the box. Then choose one of them to complete the extract below.

> off-road   mainstream   overcrowded

When you hear that China is _____, that's an understatement. I was shocked at the number of people. Even in the rural areas. I was also shocked at the poverty and at the living conditions. - Rosemary Mahoney.

Extracted from www.brainyquote.com/search_results?q=overcrowded+abroad. Accessed on January 15, 2019.

5. Complete the tag questions with one word.
   a. She is studying for her test right now, _____ she?
   b. Tina and Bob were working when their house was broken into, weren't _____?
   c. She always tells you to eat slowly, _____ she?
   d. You didn't tell Mom and Dad about me being fired, _____ you?
   e. You were driving the car when the accident happened, _____ you?
   f. Why are you reading this book now? The test is only three weeks from now, _____ it?
   g. Paul was a very good student in high school, _____ he?
   h. Pete and Gloria are writing an Italian travel guide for foreign students, _____ they?

6. Look at the pictures below and write a sentence using *need to* or *have to* for each of them.

117

7. The three tips below were extracted from "Travel tips: 11 mistakes every first-time traveler makes." Read them carefully and complete with *have to* or *don't have to*.

www.traveller.com.au/travel-tips-11-mistakes-every-firsttime-traveller-makes-1mlb2g

You're excited, obviously. You're about to head off for your first overseas trip, and it's an amazing feeling. It's inevitable that you'll make mistakes the first time you travel, just the same as you'd make mistakes in any other **facet** of life. These are the common ones that **rookie** adventurers make.

Overbooking

It's **tempting**, on that first **daunting** trip away, to get everything locked in — every hostel, every transfer, every breakfast, lunch, and dinner. That way you _____ worry about anything, right? But you'll soon come to realize that it pays to have some flexibility. Book in the big things, sure. But also leave yourself space to change your itinerary and take opportunities as they present themselves.

Using a travel agent… for everything

While it's now easy for you to book an entire trip yourself over the Internet, I can understand the wish to have the safety net of a travel agent. But that doesn't mean you _____ use them for everything. Book your flights, and maybe an accommodation package. But you'll generally save money if you look after everything else yourself.

Trying to see everything

This is why the group tours are popular, why people see things like "seven countries in 12 days" and think that's a good thing. This is your big overseas trip and you want to see as much as possible — you want to check as many boxes as you physically can. But that's a mistake. You _____ trust that you'll travel again. Instead of trying to see everywhere at once, slow down, get to know one country, or maybe two, and your appetite will be **whetted** for a lifetime of similar adventures.

Adapted from www.traveller.com.au/travel-tips-11-mistakes-every-firsttime-traveller-makes-1mlb2g. Accessed on August 21, 2018.

8. Read the sentences and complete the idioms with the words from the box.

> beaten   wheel   back   suitcase

a. OK, Dylan. I'll go with you, but only if I am the one at the _____. I drive way better than you.

b. Let's go together. Just please, don't be a _____ seat driver. I hate it when you tell me how to drive.

c. We're changing plans. I'm tired of traveling to these busy places where everyone goes. Let's travel somewhere off the _____ track.

d. My plan is to live out of a _____ for the next six months, just traveling around and getting to know new places.

9. Read the extract below and choose an idiom from activity 8 to complete it with.

> Ferðafélag Íslands (the Iceland Touring Association) runs 40 mountain huts around Iceland. Some are on popular hiking routes, such as the Laugavegur trail, while others are more _____.
>
> Extracted from www.theguardian.com/travel/2018/oct/06/europe-hut-cabin-hostel-stay-accommodation-bothy-bothies-mountain-lake-wild-remote-free-hiking-trail. Accessed on August 30, 2018.

Unit 4

10. Use the tag questions from the box to complete the dialogue. There is an extra alternative which you do not need to use.

> are you?   will you?   won't you?   do you?   aren't you?   don't I?

Jake: Wow, that's a big suitcase, Liz. You are not taking too many things, _____
Liz: Of course I am! I'm spending a year in Australia, so I have to take everything I need for a year, _____
Jake: Well, yes, but you can buy some things when you get there, too. Clothes are quite cheap in Australia. You don't want to pay an extra fee for luggage when you come back, _____
Liz: Well…
Jake: And you are planning to bring everything back home, _____
Liz: You're probably right. Help me choose between these things then, _____
Jake: OK. Let's make a list of what you need first. Then we can check the items we have already placed into your suitcase.

11. Complete the sentences below with the appropriate tag question.

a. Gloria is always talking about her amazing trips, _____ ?
b. I wasn't invited to Morgan's birthday party, _____ ?
c. Travis and Brianna didn't travel to London again, _____ ?
d. I am the only person to have access to this account, _____ ?
e. Georgia lives in the country with her husband and four kids, _____ ?
f. Malcolm would help me if I needed some money, _____ ?
g. Morty and Paula aren't taking a gap year in London anymore, _____ ?
h. Solange can speak four different languages, _____ ?
i. You shouldn't be driving your dad's car, _____ ?
j. Your mom wouldn't mind if I spent the night on your couch, _____ ?

AN EYE ON VESTIBULAR

UNESP 2017 (1º Fase)
Questão 30

Observe o cartum.

A alternativa que completa corretamente a lacuna do número 4 do cartum, sem prejuízo de sentido, é:

a. It's too hot in here.
b. I don't want to be tired all day.
c. Otherwise, I'll miss the bus.
d. I'm quite hungry.
e. Breakfast smells good.

Reasons to sleep through your alarm
1. I was having a really good dream.
2. Still so sleepy!
3. It's not even daylight yet.
4. _____
5. I've just gotten comfortable.
6. It's cold out there but warm in bed.

Reasons not to sleep through the alarm
1. I don't want to be late for work.

(www.systemcomic.com. Adaptado.)

Unit 5 — What the Future Holds

1. Read part of an article by *The Atlantic* and choose the correct alternative about the content of the text. *Understanding main ideas*

> www.theatlantic.com/business/archive/2016/09/how-can-todays-college-students-futureproof-their-careers/499244
>
> ## The Atlantic
>
> **Ask an Economist: How Can Today's College Students Future-Proof Their Careers?**
>
> **Julia Kirby**, a contributing editor at Harvard Business Review and the co-author of *Only Humans Need Apply: Winners and Loser in the Age of Smart Machines*.
> Studies are famously declaring that, with the encroachment of smart machines into knowledge work, something like 40 percent of U.S. jobs will go the way of the passenger **pigeon**. The implication: You'd better find a robot-proof line of work. Don't be **misled**. Virtually every kind of work will be affected – but every kind will still be **available**.
> **Whether** you're an actuary or an activist, a scientist or a soldier, you'll work in an augmented way, with software **relieving** you of a lot of cognitive heavy lifting and tedium, and you doubling down on the human strengths that will still be the key to moving your enterprise forward. So, the thing to focus on in college is gaining experience in working with smart machines – learning what they're capable of and what you're capable of. Choose your class projects with an eye to this. Ask: What problem could I solve in this field if I had a tireless, number-crunching **fiend** as a teammate? What if I had a partner capable of retrieving from memory instantly, and discerning patterns in seemingly chaotic information? When you arrive in the workplace, that's exactly what you'll have. And you'll rise fast if you know how to do big things with it.
>
> *Extracted from www.theatlantic.com/business/archive/2016/09/how-can-todays-college-students-futureproof-their-careers/499244. Accessed on August 1, 2018.*

a. Julia Kirby provides educators with helpful information to guide them through the process of helping students make their career choices in the world of technology.

b. The author discusses the future of the labor market, gives companies advice on what to do to be ready for the new generation of employees, and tells students to focus primarily on technology.

c. Besides informing that all types of jobs will be affected by technology, Julia Kirby goes on to tell students what they should do during college to be ready for the new labor market.

d. Julia Kirby talks about the importance of technology and smart machines in the process of changing the labor market structure and tells students that most current jobs will not be available in the near future.

e. The author is not sure of how technology will impact the labor market as it is, but she's concerned by the fact that it will take away 40 percent of U.S. jobs within the next few years.

2. Read the article again and do the following tasks.

a. Underline all structures in the future tense you can find in the text.

b. In the sentences you found, what auxiliary or modal verb is used to express future? _____

c. What is the contracted form of the auxiliary or modal verb you marked in *b*? _____

3. Read the sentences below and complete with the structures that express future from the box.

> will be   is going to move   am going to visit   won't pick   will try

a. I don't know which dress to wear to my sister's wedding tonight, but I _____ a white one. She'd be really upset.

b. As soon as she retires, Meghan _____ to Miami. She wants to live by the ocean.

c. Grace brought cookies to the meeting and they look delicious. I think I _____ one.

d. I _____ a friend from college today after work. We've been planning to see each other for months, and I miss her so much.

e. Don't worry about your brother's reaction. I'm sure everything _____ all right.

Unit 5

4. **Unscramble the words to form sentences.**

   a. his wife / move to / Mr. Packer / going / is / Oregon / to / with / .

   _____

   b. James / call / will / soon / as / I / get / as / home / I think / I / .

   _____

   c. to / you / Michigan / when / visit / sister / are / going / in / your / you're / ?

   _____

   d. Thailand / to charity / will donate / Bob / his money / all / move to / and / .

   _____

   e. give Janet / a call / and thank / for / her / I'll / maybe / the gifts / .

   _____

5. **The fragments below were extracted from original publications. To express future predictions, one of them is using *will* and the other is using *be going to*. Can you guess which fragment is using each form? Complete with your guesses.**

   a. It is by now close to certain that there are millions of people currently in high school and college who are fine-tuning their skills for steady-looking careers that _____, following technological breakthroughs, dissipate by the time they retire.

   Extracted from www.theatlantic.com/business/archive/2016/09/how-can-todays-college-students-futureproof-their-careers/499244. Accessed on August 1, 2018.

   b. Professor Richard Susskind, author of "The Future of the Professions and Tomorrow's Lawyers", echoes this distinction. "What you _____ see for a lot of jobs is a churn of different tasks," he explains.

   Extracted from www.theguardian.com/us-news/2017/jun/26/jobs-future-automation-robots-skills-creative-health. Accessed on August 2, 2018.

6. **Read the fragment below, extracted from the article "What to study in college to score the jobs of the future". Then read the tasks and check (✓) the correct alternatives.**

   One field of study that *might* seem a stretch for a list of majors that, in the future, will yield great jobs with growing salaries is Architecture. Data shows that only 9,144 students graduated with such degrees in the United States in 2014.

   Extracted from www.forbes.com/sites/karstenstrauss/2016/08/19/what-to-study-in-college-to-score-the-jobs-of-the-future/#1ef075c4567f. Accessed on August 01, 2018.

   a. In the context given, the verb *might* is used by the author to express that…

   (   ) there's a possibility his prediction will come true.
   (   ) he is sure that his prediction will come true.
   (   ) there's no possibility of his prediction coming true.
   (   ) he doesn't believe his prediction will come true.
   (   ) he wants his prediction to come true.

   b. In the fragment, the verb *might* can be replaced by other verbs without changing the main idea of the paragraph. Choose the alternative with the verbs that would best replace *might*.

   (   ) *could* and *must*
   (   ) *may* and *could*
   (   ) *should* and *could*
   (   ) *may* and *must*
   (   ) *can* and *should*

7. Choose the modal verbs that best complete the sentences below.

a. I'm calling, but Mary won't answer the phone. She _____ (may not / couldn't) be home.

b. She left about an hour ago. She _____ (may be / couldn't be) home now. Thirty minutes is more than enough to get home.

c. You're running out of alternatives. Place an order by the end of the day because these tickets _____ (might not / couldn't) be available tomorrow.

d. He _____ (couldn't be / might) Brazilian. He didn't understand a word I said.

e. Our boss _____ (couldn't / might not) be happy about it, but we are all taking the day off tomorrow.

8. Read the fragment below and complete the tasks that follow.

> **Joel Mokyr**, a professor of economics at Northwestern University and the author of *A Culture of Growth: The Origins of the Modern Economy*.
>
> There are three skills that will count in the future. One is to learn how to access information. Because no set of skills will be unaffected by continued and probably accelerating technological progress, it is important to be able to find out that what you know is obsolete, and keep updating. To do that you have to know where to find that information quickly, cheaply, and effectively, sorting the reliable from the **crackpot** websites.

Extracted from www.theatlantic.com/business/archive/2016/09/how-can-todays-college-students-futureproof-their-careers/499244/. Accessed on August 01, 2018.

a. Underline the *-ly* adverbs you find in the paragraph above.

b. Write the adjectives for the adverbs you found. _____

9. Read the definitions below and complete with the adverbs you underlined in activity 8.

a. _____ : in a way that produces the result that was intended.

b. _____ : with speed, very soon.

c. _____ : for a low price or cost.

d. _____ : likely to happen or be true.

10. Complete the sentences below with the adverbs from the box.

> academically   automatically   especially   financially   hopefully   primarily   probably   really

a. Please tell visitors not to touch the doors at our offices. They are set to open and close _____.

b. With the advances in technology, _____ in Artificial Intelligence, most low-paid workers will lose their jobs and be replaced by robots.

c. We see this agreement _____ as an alternative to reduce costs and save jobs.

d. Although he was not _____ involved in his studies, Peter was a tremendous addition to our college's baseball team.

e. Technology will _____ change the course of education and labor market within the next 10 years.

f. Diane didn't know her decision would cost hundreds of jobs in the long run, but as soon as she realized the negative impacts of her decision, she felt _____ sorry.

g. I know we don't see eye to eye when it comes to politics, but _____ we can find a solution that's best for everyone.

h. Although her plan to prevent employees from leaving the company for the competition was very impressive, her boss told her it was not _____ viable.

Unit 5

11. **Complete the sentences with your own information.**

a. I'd really like to _____
_____ when I finish school.

b. I am extremely worried about _____
_____.

c. Next year, I will probably _____
_____.

d. Hopefully, by the end of this year I _____
_____.

e. If I practice really hard, I might learn how to _____
_____ well.

AN EYE ON VESTIBULAR

2018 PUC-SP – Verão
Questão 63

Man in the mirror
Escrita por Siedah Garrett e Glen Ballard.
Gravada por Michael Jackson.

I'm gonna make a change, for once in my life
It's gonna feel real good, gonna make a difference
Gonna make it right…
I'm starting with the man in the mirror
I'm asking him to change his ways
And no message could have been any clearer
If you wanna make the world a better place
(If you wanna make the world a better place)
Take a look at yourself, and then make a change…

Esse trecho da música "Man in the Mirror" sugere que
a. qualquer pessoa consegue mudar, basta querer.
b. se queremos tornar o mundo um lugar melhor, devemos olhar para o próximo.
c. melhorar o mundo começa com nossa própria mudança.
d. fazer o bem ao próximo nos muda para melhor.

Extracted from https://vestibular.brasilescola.uol.com.br/downloads/pontificia-universidade-catolica-sao-paulo.htm. Accessed on August 3, 2018.

Unit 6 — It's Time We Reforested the Agribusiness

1. Read the title of the article below. What benefits of agroforestry do you think the article might mention? *Predicting*

HOME / BIODIVERSITY / KNOWLEDGE / AGROFORESTRY AND ITS BENEFITS

Agroforestry and its Benefits

Agroforestry is the management and integration of trees, **crops**, and/or livestock on the same **plot** of land and can be an integral component of productive agriculture. It may include existing native forests and forests established by landholders. It is a flexible concept, involving both small and large-sized land holdings.

Scientifically speaking, agroforestry is derived from ecology and is one of the three principal land-use sciences, the other two being agriculture and forestry. Agroforestry differs from **the latter** two principles by placing an emphasis on integration of and interactions among a combination of elements **rather than** just focusing on each element individually.

Agroforestry has a lot in common with intercropping (the practice of planting two or more crops on the same plot) with both practices placing an emphasis on interaction between different plant species. **Generally speaking**, both agroforestry and intercropping can result in higher overall **yields** and reduced operational costs.

[…]

Over the past two decades, a number of studies have been **carried out** analyzing the viability of agroforestry. The combined research has highlighted that agroforestry can **reap** substantial benefits both economically and environmentally, producing more output and proving to be more sustainable than forestry or agricultural monocultures. Agroforestry systems have already been adopted in many parts of the world.

[…]

As well as building on practices used in forestry and agriculture, agroforestry also works towards land protection and conservation through more effective protection of stock, control of soil erosion, salinity, and **water tables** and a higher quality control of **timber**.

Extracted from https://en.reset.org/knowledge/agroforestry-and-its-benefits. Accessed on August 29, 2018.

---

2. Read the statements below and check (✓) the ones mentioned in the article. *Understanding main ideas*

- **a.** ( ) Agroforestry is practiced in many countries around the world.
- **b.** ( ) Agroforestry integrates and combines different elements to achieve best results in the field, which is the same principle as in agriculture.
- **c.** ( ) Intercropping and agroforestry have many similarities.
- **d.** ( ) Agroforestry, agriculture, and forestry are the three main land-use sciences.
- **e.** ( ) Intercropping consists of planting the same crops in different areas.

3. According to the text, what's the main difference between agroforestry and agriculture and forestry? *Understanding details*

_____
_____
_____
_____
_____

4. Read the text once again and underline two sentences in the passive voice.

Unit 6

5. Read the extracts below. Then look at the words in bold and check (✓) the correct alternatives.

a. "[...] efficiency in agriculture **is needed** now more than ever."

Extracted from www.gamaya.com/blog-post/how-ai-in-agriculture-is-being-used/. Accessed on September 3, 2018.

( ) It shows an active voice structure.
( ) It shows a passive voice structure.
( ) It mentions the necessity of efficiency in agriculture.
( ) It mentions that to achieve efficiency in agriculture something else is needed.

b. "The world's population **is growing** at an increasing rate and there need to be enough resources to continue to support that growth [...]."

Extracted from www.gamaya.com/blog-post/how-ai-in-agriculture-is-being-used/. Accessed on September 3, 2018.

( ) It shows an active voice structure.
( ) It shows a passive voice structure.
( ) It talks about the effect the growth of the world's population is having on something else.
( ) It talks about the growth in the world's population.

c. "When there are robots [...] helping with farms and satellites in the sky scanning farms every day, a lot of data **is being collected**."

Extracted from https://gamaya.com/blog-post/how-ai-in-agriculture-is-being-used/. Accessed on September 3, 2018.

( ) It shows an active voice structure.
( ) It shows a passive voice structure.
( ) It says that robots and satellites are collecting a lot of data.
( ) It says that a lot of data is collecting robots and satellites.

6. Rearrange the words below to form sentences in the passive voice.

a. used / robots / been / have / in agribusiness / .
_____

b. conducted / were / a lot of studies / of the century / at the beginning / on agroforestry / .
_____

c. needed / to support / resources / the population growth / are / .
_____

d. in agroforestry / is / the land / protected and conserved / .
_____

e. agroforestry techniques / improved / will / we expect that / in the near future / be / .
_____

f. banned / been / has / deforestation / countries / in many / .
_____

7. Read the sentences below and cross out the verb that can't be used to complete it.

a. A book is being _____ on the use of Artificial Intelligence in the agribusiness.
published / written / reading

b. This location is _____ by hundreds of researchers every year.
visited / saw / accessed

c. The tractor was _____ in Gina's fields when no one was watching.
stolen / hit / driving

d. A movie about the importance of agroforestry is being _____ by critics all over the world.
watching / watched / analyzed

e. What questions _____ be asked by the speakers during the National Environmental Monitoring Conference?
could / will / are

f. Planting techniques _____ be improved.
can / could / was

8. **Look at the phrases in bold in the article on page 124. Which of them means that the author's statement...**
   a. describes a common feeling or opinion? _____
   b. describes an expert's point of view? _____
   c. is adding information to the subject being discussed? _____

9. **Read the following fragments and underline the discourse markers. Then identify the idea conveyed by each discourse marker.**

   a. Major obstacles to the spread of agroforestry strategies are the **lack of** support for such systems through public policies, which often take little notice of tree-based farming systems. Consequently, agroforestry is often absent from recommendations for ensuring food security under climate change, even though many practices have been shown to deliver benefits for rural development, **buffer** against climate variability, help rural populations adapt to climate change, and contribute to climate change **mitigation**.

   Extracted from www.sciencedirect.com/science/article/pii/S1877343513001449. Accessed on August 30, 2018.

   b. The world-wide **deaths** and chronic diseases due to pesticide poisoning number about 1 million per year (Environews Forum, 1999).

   Extracted from www.ncbi.nlm.nih.gov/pmc/articles/PMC2984095/. Accessed on August 30, 2018.

   c. However, despite these high costs, farmers continue to use pesticides and in most countries in increasing quantities.

   Extracted from www.sciencedirect.com/science/article/pii/S0921800901002385. Accessed on August 30, 2018.

10. **Complete the sentences below with the discourse markers from the box.**

    > due to   since   in addition   consequently   thanks to   however

    a. She was hired to help during the harvest. _____, I don't think she has any experience in the agribusiness.
    b. _____ the agribusiness has been growing, a lot of Artificial Intelligence tools are being produced.
    c. We are hiring people to support us during peak season. _____, every employee will get a bonus for working overtime in this period.
    d. _____ a lot of hard work, our country has achieved great improvements in the agroforestry field.
    e. In the last century, a lot of trees were cut down. _____, the importance of planting new trees is greater than ever.
    f. Excuse me, Ma'am. I would like to inform you that, _____ the weather conditions, your visit to the gardens must be canceled. We apologize for that.

11. **Complete the extracts below with the correct form of the verbs *get* or *set*.**

    a. "[...] As agroforestry tries to _____ closer to the way nature works, it is intrinsically related with agroecology."

    Extracted from www.fcrn.org.uk/interviews/perspectives-agroforestry-model-sustainable-intensification-agriculture. Accessed on September 3, 2018.

    b. "The Rainforest Alliance _____ standards for sustainability that conserve wildlife and wildlands and promote the well-being of workers and their communities. [...]"

    Extracted from www.rainforest-alliance.org/business/climate/documents/coffee_carbon_guidance.pdf. Accessed on September 3, 2018.

    c. "Small employers need to _____ ready for super payment changes in the agribusiness."

    Extracted from www.sheepcentral.com/agribusiness-small-employers-need-to-get-ready-for-super-payment-changes/. Accessed on September 3, 2018.

Unit 6

12. **Complete the questions using the verbs *get* and *set* in the correct form. Then answer them with your own opinion.**

a. What could the government in your country do to make sure people _____ the message about the importance of agroforestry and ecology?

_____
_____
_____

b. Do you know how someone in your country can _____ permission to cut down trees?

_____
_____
_____

c. Do you think your school _____ an example on sustainable habits? If so, what does it do? If not, how could this be changed?

_____
_____
_____

AN EYE ON VESTIBULAR

FUVEST 2015 – 1º fase (Prova V)
Questão 43

Between now and 2050 the number of people living in cities will grow from 3.9 billion to 6.3 billion. The proportion of urban dwellers will swell from 54% to 67% of the world's population, according to the UN. In other words, for the next 36 years the world's cities will expand by the equivalent of six São Paulos every year. This growth will largely occur in developing countries. But most governments there are ignoring the problem, says William Cobbett of the Cities Alliance, an NGO that supports initiatives such as the one launched by New York University to help cities make long term preparations for their growth. "Whether we want it or not, urbanization is inevitable," say specialists. "The real question is: how can we improve its quality?"

The Economist, June 21st 2014. Adaptado.

De acordo com o texto

a. A população rural crescerá na mesma proporção que a população urbana nos próximos 20 anos.
b. A população, nas cidades, chegará a mais de 6 bilhões de pessoas até 2050.
c. A expansão de cidades como São Paulo é um exemplo do crescimento global.
d. A cidade de São Paulo cresceu seis vezes mais, na última década, do que o previsto por especialistas.
e. O crescimento maior da população em centros urbanos ocorrerá em países desenvolvidos.

Unit 7 — The Economic Effects of Globalization

1. **Read part of a news report and check (✓) the most appropriate headline.** *Skimming*

   > Business leaders around the globe have said the rise of economic nationalism **triggered** by Brexit, Donald Trump, and populist politics poses the greatest **threat** to their growth.
   >
   > According to a **survey** of 1,300 chief executives from some of the world's biggest companies, carried out by the accountancy company KPMG, British business leaders are notably more pessimistic than their peers.
   >
   > Two-thirds of U.K. CEOs said they were most worried about the growing use of protectionism, which includes measures such as tariffs and quotas on imports, compared with just over half of their international counterparts.
   >
   > Such barriers have the potential to protect jobs in the countries that put up trade barriers, but business leaders argue the benefits are **outweighed** by higher prices for consumers.
   >
   > Extracted from www.theguardian.com/business/2018/may/22/economic-nationalism-biggest-threat-growth-business-leaders-poll-political-populism. Accessed on August 4, 2018.

   a. ( ) Donald Trump's election and its impact on global economy.
   b. ( ) Business leaders say Brexit might affect economic growth.
   c. ( ) Business leaders blame politics for global economic problems.
   d. ( ) Why isn't the economy getting better?
   e. ( ) Business leaders say economic nationalism is the biggest threat to growth.

2. **Find the following information in the article.** *Scanning*

   a. the nationality of the business leaders who took part in the survey: _____
   b. the number of CEOs who took part in the survey: _____
   c. ratio of British chief executives worried about the growing use of protectionism: _____
   d. protectionism measures: _____

3. **Read the fragment below, extracted from the article in activity 1. Circle the verb tense of the phrase in bold.**

   > Business leaders around the globe **have said** the rise of economic nationalism triggered by Brexit, Donald Trump, and populist politics poses the greatest threat to their growth.

   a. simple present
   b. simple past
   c. present continuous
   d. present perfect
   e. past perfect
   f. past continuous

4. Check (✓) the alternative that completes the sentence below.

The _____ in the affirmative form is formed using the auxiliary verb _____ and the main verb in the _____ form.

a. ( ) present perfect / have / past participle
b. ( ) simple present / be / infinitive
c. ( ) present perfect / be / past participle
d. ( ) simple present / have / present participle

5. Read the fragment below and underline the statements in the simple past and in the present perfect. Then read the sentences that follow and mark SP for simple past and PP for present perfect.

> […]
> In declaring that the U.S. economy has entered a new era of faster growth, President Donald Trump is dismissing signals from financial markets and the outlook of economists from Wall Street to the Federal Reserve.
>
> Flanked by his top economic advisers, Trump delivered remarks on the South Lawn of the White House on Friday to celebrate a report that the economy expanded in the second quarter at the fastest pace in four years. He said the economy is on track to reach an annual growth rate of more than 3 percent.
> […]
>
> Extracted from www.chicagotribune.com/business/ct-biz-trump-gdp-economists-20180727-story.html#. Accessed on August 05, 2018.

a. ( ) The U.S. economy has entered a new era.
b. ( ) Donald Trump won the presidential elections in 2016.
c. ( ) President Trump delivered remarks on the South Lawn of the White House on Friday.
d. ( ) It is believed that the economy has already expanded substantially.
e. ( ) He said the economy is on track to reach a 3% annual growth rate.

6. Complete the sentences below with the words from the box in the simple past or present perfect.

> be   tell   apply   discuss   not be

a. _____ for that job yesterday? When I saw the job post, I knew you would consider filling in an application.
b. I _____ her not to come in before dinner time because I would be studying.
c. _____ she able to explain the economic situation during the meeting?
d. _____ these topics with your classmates?
e. I _____ to your house in years. The last time I was there was in 2011.

7. Read the statements below and complete them with *for* or *since*. Then complete the rule about the use of *for* and *since*.

a. I've had this car _____ two years.

b. We've lived alone _____ our parents moved to the countryside.

We use _____ to stress the idea that something started at a given point in time in the past and still takes place in the present, whereas _____ is used to stress the duration of an activity or situation.

8. Read the extract below and complete with *for* and *since*.

All of that slower growth last year, then, means that the economy is probably chugging along at the same 2 to 2.5 percent annual pace that it has been _____ most of the recovery. That makes sense when you consider that job growth hasn't sped up _____ Trump took office but has slowed a little.

Extracted from www.washingtonpost.com/news/wonk/wp/2018/05/02/trump-has-not-made-the-economy-great-again/?utm_term=.9a35dfa98ff8. Accessed on August 5, 2018.

9. Complete the sentences below with *just*, *for*, or *since*.

a. Joshua and Miranda have lived in this house _____ five years now. They want to sell it and move to a penthouse.

b. What have you done for Anna _____ she lost her job? Maybe she needs some extra help finding something new.

c. I have seen a lot of people going through customs _____ the last plane landed.

d. She had been looking for a job for months, but she has _____ found one now.

e. I've worked at the same company _____ 32 years.

f. Our economical welfare has been at stake _____ 2016.

g. Louise has _____ arrived! She arrived about five minutes ago.

10. Answer the questions with your own information. You can use *for* and *since*.

a. How long have you studied at this school?
_____

b. How long have you lived in your house / apartment?
_____

c. How many English tests have you had this year?
_____

d. Have you written in your book today?
_____

e. Can you think of an activity you have just done? Write about it.
_____

11. The fragment below analyzes the economic growth in the USA during Trump's election campaign for president of the United States. Complete it with the verb *be* in the simple past or present perfect.

www.macleans.ca/economy/economicanalysis/trumps-economy-looks-just-like-obamas-except-for-one-important-thing/

"I will be the greatest jobs producer that God ever created" - Donald Trump, Jan. 11, 2017

Jobs might _____ the dominant **plank** in Trump's election campaign, but employment _____ growing at a slightly quicker pace by this point in Obama's second term. The challenge for Trump going forward is that **unemployment** in the USA is already at such a low level, at just 4.1 percent, that the easy gains have been had. On the campaign trail Trump regularly stated that 96 million American workers _____ shut out of the economy. But while there _____ indeed 96.2 million people not in the labor force in December – a new all-time high – that figure includes retirees, students, people with family responsibilities, and people with disabilities.

Adapted from www.macleans.ca/economy/economicanalysis/trumps-economy-looks-just-like-obamas-except-for-one-important-thing/. Accessed on August 7, 2018.

AN EYE ON VESTIBULAR

2018 – UNICAMP
Vestibular de Verão
Questão 33

ZOMBIE NEUROSCIENCE
I don't know if cockroaches dream, but I imagine if they do, jewel wasps feature prominently in their nightmares. These small, solitary tropical wasps are of little concern to us humans; after all, they don't manipulate our minds so that they can serve us up as willing, living meals to their newborns, as they do to unsuspecting cockroaches. The story is simple, if grotesque: the female wasp controls the minds of the cockroaches she feeds to her offspring, taking away their sense of fear or will to escape their fate. What turns a once healthy cockroach into a mindless zombie is its venom. Not just any venom, either: a specific venom that acts like a drug, targeting the cockroach's brain.

(Adaptado de Christie Wilcox, Zombie Neuroscience. Scientific American, New York, v. 315, n. 2, p. 70–73, 2016.)

De acordo com o autor,
- **a.** certas baratas conseguem escapar de ataques de vespas comportando-se como zumbis.
- **b.** baratas são capazes de ações predatórias que mal podemos imaginar.
- **c.** vespas fêmeas de uma certa espécie podem controlar a mente das baratas.
- **d.** uma barata pode inocular um veneno que transforma uma outra barata em um zumbi.

Unit 8 — Spotting Fake News Among the Real Stories

1. **Read part of a news report by the National Democratic Institute (NDI). Check (✓) the alternative that describes its main purpose.**
   Identifying the main purpose of a text

   a. ( ) To discuss the problems caused by incorrect reporting of facts in politics.

   b. ( ) To present the topics of an NDI's annual dinner concerning false news and the reasons why this is an issue.

   c. ( ) To present NDI and its fight against false news together with three other organizations.

   ---

   https://www.ndi.org/our-stories/disinformation-vs-democracy-fighting-facts

   ## DISINFORMATION VS. DEMOCRACY: FIGHTING FOR FACTS

   TWEET   SHARE   +

   Thursday, October 26, 2017

   NDI's annual Democracy Dinner will be **held** November 2nd at the Fairmont Hotel in Washington, DC. This year, NDI will honor three organizations on the front lines of fighting the global challenge of disinformation and false news. In addition, Senator Chris Murphy will provide a perspective from the U.S. Congress on this important topic and efforts that are being taken to counter disinformation. […]

   The global **reach** of social media platforms, coupled with the rise of artificial intelligence and machine learning, has provided a powerful suite of new tools that are increasingly used by autocratic regimes seeking to control the information space. While control of information has long been a key feature of autocracies at home, the rise of social media platforms and online political discourse now **provide** new opportunities for autocracies to manipulate public opinion abroad and disrupt domestic politics in geopolitical adversaries. The **weaponization** of social media is a global challenge, both during and between elections. Emerging democracies have often been used to "weapons test" new approaches to computational propaganda and disinformation, and the work being done to counter it is critical to the future of democracy.

   At the dinner, NDI will recognize three organizations that have demonstrated a deep and **abiding commitment** to democracy and human rights:

   - **StopFake.org** – StopFake.org in Ukraine works with journalists and citizen groups to monitor and uncover false news sources, and has created tools on "how to identify a fake" on its website. It checks facts and verifies information in media to help consumers obtain objective news that is free from distorted information, specifically on events in Ukraine. Long before most were aware of the use of false media to manipulate public opinion, StopFake was on the front lines exposing these tactics in a very **tough** neighborhood in which Ukraine is facing lots of outside pressure. One of the challenges of "fact checking" approaches to disinformation is that in correcting the record, after the fact, it is difficult to displace opinions or ideas that have already been formed or reinforced by disinformation. […]

   - **Rappler** – Rappler is an online social news network based in the Philippines. It holds public and private sectors accountable, **pursuing** truth and transparency for the people served. It encourages its readership to be aware of the spread of disinformation and propaganda, and exposes the hidden social media "machines" or bots that distort the truth. […]

   - **The Oxford Internet Institute's Project on Computational Propaganda** – The Oxford Internet Institute (OII), a multi-disciplinary research teaching department of the University of Oxford, has been at the **forefront** of research in the field of disinformation. In early 2017, OII's Project on Computational Propaganda issued a **groundbreaking** study on the use of social media and computational propaganda to manipulate public opinion in nine countries. […]

   Extracted from www.ndi.org/our-stories/disinformation-vs-democracy-fighting-facts. Accessed on September 18, 2018.

Unit 8

2. Read the news report again and answer the questions. *Understanding details*

a. How many organizations will be honored in this NDI meeting? What are they?
_____

b. Who is going to talk about the efforts being made to fight misinformation?
_____

c. What is considered a global challenge in election times?
_____

d. Which organization has a tool to identify false news?
_____

e. Which organization works with research and has recently conducted a study on the use of social media to manipulate opinions?
_____

3. Read the extracts below and check (✓) the correct alternative regarding the verb tenses of the words in bold.

a. "'Fake news' **was not** a term many people used two years ago, but it **is** now seen as one of the greatest threats to democracy, free debate, and the Western order. [...]

Governments and powerful individuals **have used** information as a weapon for millennia, to boost their support and quash dissidence. [...]"

Extracted from www.telegraph.co.uk/technology/0/fake-news-exactly-has-really-had-influence. Accessed on September 18, 2018.

(   ) simple past – present perfect – simple present

(   ) simple past – simple present – present perfect

b. "Students often look to teachers for information about how the Internet **works**. 'If they **don't get** it from teachers, they'**re not getting** it anywhere else,' **said** Matthew Johnson, director of education at MediaSmarts, an Ottawa-based organization that provides media literacy resources. [...]"

Extracted from http://teachmag.com/archives/9860. Accessed on September 18, 2018.

(   ) simple present – present continuous – simple present – simple past

(   ) simple present – simple present – present continuous – simple past

4. Complete the sentences with the verbs from the box in the correct form. Pay attention to the verb tense used in each sentence.

> convince   access   realize   tell   be   check   try   share   visit

a. I am not _____ that website. Almost 50% of the information on it is fake news!

b. Margaret is sure that you _____ that web page yesterday. She was just _____ me that she saw your navigation history this morning.

c. Don has _____ online for too long. Could you ask him to be careful about what he reads on the Internet?

d. She didn't _____ me this is real news. I'm sure she's _____ to pass on fake news.

e. When I was _____ my Facebook page I _____ that my friend was _____ a lot of news from an unreliable website.

5. Complete the questions below with one word.

a. _____ you ever shared news without checking its veracity?

b. _____ you try to send me a link by WhatsApp yesterday? I couldn't open it.

c. _____ you still want to report that piece of news you got yesterday by e-mail?

d. _____ you telling me that I should just stop reading online news?

e. _____ you at the lecture about spreading false news yesterday? I didn't see you there.

f. _____ Sarah know that people are saying things about her? I really don't think they are true.

6. Complete the following sentences with the affirmative or negative form of *will* or *be going to*.

a. I _____ tell anyone about your secret. You can trust me.

b. Louise _____ report that fake news to Facebook. She is already writing an e-mail to them.

c. Maybe the president _____ show his support to our commission against spreading false information during the annual meeting.

d. I can't find any information about yesterday's accident in the newspaper. I think I _____ check online.

e. Apparently, the conservative candidate _____ win the election. Polls show that 54% of voters prefer him over the other candidate.

7. Read the excerpts below and check (✓) the alternative that best completes them. Then write the missing word in the blank.

a. "NEW DELHI: Under fire over fake and provocative messages being circulated on its platform, WhatsApp on Tuesday began an awareness campaign to help users identify and prevent the spread of false information, _____ and fake news. […]"

Extracted from http://timesofindia.indiatimes.com/articleshow/64930914.cms?utm_source=contentofinterest&utm_medium=text&utm_campaign=cppst. Accessed on September 18, 2018.

( ) web crawler   ( ) hoax   ( ) bot

b. "Use a mobile antivirus – Keep a proactive defense on your Android so that if any malware, ransomware, adware, or _____ try to infiltrate, it'll be blocked and rejected. […]"

Extracted from https://blog.avast.com/fake-apps-android-spyware. Accessed on September 18, 2018.

( ) spyware   ( ) bot   ( ) slander

c. "The production values are high and the message is compelling. In an 11-minute mini-documentary, Facebook acknowledges its mistakes and pledges to 'fight against _____.' […]"

Extracted from www.theguardian.com/commentisfree/2018/jul/20/facebook-pledge-to-eliminate-false-information-is-itself-fake-news. Accessed on September 18, 2018.

( ) misinformation   ( ) bot   ( ) spyware

d. "_____ have become one of the biggest threats to security systems today. Their growing popularity among cybercriminals comes from their ability to infiltrate almost any internet-connected device […]."

Extracted from www.pandasecurity.com/mediacenter/security/what-is-a-botnet/. Accessed on October 10, 2018.

( ) Spyware   ( ) Botnets   ( ) Misinformation

8. Unscramble the words to form embedded questions.

a. news / fake / ? / how to / know / do / you / identify

_____

b. tell / ? / can / me / you / what / is / a web crawler

_____

c. if / do / know / you / this antivirus / the phone / protects / ? / from spyware

_____

d. this website / I / is / wonder / reliable / . / if

_____

9. Match the parts of sentences to form embedded questions.

a. Can anybody tell me…   ( ) the information on this website is reliable.
b. What I really need to know is if… ( ) where the bathroom is?
c. Could you tell us when…   ( ) her students can't use reliable sources in their school projects.
d. Do you think you can figure out what… ( ) the information will be available for students?
e. She wonders why…   ( ) Anna ever checks before passing on news?
f. Do you know if…   ( ) we must do to put the system back in place?

10. **Read the direct questions and complete the questions and sentences that follow.**

   a. Is this the most expensive ring in this jewelry store?

   Do you know _____ ?

   b. Where do you want to go on your vacation?

   Can you tell _____ ?

   c. When is Mona's birthday?

   Can you remember _____ ?

   d. What's the most important thing about this project?

   I wonder _____ .

   e. Did Anthony tell anyone about the false information on this link?

   Does anybody know _____ ?

11. **After everything you read throughout this unit, can you summarize what fake news is and what problems it can cause?**

_____

_____

_____

AN EYE ON ENEM

ENEM 2010 – Prova Azul
Questão 91

The record industry

The record industry is undoubtedly in crisis, with labels laying off employees in continuation. This is because CD sales are plummeting as youngsters prefer to download their music from the Internet, usually free of charge. And yet it´s not all gloom and doom. Some labels are in fact thriving. Putumayo World Music, for example, is growing, thanks to its catalogue of ethnic compilation albums, featuring work by largely unknown artists from around the planet.

Putumayo, which takes its name from a valley in Colombia, was founded in New York in 1993. It began life as an alternative clothing company, but soon decided to concentrate on music. Indeed its growth appears to have coincided with that of world music as a genre.

Speak Up. Ano XXIII, nº 275 (fragmento).

A indústria fonográfica passou por várias mudanças no século XX e, como consequência, as empresas enfrentaram crises. Entre as causas, o texto da revista *Speak Up* aponta

   a. o baixo interesse dos jovens por alguns gêneros musicais.

   b. o acesso a músicas, geralmente sem custo, pela Internet.

   c. a compilação de álbuns com diferentes estilos musicais.

   d. a ausência de artistas populares entre as pessoas mais jovens.

   e. o aumento do número de cantores desconhecidos.

AUDIO SCRIPTS

Unit 1

Track 02 – Activity 2

Five apps to help social media addicts fight Fomo

Some teens are glued to social media feeds, and research suggests it's causing anxiety and sleeplessness, but there are ways of taking back control.

Fomo (Fear Of Missing Out) may sound like a silly acronym, but it can drive people to spend excessive time staring at social media feeds, anxious that they may miss a social opportunity or be left out.

The advent of Facebook in 2004 followed by other big social networks over the past decade means the amount of time children spend online has skyrocketed.

[…]

Extracted from www.theguardian.com/sustainable-business/2016/may/18/five-apps-help-smartphone-addicts-fight-fomo. Accessed on November 19, 2018.

Track 03 – Activity 3

"Research clearly shows that the amount of time British children and adolescents spend on social media has more than doubled in the past 10 years," says Dr Andrew Przybylski, research fellow at the Oxford Internet Institute. While in the USA, a quarter of teens are online "almost constantly", according to the Pew Research Centre, with 71% using multiple social networks.

Research suggests there are negative impacts to this increase in young people's time spent online. The Australian Psychological Society surveyed teens aged 13 to 17 at the end of last year and reported that half suffer from FOMO and feel anxious because of it.

Alongside potentially increasing the risk of anxiety and depression, a University of Glasgow study found using social media late at night could lead to less, and lower-quality, sleep. This result chimes with research from the University of Pittsburgh on young adults, which found that participants who were on social media the most had three times the level of sleep disturbance compared with those who checked least frequently.

[..]

But it's not all bad news: the teens surveyed by the Australian researchers said social media helped them to build stronger relationships, set better goals, seek help and guidance, and feel "part of a global community".

Adapted from www.theguardian.com/sustainable-business/2016/may/18/five-apps-help-smartphone-addicts-fight-fomo. Accessed on November 19, 2018.

Unit 2

Tracks 04 and 05 – Activities 1 and 2

A self-driving car has killed a pedestrian for the first time ever.

The autonomous car, operated by Uber, struck a pedestrian and killed them in what is thought to be the first death of its kind. The autonomous taxi was operating as part of a trial that Uber hoped would represent the future, but has now been suspended.

At the time of the accident, the car was driving itself in autonomous mode, Tempe police said. There was a vehicle operator behind the wheel, but they weren't in control of the car at the time of the crash.

[…]

A spokesman for Uber Technologies Inc. said the company was suspending its North American tests.

People have died in crashes involving vehicles that are driving themselves before. But this is thought to be the first time that a pedestrian has died after being hit by a self-driving vehicle.

Uber's autonomous taxis, like the self-driving cars made by other companies, use a series of sensors built into the car to spot pedestrians, cyclists, and other cars, feeding that into a computer that is able to steer and accelerate. Until recently, they have required a real person to be sat in the front of the car and ready to take over – but recently California officials approved the testing of such vehicles without humans in the front seats.

[…]

The cars have also been involved in smaller issues, such as running red lights.

Extracted from www.independent.co.uk/life-style/gadgets-and-tech/news/uber-self-driving-car-killed-pedestrian-death-tempe-arizona-autonomous-vehicle-a8263921.html. Accessed on September 20, 2018.

Unit 3

Tracks 06 and 07 – Activities 2 and 3

Gen Z, Gen Y, baby boomers – a guide to the generations

As a new report says Generation Z is smarter and more prudent than Gen Y, here's a guide to all those complex generational labels.

[…]

Generation Z

[…]

They have grown up in a world in political and financial turmoil. As a result, they are keen to look after their money, and make the world a better place. A report by Sparks & Honey, a U.S. advertising agency […], describes this generation as the "first tribe of true digital natives" or "screenagers". But unlike the older Gen Y, they are smarter, safer, more mature, and want to change the world.

Generation Y

Also known as Millennials, born between about 1980 and 2000.

Born between the advent of the Walkman and the founding of Google, the members of Gen Y are unsurprisingly shaped by technology. Some have made fortunes from it. […]

Generation X

Gen X are those born between the early 1960s and the early 1980s. [...]

This generation has been characterized as being saddled with permanent cynicism. Too young to have fought in any major war, old enough to have enjoyed a free education – they have spent too much of their adulthood sitting around in coffee shops trying to set the world to rights. And failing.

[...]

Adapted from www.telegraph.co.uk/news/features/11002767/Gen-Z-Gen-Y-baby-boomers-a-guide-to-the-generations.html. Accessed on November 19, 2018.

Unit 4

Track 08 – Activity 1

Jason: Very excited to welcome Tim Leffel to the show. Tim, welcome to the "Zero to Travel" podcast my friend.

Tim: Thank you so much for having me, Jason. It's good to talk with you again.

Jason: No problem. When we connected for the first time you were part of the "Paradise Pack" and this book that we're talking about today – "A better life for half the price" was one of the books in the pack. I'm really blown away by the content in here and I just want to preface this whole conversation by letting you, the listener, know that Tim is from the U.S.A. so, we're coming from, the perspective, I guess, but Tim would you say that maybe this perspective applies to all sort of Western cultures?

Tim: Yeah, I think I tried to cover that in the book too, by interviewing a lot of people that were from England, or Australia, or New Zealand. Basically, whenever you move from a really expensive country, to a much cheaper country you're going to get that benefit of a lower cost of living, so while the specifics may vary from, you know, place to place, depending on where you came from, the visa situation might be different. In general if you move from a more developed country to a less developed country, you're just going to be able to cut your expenses in half pretty easily if you do it right.

Jason: So, what prompted you to move abroad at first and why is this something somebody should consider?

Tim: Well, I actually lived abroad when I was back in my backpacking days and traveling around the world we actually lived in Turkey for a while, and we lived for more than a year in Seoul, South Korea. I say we – it was my wife and I, and we were teaching English as second language teachers. [fade out]

Adapted from http://zerototravel.com/podcast/living-abroad-tim-leffel/. Accessed on October 2, 2018.

Unit 5

Track 09 – Activity 2

Hi. I'm Josh, I am a third year primary education student here at Macquarie and I'm here today to talk to you a little bit about a gap year. You might ask what is a gap year and it's, um, it's just time between school and college, where usually you go away or some people work for the year, but it's a time when you kind of you learn more about what you wanna do in your career, what you wanna do once you leave school, university life, those kinds of things.

Adapted from www.youtube.com/watch?v=oJTwlOHk9Ro. Accessed on July 20, 2018.

Track 10 – Activity 3

So, I finished school, I was only 17 at the time, I was under age and I was really young. I had no idea what I wanted to do for a career. I went away for a year, I worked in a school in England just south of Manchester, a place called Alderley Edge, so we were living there, we were working there and then we were able to go into Manchester and the local towns. I started off being the music gap student, so that meant working in the music department filing music, running classes, being involved in the choir and the orchestra, which I was really keen on doing because I was big singing, big on singing. My mate here in Sydney, they decided to put him in the office and so what we figured out really quite early on and what the teachers and the headmaster of the school figured out was that I wasn't so good at the music and my mate wasn't so good at the office and so that was a bonus of a gap year: learning what your strengths are, where they are. Later on in the year I decided that, you know, what I would like to have a bit of a go at was some teaching and I was able to teach a computer class, so we were teaching them you know Word, PowerPoint, those skills and these kids we knew too so they were like seven or eight and they'd never done anything like that, so it was a great experience because I was teaching them something that they had never done before, they hadn't got at school before and it was something that they were really going to use and they were able to go home and show their parents, "Hey, guess what I can do". So I came back and I had deferred a Bachelor of Arts here at Macquarie University and so I am, I switched my degree into a Bachelor of Arts with the Diploma of Education, which is the degree to become a primary school teacher. In your third year here at Macquarie University you get to go to a school and so I went up to school in Pennant Hills and it was an incredible experience. I had a year three and they were fantastic. I feel that Macquarie did support me through my gap year because I was able to defer my course, I felt a lot more comfortable about, about going away knowing that I had a position still here.

Transcribed from www.youtube.com/watch?v=oJTwlOHk9Ro. Accessed on July 20, 2018.

Track 11 – Activity 4

So, guys, a gap, a gap year is good because it teaches you more about yourself, you develop a self-understanding and a self-awareness, you learn what your strengths are and through that understanding you're able to kind of figure out what you want to do with the rest of your life. So that's why I chose a gap year and if it's right for you that's why you should too.

Transcribed from www.youtube.com/watch?v=oJTwlOHk9Ro. Accessed on July 20, 2018.

Unit 6

Tracks 12 and 13 – Activities 1 and 2

Brazil has progressively emerged as a major agricultural powerhouse during the past few years: A net importer of agricultural products in the 1970s, the country now ranks among the world's five largest agricultural producers and exporters. The world's largest country in terms of land size and South America's largest nation in terms of land and population size, Brazil is currently a key player in the international arena and a great power among emerging countries.

As the world's sixth largest economy, Brazil ranks third among the world's major agricultural exporters and fourth for food products. With 25 percent of global investment, the country is the principal recipient and source of foreign direct investment in Latin America and fifth recipient nation in the world. Thanks to its agricultural and oil resources, Brazil also ranks second worldwide for bioethanol production.

Blessed with the world's largest reserves of farmable and not cultivated land, Brazil has carved out its regional and international rank thanks to strong exporting agricultural activities, radical economic reforms, and an aggressive trade and influence policy.

Even while manufacturing and services are showing a steep growth, agriculture is still a driving force of the Brazilian economy with 5.8 percent of GDP (against 2 percent in France), and with the agribusiness share reaching 23 percent. In 2009, agriculture accounted for 19.3 percent of the labor force, or 19 million people, thus strongly contributing to poverty reduction. Agribusiness employment accounted for 2.7 percent of the labor force.

Extracted from www.momagri.org/UK/focus-on-issues/Agriculture-a-strategic-sector-for-Brazil-s-economic-growth_1089.html. Accessed on August 31, 2018.

Unit 7

Track 14 – Activity 2

SHARMINI PERIES: It's The Real News Network. I'm Sharmini Peries, coming to you from Baltimore. Will there be another financial crisis, or even another great recession like that of 2007 and 2008? A new report issued by the Next Systems Project argues that it is almost inevitable that there will be another major financial crisis. The report, titled "The Crisis Next Time: Planning for public ownership as an alternative to corporate bank bailouts," looks at the history of financial crises over the past 70 years, and it predicts that another major crisis is very likely. Secondly, the report outlines a plan for how to deal with the next crisis. The calculated guess is that the next financial crisis could even be worse than the last one we experienced. And the report's main recommendation is to create a public banking sector not only to cope with the next crisis when it happens, but also to prevent future crises.

Joining me now here in our Baltimore studio is the report's author, Thomas Hanna. And Thomas is the research director at the Democracy Collaborative, to which the Next Systems Project belongs.

Extracted from https://therealnews.com/stories/the-next-global-financial-crisis-is-inevitable-pt-1-2;. Accessed on July 24, 2018.

Track 15 – Activity 3

THOMAS HANNA: Thank you very much for having me.

SHARMINI PERIES: Thank you for joining us here. All right, Thomas, let's take up this very important issue, because it is very solution-oriented. But let's step back a bit and first, in our first segment, discuss, looking at history, why you think that there is a next crisis pending, and what are the indicators, what does history tell us. And then in the second segment we'll take up what the potential solution that you're proposing is here, which is public banking. But let's start with the first issue, which is you went back 70 years, and you took a look at the history of crises. And so, based on that, tell us why there's another crisis pending.

THOMAS HANNA: Well, I think the first thing that we need to understand is that we are exactly 10 years from the last major financial crisis, which was essentially the biggest financial crisis in this country in 70 years, since the Great Depression. And if you look at history in the post-1970 period, what we call the neoliberal period, crises happen on average about once every 10 years. So, 10 years from the financial crisis, we're looking at a time when there should, or probably would be, another financial crisis just based on history alone. That's not taking into account what has happened in the intervening 10 years since the financial crisis. And essentially what has happened is nothing. We've had very little movement on addressing or changing any of the underlying basis of the financial sector that caused the crisis.

[...]

Extracted from https://therealnews.com/stories/the-next-global-financial-crisis-is-inevitable-pt-1-2. Accessed on July 24, 2018.

Unit 8

Tracks 16 and 17 – Activities 1 and 2

Real News Can be Confirmed in Four Steps

Teaching with current events has always been a vital way to help students become informed and engaged citizens. But the importance of news literacy has perhaps never been as critical as it is today, with the pronounced rise of deliberately misleading and patently fake news.

[...]

As educators, we have a role to play in equipping our young adults with the critical thinking skills necessary to assess the credibility of news reports as they make their own informed opinions about the day's topics.

Reliability: Determine if a source is trustworthy

We now know that there are intentional efforts to widely disseminate false content on social media channels, blogs, and other websites. Making sure students know how to measure the reliability of a source is a critical first step to helping them spot fake news.

[...]

Evidence: Check sources, citations, and facts

As students learn to discern real from fake news, it is important to remember that there is a difference between fake news and inaccurate information. Reliable news sources will include links to professional sources, fact-based evidence, and will present multiple sides of an issue. Train students to check the evidence within the article they are reading.

[...]

Argument: Identify the two sides in every story

This step can be tricky, as even the most factual news outlets can still have a bias or unique perspective on a topic. A biased article does not inherently imply that it's fake news; rather, it's part of the overall formula (along with reliability and evidence) that can help students. A well-written article is balanced, representing many sides of a story. Recognizing that there are, more often than not, multiple perspectives of an event or a political issue, can lead students to better understand their community and the world as a whole.

[...]

Language: Show how words and tone matter

The final step of identifying real news is to evaluate the tone and level of sensationalism of an article. Incorporate analysis of word choice in evaluating the reliability of a news source.

[...]

Extracted from www.amle.org/BrowsebyTopic/WhatsNew/WNDet/TabId/270/ArtMID/888/ArticleID/878/Fight-Fake-News.aspx. Accessed on October 8, 2018.

NOTES

NOTES

NOTES

STICKERS

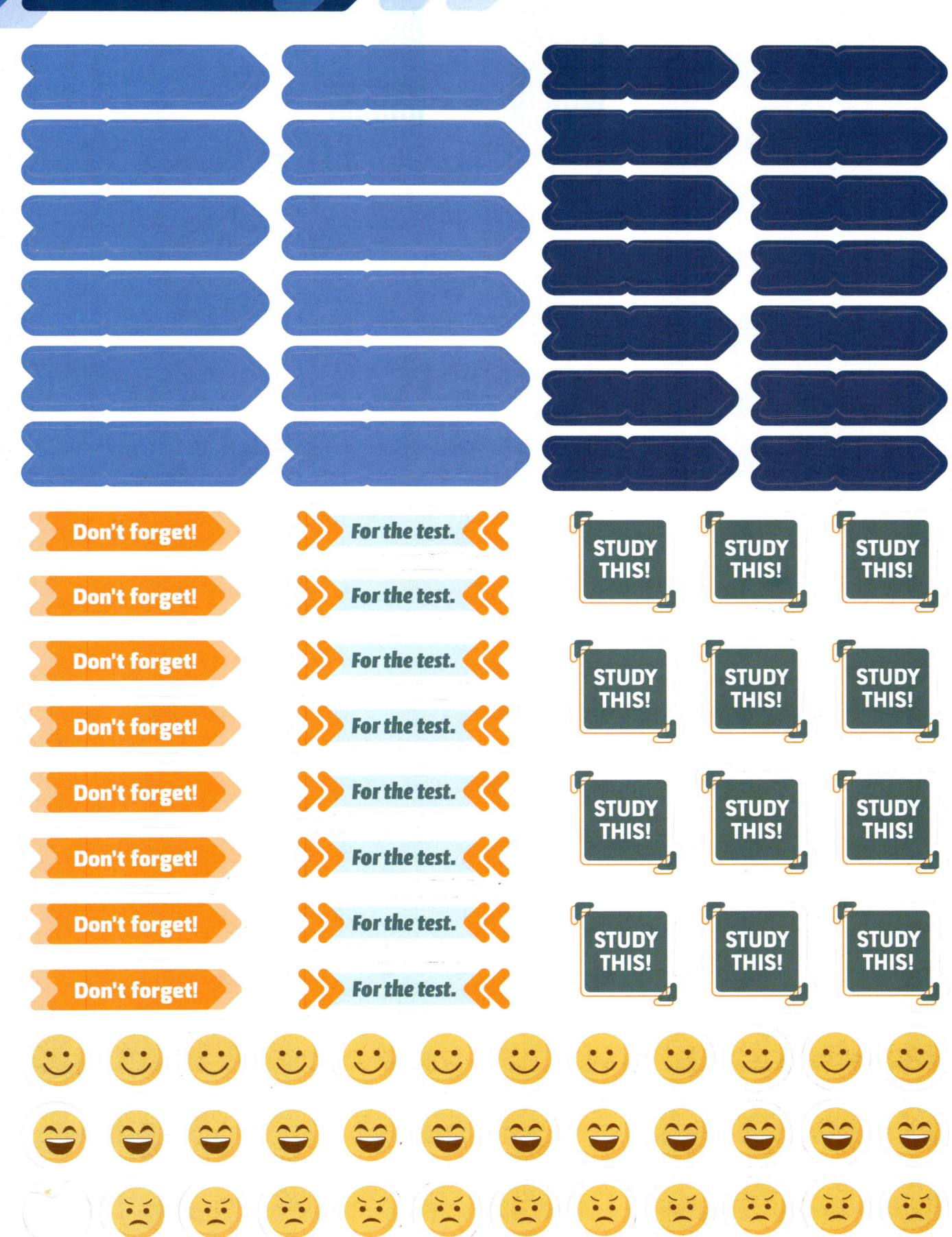

Don't forget!

For the test.

STUDY THIS!